Middle East

C000245689

Series Editors
Fawaz A. Gerges
Department of International Relations
London School of Economics
London, UK

Nader Hashemi
Center for Middle East Studies
Josef Korbel School of International Studies
University of Denver
Denver, CO, USA

The Iranian Revolution of 1979, the Iran-Iraq War, the Gulf War, and the US invasion and occupation of Iraq have dramatically altered the geopolitical landscape of the contemporary Middle East. The Arab Spring uprisings have complicated this picture. This series puts forward a critical body of first-rate scholarship that reflects the current political and social realities of the region, focusing on original research about contentious politics and social movements; political institutions; the role played by non-governmental organizations such as Hamas, Hezbollah, and the Muslim Brotherhood; and the Israeli-Palestine conflict. Other themes of interest include Iran and Turkey as emerging pre-eminent powers in the region, the former an 'Islamic Republic' and the latter an emerging democracy currently governed by a party with Islamic roots; the Gulf monarchies, their petrol economies and regional ambitions; potential problems of nuclear proliferation in the region; and the challenges confronting the United States, Europe, and the United Nations in the greater Middle East. The focus of the series is on general topics such as social turmoil, war and revolution, international relations, occupation, radicalism, democracy, human rights, and Islam as a political force in the context of the modern Middle East.

More information about this series at
http://www.palgrave.com/gp/series/14803

Mustafa Menshawy

Leaving the Muslim Brotherhood

Self, Society and the State

Mustafa Menshawy
Doha Institute for Graduate Studies
Doha, Qatar

Middle East Today
ISBN 978-3-030-27862-5   ISBN 978-3-030-27860-1   (eBook)
https://doi.org/10.1007/978-3-030-27860-1

This Palgrave Macmillan imprint is published by the registered company Springer Nature
Switzerland AG
The registered company address is: Gewerbestrasse 11, 6330 Cham, Switzerland

ACKNOWLEDGEMENTS

From the bottom of my heart, I would like to thank Professor Fawaz Gerges, of the London School of Economics, who played a pivotal role in helping me convert the idea for this book into reality. Professor Gerges, one of the world's leading authorities on the Middle East, was incredibly generous with his time, providing input and asking questions that were vital. I am eternally grateful for him being an inspiration. Dr. Khalil Al-Anani, the chair of Politics and International Relations Program at the Doha Institute for Graduate Studies, helped in making this book possible. He forced me to take into consideration certain nuances I might have overlooked otherwise and provided critical comments on various iterations of the draft manuscript.

After a long conversation with Professor Nathan Brown, at George Washington University, I felt my ideas were massively refined. I benefitted greatly from his comments and constructive criticism. The final product was improved as I meticulously tried to grapple with suggestions coming from Dr. Erika Biagini of the School of Law and Government at the Dublin City University, Professor Lawrence Pintak who is the founding dean of The Edward R. Murrow College of Communication at Washington State University (2009–2016), and Dr. Dalia Abdelhady at the Centre for Middle Eastern Studies in Lund University, Lund, Sweden. I appreciate the support of Dr. Diala Hawi, the chair of Psychology Program at the Doha Institute for Graduate Studies. Dr. Hawi suggested literature to read and gave her valuable comments on Chapter 2 on the 'affective disengagement' stage of the exit process.

Dr. Eid Mohamed of the Doha Institute for Graduate Studies and the University of Guelph allowed me to present my rough thoughts in front of scholars and students at one of the seminars which he kindly organized in 2017. My friend Hossam El-Sayyed was so generous to read all of the draft manuscript tirelessly. I am the fortunate recipient of great support from him as a mentor and I owe him a huge debt of gratitude as a specialist on the Brotherhood. Thanks are extended to Dr. Mahmoud El-Tahawy who also read different drafts of the manuscript and offered his valuable thoughts. Professor Dibyesh Anand and Dr. Raouf Tajvidi of the University of Westminster, London, believed in me and offered motivation and immense knowledge. Professor Abdelwahab El-Effendi and Dr. Mohamad Hamas Elmasry, Raed Habayeb, Eric Faust, and Amal Khayat from the Doha Institute supported me and made available all facilities that have made any delay in completing the manuscript simply unjustifiable. I cannot forget the massive support of my friend Dr. Emad Abdel-Latif, who moved from Lancaster University to Qatar University without losing the passion of tracing the interplay between language and politics in the Arab region. There are many other people whom I must acknowledge for their support of this project, including Professor Nabil Khattab at the Doha Institute for Graduate Studies. His input to develop my career and life is invaluable, and his support constant.

I thank my assistants who helped me ensure the manuscript was up to date and correctly referenced according to Palgrave's designated style: Jonathan Miseroy and Yasser Al-Wasabi were indispensable. The list includes Rababe Kardellass, Yousra Sabri, Mohamed Al-Agha, Issa Youssouf, Zainab Hajjar, Lahcen Sakour, Mohamed Meska, Oumnia Rais, Joseph Devine and Noureddine Radouai. Mahmoud Sha'ban, a prolific journalist and expert on the Brotherhood, was patient with my repeated questions during my visits to Turkey on a regular basis. Thanks extend to Ahmed Mohsen for networking and good manners while introducing me to many Brotherhood exiters in Qatar and Turkey. Ahmed Nazily played a major role in getting her, as he accepted to meet every time I had questions without answers. Abdel-Rahman Youssef also made it happen with all fruitful discussion with him in the initial stage of the project. Thanks to everyone on the Palgrave team who helped me so much. Special thanks to Alina Yurova, John Stegner, and Mary Fata for being patient. Special thanks to the fully diligent and enthusiastic Mary who was a key part of my getting there.

I owe much to Zeynep for coping with working on weekends and for understanding my whimsical shifts in mood correlating with shifts at levels of producing this manuscript. In the long hours spent in the office working on one single project, or one single thought, I missed the cosy atmospherics of sharing simpler and more interesting thoughts with Emir. As Bilal joined us at the end of this second book of mine, exactly as Emir did at the end of my first book (a random coincidence!), I am grateful to him as well. Finally, I express appreciation for any individual who did not question the wisdom of my academic pursuits.

A NOTE ON TRANSLITERATION

The study follows a simplified form adopted by the International Journal of the Middle East Studies (IJMES). The letter ayn is transliterated as [']. However, hamza, the Arabic alphabet letter representing the glottal stop, is not transliterated but represented by an [a], for the sake of convenience for non-specialists. The study uses [al] as a prefix in words referring to non- humans and [el] to humans.

CONTENTS

LIST OF TABLES

CHAPTER 1

Introduction

On 13 November 2014, Zainab El-Mahdy, a 22-year-old woman and former member of the Muslim Brotherhood, committed suicide after a series of difficulties she experienced following her disengagement from the group. She had removed her headscarf, and adopted daring hairstyles whose colors she would sometimes change. She also joined the campaign team of a presidential candidate, former Brotherhood leader 'Abdel-Mon'im Aboul-Futouh, who faced the Brotherhood's candidate, Mohamed Morsi, in the 2012 elections. I was so struck by the tragic loss of this lovely, active young girl, that I arranged to speak with her friends who had first announced her suicide. One of them attributed it to the 'emotional pain' and 'psychological pressures' that El-Mahdy had endured since her disassociation from the group.[1] This was my first clue that there is something about the Brotherhood and the demands it makes on members that can make the experience of disengagement personally very difficult.

I became further attracted to disengagement as a research topic as I noticed a growing number of people departing from the group. Through further preliminary research and initial interviews, I became aware of how many people belonging to various levels of membership had left the Brotherhood after 2011.[2] There were a number of high-level

---

[1] Nouh, A. (2014).
[2] Sha'ban, M. (2017).

© The Author(s) 2020
M. Menshawy, *Leaving the Muslim Brotherhood*, Middle East Today,
https://doi.org/10.1007/978-3-030-27860-1_1

1

officers among them, including Mohamed Habib, Ibrahim El-Za'frany, Kamal El-Helbawy, and Aboul-Futouh, who were all members of the organization's *Shura* or Guidance Council (the group's legislative and executive bodies, respectively). The list of leavers also includes many who are part of the middle and lower levels inside the group. The wave of departures sounds as a general phenomenon. Most departures occurred between 2011 and 2015, and those who left came from all over Egypt. Beginning with the group's foundation in 1928, there had been noted cases of prominent leaders departing due to some disagreement.[3] This recent wave was different from all of these cases, as it involved persons of disparate backgrounds from every level of the organization. What needs to be explained is not an action, but a pattern.

Seeking to trace this pattern, it is hard to speak by numbers. While it may seem that cases of disengagement before 2011 were few in number, exact figures are unavailable, just as it is difficult to know the precise number of persons who are, or were at any given time, members of the Brotherhood.[4] Adding to these uncertainties is the organization's secrecy. In 2008, as I began studying the Brotherhood at the University of London, I innocently asked a Brotherhood leader, Sa'd El-Katatny, after a lecture he had given, how many members they had. Laughing, he turned to those around him and remarked, 'He is asking me about figures that only God knows.' El-Katatny had a reason to keep this information secret. Officially banned yet sometimes tolerated, the Brotherhood always feared that disclosing information could jeopardize

---

[3]Disagreements have been mainly political or organizational since the group's foundation in 1928. Examples include Ahmed El-Sukkary, the deputy of the founder Hassan El-Banna, who exited the group in 1947, after a scathing diatribe against El-Banna in what can be considered a power struggle (see Lia, B. [2006]. *The society of the Muslim Brothers in Egypt: The rise of an Islamic mass movement 1928–1942*. Reading, UK: Ithaca Press). Another example is Ahmed Hassan El-Baquri, who resigned from the group in 1953 after he took over the post of the Minister of Religious Endowments without the approval of the Brotherhood's leaders, who were engaged in a political contestation with the ruling Free Officers including Gamal 'Abdel-Nasser, who appointed El-Baquri (see El-Baquri, A. H. [1988]. *Baqayya Zekrayat* [Residues of memories]. Cairo: Al-Ahram Centre for Translation and Publishing). In addition, these cases of disengagement were few in number and were disparate and not frequent as they occurred in different periods of time and under different circumstances.

[4]See Trager, E. (2011). *The unbreakable Muslim Brotherhood: Grim prospects for a liberal Egypt*. The Washington Institute. Available via: https://bit.ly/2FZzBR7. Accessed 18 September 2018.

its security.[5] Nevertheless, by 2011, this earlier caution had somewhat dissipated, allowing for figures on disengagement to be estimated. The reason was a new 'documented' publicity, which awaited deeper research and more investigation.

This 'documented' publicity is evident in the cases of those who have exited the Brotherhood. Beginning in 2011, disengagements from the group began to be publicly announced on television or in resignation letters sent to newspapers.[6] Dozens of ex-members described their involvement with, and departure from, the group in autobiographies or on television, while sometimes analyzing the conduct of former comrades in the process. In Egypt, much attention was given to the manner in which ex-members explained their participation in the so-called 'spectacle of disclosure' drawn on their departure from the group. Some autobiographies by those ex-members even topped the bestsellers list.[7] The 'spectacle' frequently involved former members deliberately revealing various organizational secrets publicly, which was again a new phenomenon in the organization's history and its interaction with the outside world.

Still, what drove me more into deciding to research the topic was the gaps in the literature on the Muslim Brotherhood, which was the founding Islamist group from which other such groups have emerged in recent decades. Many scholars drove their interest toward the Brotherhood as a 'social movement,'[8] which means analysis gets further limited to its 'collective actions' and politicized 'networks and resources' made available to face its 'political opponents.'[9] Missing from these analyses is the *individual* as a member of the group. As an exception, the mostly

[5] York, E., Martini, J., & Kaye, D. (2012). *The Muslim Brotherhood, its youth, and implications for U.S. engagement.* Santa Monica: RAND Corporation.

[6] El-Helbawy, K. (2012). *El-Helbawy announces his resignation on air.* Available via: https://bit.ly/2G0KYbE. Accessed 19 September 2018.

[7] Samir, I. (2015). Asrar tard Hassan El-Banna wa Sayyed Qutb min al-maktabat [The secrets of dismissing Hassan El-Banna and Sayyid Qutb from bookships], *Al-Bawabh News.* www.albawabhnews.com/1056377. Accessed 10 March 2019.

[8] Mellor, N. (2018). *Voice of the Muslim Brotherhood: Da'wa, discourse, and political communication* (p. 2). London: Routledge; see also Tarrow, S. (2011). *Power in movement: Social movements and contentious politics.* New York: Cambridge University Press.

[9] Mellor, N. (2018). *Voice of the Muslim Brotherhood*, p. 2. See Munson, Z. (2001). Islamic mobilization: Social movement theory and the Egyptian Muslim Brotherhood. *The Sociological Quarterly*, 42(4), 487–510; Wickham, C. R. (2013). *The Muslim Brotherhood: Evolution of an Islamist movement.* Princeton, NJ: Princeton University Press.

individual-based analyses gave researchers the opportunity to reveal some of the ideological and internal workings of the group in terms of relationships between members and leaders. Nevertheless, such works still restricted their enquiry to who and what is *inside* the Brotherhood.[10] This literature, as informative and insightful as it is, ends up discriminating against dissenting voices inside the Brotherhood as it focuses on what is 'visible,' 'common,' and 'ordinary' about the group.[11] Strikingly, and perhaps ironically, the Brotherhood itself reacted to the wave of dissent through a 'symbolic annihilation,' which included condemning or trivializing the dissidents, or even denying that they had been members of the group in the first place. The focus of the scholarly literature on 'what and who is inside' inadvertently supports the Brotherhood's attempts of 'omission.'

In light of these gaps in the literature and based on my interest drawn on the growing number of disengagements at different levels, this study seeks to understand:

- How do individuals leaving the Brotherhood describe and explain their disengagement?

I consider disengagement to be a *discourse*, including narrative episodes as tools of description, and comprised of 'frames' that determine the meaning of the objects and events represented, and 'macro frames' that broadly function to organize the whole experience and guide the action of exiting the group.[12] The study investigates reasons which former Brotherhood members give for departing the group and discern recurring *patterns* that appear in the explanations of those leavers.

As accounts are analyzed into patterns of frames and patterns making up the 'discourse of ex-hood,' as to be detailed in the methodology

---

[10]Zollner, B. (2009). *The Muslim Brotherhood: Hasan al-Hudaybi and ideology*. New York: Routledge; Kandil, H. (2014). *Inside the Brotherhood*. Cambridge, UK: Polity Press; Al-Anani, K. (2016). *Inside the Muslim Brotherhood: Religion, identity, and politics* (p. 4). Oxford University Press.

[11]Williams, R. (2016). *Resources of hope: Culture, democracy, socialism* (pp. 3–14). London: Verso.

[12]Snow, D. A., Rochford, Jr., E. B., Worden, S. K., & Benford, R. D. (1986). Frame alignment processes, micromobilization, and movement participation. *American Sociological Review, 51*(4), 464–481.

section below, the book seeks to set another related goal: Understanding disengagement as a *process*. Tracing this process while it unfolds through interactions and interpretations manifesting in discourse is necessary for three main reasons. First, I can avoid any claims of causality when it comes to inferring from the data I am using and which are mainly subjective and admittedly biased narratives of members who specifically left the group within a specific 2011–2017 time frame. Second, there can be no inference about a cause (e.g., 'why') as there's no comparison of current Brotherhood members (i.e., those who remain). In other words, and as it is important to be clear about the book's claims, I am not concerned why members exit the Brotherhood at a certain time more than any other times, or why certain members exit it while others do not (which could be legitimate goals in future research). Third, the analysis stops short of throwing any of these claims of causality on the case under analysis. I do not compare the Brotherhood with other movements that witness similar, larger, or smaller waves of disengagement. Rather, the research situates the Brotherhood itself equally as the phenomenon of disengagement from it: Being a process. No time, effort, or space wasted on validating or questioning descriptors for the movement itself as other scholars have done, for example, as 'terrorist,' 'radical,' 'violent radical,' 'moderate' or 'extremist,' 'pro-democracy,' or 'anti-democracy.'[13] All these classifications are problematic since they treat the Brotherhood as unitary, which has not been the case since 2011, when the group has been factionalized and its dominant discourse fragmented and destabilized. Furthermore, this holistic approach also traces the movability between states which the Brotherhood has gone through such as 'moderation' and 'radicalism' within a linear causality and on the basis of particular structural, social, and political criteria such as electoral participation, and it thus ignores the *individual* inside or outside the group. In the book, what does matter is the Brotherhood the process, that is,

---

[13]See Ehud, S. (1991). The process of delegitimation: Towards a linkage theory of political terrorism. *Terrorism and Political Violence, 3,* 50–68. https://doi.org/10.1080/09546559108427092; 'Abdelrahman, M. (2009). 'With the Islamists?—Sometimes. With the state?—Never!' Cooperation between the left and Islamists in Egypt. *British Journal of Middle Eastern Studies, 36*(1), 37–54 (49–52). https://doi.org/10.1080/13530190902749556; and Denoeux, G. (2002). The forgotten swamp: Navigating political Islam. *Middle East Policy, 9*(2), 56–81. https://doi.org/10.1111/1475-4967.00057.

interactions, dynamics, tactics, routes, relations, and rules affecting engagement and disengagement from it.[14]

As part of discourse construction and process tracing drawn on it, disengagement includes 'stages' analyzed as these three (methodologically distinguishable) levels of micro-, meso-, and macro-:

- The micro-level stage focusing on what I call 'affective disengagement': the emotions, sentiments, and moods related to the disengagement process and dis-identification from the tight social circles, sometimes considered family, in which the engagement of individuals was embedded.
- The meso-level stage that I call the 'ideological' disengagement, including changing understandings of pre- and post-disengagement of the Brotherhood's ideology, as set by the organization's founder, Hassan El-Banna, and subsequent and current leaders. Relevant here are the ways the group's organizational style affects an individual's manner of engagement or disengagement.
- The macro-level stage linking what is individual and ideological/organizational to the socio-political, and thus enables an understanding of the concerns of individuals and their consequences within a context of broader developments such as the rise of the Brotherhood to power and its meteoric fall not long after.

To reiterate, these stages are neither meant to identify nor test a theory of the conditions under which individuals do disengage with organizations like the Brotherhood. Rather, they generate a very limited scope of conditions related to the Brotherhood and to the post-2011 era in which Egypt and the group has witnessed unprecedented transformations. The scope is a very narrow one, that is, how disengagement unfolds as *process* and *discourse*. Having said so, this limitation does not have to be defensive. The approach of building theory via discourse analysis and process

---

[14] McAdam, D., Sidney, T., & Charles, T. (1996). *Towards an integrated perspective on social movements and revolution.* Lazarsfeld Center at Columbia University; Tilly, C. (2017). From mobilization to revolution. In E. Castañeda & C. L. Schneider (Eds.), *Collective violence, contentious politics, and social change* (pp. 71–91). Routledge; Tarrow, S. (1996). States and opportunities: The political structuring of social movements. *Comparative perspectives on social movements: Political opportunities, mobilizing structures, and cultural framings* (pp. 41–61).

tracing based on it proved an entirely valid and useful exercise. For example, I found at the end of the project that disengagement is a point of rupture or incongruence in discourse between the dominant frames of the Brotherhood and the 'resistant' frames of individuals exiting it. Former members of the Brotherhood can now articulate a consistent, coherent, and resonant 'alternative' discourse that can effectively resist and seriously challenge the dominance of the Brotherhood's discourse long established, fixated, and unquestionably sanctified. Another finding that disengagement is processed as exiting members have been accumulating at every 'stage' benefits from opportunities and as they maximize their utility of resources in order to articulate as well as materialize their discourse. It is within the struggles, workings, intricacies, transformations, and opportunities at those two levels of discourse and process that engagement ends.

The time frame of this study, from 2011 to 2017, is significant in order to understand and contextualize how disengagement is constructed as discourse and developed as process. For example, two sub-divisions are made within this period, marking the dramatic rise and fall of the Brotherhood from power. The first is the moment in 2011 marked by the resignation of President Hosni Mubarak and the rise of the Brotherhood during the following year, leading to the election that year of Mohamed Morsi. Among the questions that are asked in the book: Did the replacement of Mubarak by the Brotherhood provide an opportunity to facilitate individual disengagements from the group? Did this make 'ex-hood' more acceptable by offering alternative 'mediated spaces' and political opportunities to articulate and materialize it? The second event was the end of the Brotherhood's rule on June 30, 2013. Among the questions that are asked in the book: Did the fall of the Brotherhood serve as an additional background against which to view the wave of disengagements expanding? The years 2011–2017 also witnessed widening divisions inside the Brotherhood. This left the organization with two advisory councils for the first time since its foundation in 1928. Members of the two councils engaged in several disputes by way of media statements, with each claiming to be the legitimate representatives of the organization.[15] Did these disputes stand as an opportunity

[15]Aziz, M. (2017). *Divisions widen between Muslim Brotherhood factions after policy reassessment initiative.* Available via Ahramonline: https://bit.ly/2Uo27PI. Accessed 19 September 2018.

for exiting members feeling further disillusioned with the group and its divided leadership? In this sense of tracing disengagement across some of these specific time pointers, my interest is not time as a chronological unit (i.e., what events happen before others or along with others). Away from any 'linear succession of instants,'[16] time is about a relational construction between some of these past events or pointers and present situation. It is about how members interact with and interpret these events while narrating their disengagement. On some occasions, what also does matter is how the past is re-ordered for the sake of highlighting or suppressing certain events in order to validate the disengagement-related accounts.

DISENGAGEMENT: LANGUAGE AND IDENTITY

The book seeks to give a central position to language 'in use' as the main unit of analysis to analyze the discourse of disengagement. The language, or so I argue in this study, is not treated as other scholars have done; that is being a mere representational tool describing the process or events that constitute it.[17] Language plays a central role as an agent infusing the stages of the process and these events with 'meaning,' and the constitution of an image of disengagement as a 'reality' in consequence.[18] As such, language *creates* disengagement itself as well as being *created* by it. As George Herbert Mead puts it, language 'does not simply symbolize a situation or object which is already there in advance; it makes possible the existence or the appearance of that situation or object, for it is part of the mechanism whereby that situation or object is created.'[19] As next chapters indicate, disengagement is made in the functionality of this language and its manifestations such as repeating linguistic formulations

---

[16] Mishler, E. (2006). Narrative and identity: The double arrow of time. In A. De Fina, D. Schiffrin, & M. Bamberg (Eds.), *Discourse and identity* (23rd ed.) (pp. 30–47 [32]). Cambridge, UK: Cambridge University Press.

[17] See Wickham, C. R. (2004). The path to moderation: Strategy and learning in the formation of Egypt's Wasat Party. *Comparative Politics, 36*(2), 205–228; Horgan, J. (2014). *The psychology of terrorism* (p. 139). London and New York: Routledge.

[18] Hodges, A. (2011). *The 'war on terror' narrative: Discourse and intertextuality in the construction and contestation of sociopolitical reality* (p. 5). Oxford, UK: Oxford University Press.

[19] Mead, G. H. (2015). *Mind, self & society* (p. 78). Chicago: The University of Chicago Press.

such as metaphors of 'slavery,' 'imprisonment,' and emancipation as well as the dichotomy between the pronouns of 'I' and 'we.' On some occasions, disengagement appears as part of a 'war of words' between the group imposing a dominant language to consolidate the full obedience of its ranks and disgruntled members resisting or challenging this dominance with their own 'alternative language' that have its rules, relations, and uses. It is also through language that those members can also construct and reconstruct as a totality of their experience. They found the opportunity to use their own 'language' to narrate disengagement and have this narrative published in different formats such as autobiographies with no censorship or prior approval obtained from Brotherhood leaders according to the group's rules.

The book also gives a central position to identity as part of disengagement. If, as Roberto Melucci contends, identity is 'inherent in all social movements' framing activities'[20] related to engaging members, it holds true identity is also inherent in all framing activities related to disengaging members. Furthermore, identity fits in with the process–discourse understanding of disengagement as it emerges in both individual and collective shapes while both actors, the movement, and the individual members of it 'assess their environment' and 'calculate costs and benefits of their actions.'[21] Out of assessment and calculation done by both sides, identity appears contested, fragmented, and contradictory. In this sense identity is a process of representation, that is, how the group and its (exiting) members 'see themselves and are seen by others'[22] (which fits in with the sampling style and method of analysis based on personal testimonies as to be explained below). Analysis has found that exiting members seek to replace a largely collective identity with a more personal one. The Brotherhood tended, unsurprisingly, to work in the opposite direction, to subsume personal identity within a largely collective one. To this extent, disengagement operates in reverse of that logic, effectuating an undoing. This movability between a member

[20] Hunt, S. A., Benford, R. D., & Snow, D. A. (1994). Identity fields: Framing processes and the social construction of movement identities. *New social movements: From ideology to identity* (pp. 185–208).

[21] Melucci, R. (1989). *Nomads of the present: Social movements and individual needs in contemporary society* (p. 35). Philadelphia: Temple University Press.

[22] Polletta, F., & Jasper, J. M. (2001). Collective identity and social movements. *Annual Review of Sociology, 27*(1), 283–305.

and the Brotherhood as well as their identities makes identity more of a 'process' through which 'individuals or groups define the meaning of their action and the field of opportunities and constraints of such an action.'[23] Within this process, identity is 'constructed' within different levels of interactions between the individual and the group and is shaped by resources, opportunities, and constraints in the external world.[24] As such, the identity process also involves a 'discursive work' including prioritizing or de-prioritizing specific linguistic features to demonstrate identification or dis-identification with the group or the individual. These features are symbolized in the book through the extensive use of pronouns such as 'we,' 'I,' and 'they' to reflect the positionality of the individual inside and outside of the group.[25] Within this complexity of various features of identifications, this book found an interesting territory for drawing correlations and accentuating other findings. While scholars have sought to confirm that a strong and exclusive identification with the group makes engagement more likely and more enduring,[26] I complete the picture by moving in the other direction to reach the same conclusion: A weaker identification with the group and the rise of competing inclusive identities make disengagement from this group more likely. Among the many theories of identity, I shall focus on identity process theory (IPT) in particular. The theory, concerned with the 'holistic analysis of the total identity of the person,'[27] encompasses elements that derive from every aspect of the person's experience, including her or his membership in the Brotherhood, interpersonal relationships inside the group, exposure to the outside world, and her or his political activities. Secondly, the IPT includes a number of principles that fit the exploration of ex-hood as process and discourse. Glynis Blackwell theorized these principles as 'evaluation,' 'accommodation,' 'uniqueness' or distinction

[23] Melucci, A. (1996). *Challenging codes: Collective action in the information age* (pp. 76–77). Cambridge: Cambridge University Press.

[24] Al-Anani, K. *Inside the Muslim Brotherhood*, pp. 42–44.

[25] Zimmerman, D. H., & Wieder, D. L. (2017). Ethnomethodology and the problem of order: Comment on Denzin. In J. D. Douglas (Ed.), *Understanding everyday life: Toward the reconstruction of sociological knowledge* (pp. 285–298). Chicago: Aldine Publishing.

[26] Huddy, L. (2001). From social to political identity: A critical examination of social identity theory. *Political Psychology, 22*(1), 127–156.

[27] Jaspal, R., & Breakwell, G. M. (Eds.). (2014). *Identity process theory: Identity, social action and social change* (p. 250). Cambridge, UK: Cambridge University Press.

from others, feelings of 'personal worth,' and 'self-efficacy.' Accounting for these principles renders identity a dynamic product of interaction with the self, the structures of surrounding environment, and the social or representations thereof.

SOURCES OF DATA

Researching the Brotherhood is a difficult task in the best of times, and it is significantly complicated in the post-2013 Egypt, thus below I describe the challenges to research and data gathering in this environment and how to deal with them.

The book combines different data sources and methods in the study of the disengagement phenomenon. The data includes autobiographies written by exiting members and published between 2011 and 2017, and transcribed interviews conducted with 32 other exiting members and who announced their departure from the group within the same period (see Appendix, Table A.1). I adopt this 'triangulation,' that is, the combination of data sources in the study of the same phenomenon,[28] for a number of reasons. Firstly, it secures a richer and thicker data grounded in a more well-rounded investigation of a topic considerably under-explored in literature. Secondly, each medium can include, or so I hypothesize, different frames encompassing 'thematic meanings' of a subjective nature and which are mainly constructed in the 'minds' of exiting members. This means that the combination of the sources helps us present a full-fledged framing and all angles of meanings constituting it. The method also adds 'truthfulness' created by the confirmation and corroboration among frames which cover all domains of the disengagement phenomenon and which could be contradictory or conflictual.

On many occasions, I cannot independently or separately verify these accounts or events on which the framing process is drawn. Therefore, the best option is to compare and contrast the frames as multiple outcomes of different departure narratives. The bias inherent in any one particular data source can be canceled out (or perhaps confirmed) when used

---

[28] For some essential readings on triangulation, see Denzin, N. K. (1978). *The research act: A theoretical introduction to sociological methods.* New York: Praeger; Denzin, N. K., & Lincoln, Y. S. (2005). Introduction: The discipline and practice of qualitative research. In N. K. Denzin & Y. S. Lincoln (Eds.), *The Sage handbook of qualitative research* (3rd ed., pp. 1–28). Thousand Oaks, CA: Sage.

in conjunction with the other source. Analysis also adds another layer of verification, this time beyond the level of texts of narrativization. I go with the 'original' and 'independent' sources. Once an exiting member refers to an idea or a notion related to the Brotherhood and which she or he observes and 'is conscious of having in his mind,' again to borrow from John Locke, I go to the 'origin' of these notions or ideas by tracing their meanings in the literature of the Brotherhood, and by also evidencing them independently.[29] This search for independent sources led me to regularly talk to and consult with some impartial scholars, academics, or journalists who are specialized in the Brotherhood or closely follow the disengagement phenomenon.[30] I do hope that such an approach brings me closer to the attempted 'truthfulness' in the research.

As I combine autobiographies and interviews as two 'sets' of items equally studied in the book, the findings will enjoy *reliability*. That a frame, such as the one evolving in 'Gaining the I' in Chapter 2, is repeated frequently and resonantly in both autobiographies and interviews and by individuals (i.e., the producers of these texts) who differ in age, gender, and geographic location. It is a reliability based on 'internal consistency' drawn on the repetition of the frame across more than one genre of texturing. This makes me as a researcher more confident that the frames that I admittedly and intuitively selected at the beginning of research as the more 'salient' ones in the texts are not a matter of personal preference. It is what exiting members themselves choose, select, and emphasize across different texts as part of drawing our attention to specific areas of their own experience of disengagement. Nevertheless, the triangulation of data sources runs risk of making it a search for similarities and continuities in meanings and inter-frame correlations drawn on their recurrence in texts. In other words, we do care about a frame only when it is mentioned again and again across autobiographies and interviews. Fully aware of such a risk, the book does not ignore inconsistencies, paradoxes, or contradictions that can emerge by virtue of pluralism in the data sources.

---

[29] Locke, J. (1817). *An essay concerning human understanding, Book I, Chapter I & IV*. Rivington.

[30] For example, I am grateful to my repeated conversations over the past three years with Dr. Khalil Al-Anani, an authority on the Muslim Brotherhood and an author of some seminal works on the movement. I also chatted with Professor Nathan Brown of the George Washington University, Raed El-Samhouri of the Arab Center for Research and Policy Studies, and senior independent researchers Hossam El-Sayyed and Mahmoud Sha'ban.

More challenges still emerge on the selection of the sample. All auto-biographies published since 2011 have been included in this study, which helps the sampling with fair and accurate representation of this genre of texturing. Still, questions have to be answered on the selection of inter-viewees. The question remains on why 32 interviewees were selected and others not (especially as I ran the abovementioned argument that there are many of them). Admittedly, the sampling in interviews is subjected to biases as the 32 individuals were selected on a 'snowballing' basis. For example, in Turkey, ex-members whom I interviewed on the first day of my arrival in Istanbul introduced me to their friends and acquaintances who also departed from the same group and who could share the same characteristics. As the sample builds up in this 'non-probability' tech-nique, also adopted in Egypt, the UK, and Qatar, the data was gathered. However, the technique can be justified as I was looking for a variety of exiting members including those who were 'hidden' and difficult to locate, especially in Egypt's 'conflict environment' full of suspicion and mistrust drawn from the official anti-Brotherhood hostility and public outrage. The 'snowballing' technique is justified to avoid more problems in this kind of research, problems that also have to do with the charac-teristics of exiting members who are ready to talk to researchers and the public in general.

The interviewees who are ready to talk are mostly those of the 'apos-tate' type that is, those who have 'louder' voices as they can dramatically and publicly narrate their experiences, 'reverse' their loyalties and even become 'professional enemies' of the movement they have left.'[31] I was not the first one to talk to those exiting members of the 'apostate' type as they enjoy a wider access to other researchers and media outlets in and out of Egypt. Benefitting from contextual shifts such as the Egyptian

---

[31] Introvigne, M. (1999). Defectors, ordinary leave-takers, and apostates: A quanti-tative study of former members of New Acropolis in France. *Nova Religio: The Journal of Alternative and Emergent Religions, 3*(1), 83–99; Bromley, D. G. (1998). The social construction of contested exit roles: Defectors, whistle-blowers, and apostates. In D. G. Bromley (Ed.), *The politics of religious apostasy: The role of apostates in the transformation of religious movements* (pp. 19–48). London: Praeger. In the case of the Muslim Brotherhood, the 'apostasy' can even take a radical form as members of the group are mostly well-trained on activities such as public speaking as part 'tarbiya' which implies that the 'movement educates and fosters the development of its members,' Brown, N. J. (2012). *When victory is not an option: Islamist movements in Arab politics* (p. 69). Ithaca and London: Cornell University Press.

state's attempts to use every tool to crack down on the Brotherhood and its existing members, some of those 'apostate' ex-members found additional reasons to enhance their 'visibility.' They not only narrate their experiences, but also share the regime's goals of 'exposing' their former group. As to be detailed in Chapter 4, one can even suspect this 'visibility' and ubiquity in the 'quit literature' that abounds in the literature on the Brotherhood within a short space of time could not have been possible without the tacit approval, if not outright encouragement, of the regime of Abdel-Fatah El-Sisi. The latter is interested in doing so as he took over power after a coup on the rule of the Brotherhood leader and president Mohamed Morsi, and has taken it upon himself to clamp down on the Brotherhood and 'weed out' its ideology. Indeed, the 'apostate' exiting members in the interview list such as Tareq Aboul-Sa'd can be easily recognized by their intensive presence in media as writers, experts, guests, and TV hosts in Egypt at a time of strict state censorship that would never allow any pro-Brotherhood sympathizers to have the same windows of opportunity. Therefore, the snowballing in sampling has allowed me to get in touch with hard-to-reach exiting members who could never have participated in or contributed to my study were it not for the social networks referring to them under this technique of data gathering. The list of interviewees thus includes 'ordinary leavers' who had never narrated their disengagement publicly and those who have drifted away quietly, without fanfare or revealing themselves to the media or researchers. It was significant to enroll in the study those voices that are 'most common and least often discussed' and which have long been 'marginalized' at the expense of the louder voices of the 'apostate' type. Again, this helped boost the reliability of my findings as the frames of interviewees of the 'quiet' individuals always stand as a tool corroborating the frames of louder 'apostate' type of ex-members who could hold stronger feelings, radical views, and revengeful attitudes when they narrate their past. I changed the first name of some of the 'ordinary leavers' for the sake of their own safety, even they have consented to have their full name used at the time of the interviews. After a period of thinking through the potential consequences, I found it wise to hide the full names of those who have never 'exposed' themselves to the public as they could be the most vulnerable amidst the growing hostilities against the Brotherhood. On the opposite, I left the full names of the 'apostate' leavers as they have maintained, if not encouraged, their public exposure as such through talking to other scholars or regularly appearing in the media. Still, as another layer of precaution, I resorted to hiding the name of the apostate if she or he mentioned a piece of information which I assessed as sensitive or risky to them or their social circles of family and friends.

Meanwhile, and since we do not know the exact number of ex-members from the Brotherhood, the research adds another layer of sampling validity. The representation of exiting members somehow correlates with the representation of existing members in the Brotherhood itself. It is a reflection of the original population makeup from which this sample is drawn and on which more data is already available. For example, members of the Brotherhood dominantly belong to the 'middle class,'[32] exiting members were equally supposed to come from this category which has 'greater aspirations concerning policy and a better life' than other classes.'[33] The group also said it 'prevails in the educated circles' and takes 'university students' as an important category in its recruitment. The list of interviewees can thus stand as a reflection of the original population to which the exiting members belonged to prior to their disengagement. According to Table A.2 (see Appendix) on the profession of the interviewees, 37% of them are writers or journalists and 16% are students. The sampling validity increases as the list also includes professionals, politicians, and petty or big businessmen, and these are all categories representing the broad range of 'middle class' to which most Brotherhood members belong. As the Brotherhood's recruitment also 'targets children' especially 'kids of its members,' the sampling also reflects this tactic. According to Table A.5 (see Appendix), 44% of the sample joined the Brotherhood when they were less than 16 years old and 53% when they were between 17 and 24 years old. Only 3% of the interviewees had been recruited into the movement when they had been 25 years old or more, which again accords with the dynamics of recruitment. In addition, the fact is that the recruitment is just the beginning of a much longer, multistage process that turns a hopeful new recruit into a fully-fledged Brotherhood member and which can take years. This reflects on my sampling as Table A.3 (see Appendix) demonstrates

---

[32]On the Brotherhood's official website, it explains its structure as follows: 'The MB group does exist in all the classes, from the upper one to the lower, but it's mostly dominant in the middle one, which is the main source for recruitment,' No author, *Muslim Brotherhood: Structure & Spread*. http://www.ikhwanweb.com/article.php?id=817.

[33]Ibid.

that the groups of those who stayed in the Brotherhood for less than 10 years, for less than 20 years, and for less than 30 years are almost equally represented in the sample in order to reflect all of the stages of this process as a whole. However, this leaves the research with another dilemma, exiting members under analysis joined the group in different times. As Table A.4 (see Appendix), interviewees joined the group across 1970s, 1980s, 1990s, and 2000s. This signals that any framing identified in the 'presentist' texturing or narration has to be contextualized against the internal dynamics of continuity and change inside the Brotherhood across these decades. For example, the frame of the 'group's anti-intellectualism' (Chapter 3) is based on meanings in which ex-members evoke previous incidents showing the group's 'stagnation' and resistance to change occurring around it during earlier decades. The sample can grab this intersection between the past and the present as they had witnessed events across all these different decades. As the book takes geographic spatialization into consideration of the construction of frames, the interviews were conducted beyond Egypt. As shown in Table A.6 (see Appendix), I held interviews in Turkey, where thousands of Brotherhood members, some of whom disengaged in association during or after this dislocation, found sanctuary after the coup against Morsi in 2013. On the basis of this 'spatial' expansion of the interviews, the book found some interesting phenomena in which spaces can play a role in the articulation and materialization of specific frames which can inhibit or precipitate departure from the group.

Having centralized the role of language in analysis as highlighted above, the book carefully describes all acts of disassociation from the Brotherhood as a 'disengagement' in order to deal with more challenges in data and sampling. Departing from the Brotherhood is based on claims of individuals making them that they had been members of it. They are self-proclaimed members and also self-proclaimed ex-members. Some people who left the Brotherhood were reportedly expelled from it, and the organization sometimes denies they had been members of it in the first place. Other people claim that they took the decision and left the group voluntarily. 'Disengagement' thus comes as a middle ground avoiding getting into the uncharted territory of verifying who left the other (the individual or the group) and how this happens (voluntarily or by expulsion). The act of disengagement typically involves a 'mutual withdrawal' that includes both 'the individual's decreased association with a group, and, simultaneously, the group's decreased demands or involvement with the individual.'[34] The concept also fits with our understanding of disassociation from the group as process based on interactions between the individual and the group.

METHODOLOGY

Once the interviews were conducted, they were transcribed, and the data from them, along with the autobiographies, is analyzed for identifying frames and reporting patterns within it. A frame is identified in the use of specific textual devices such as metaphors, catchphrases, associations, depictions, keywords, or sentences to convey a specific 'selected' idea, message, or 'aspect of the perceived reality.' Any of these devices need to gain 'salience' in order to turn into a frame. As Entman put it, this 'salience' (a description which I will use at a regular basis in the book) is obtained by 'placement or repetition, or by associating them with culturally familiar symbols.'[35] As there were numerous frames, and most were interrelated, I have to collate them into superordinate frames holding the same thematized meanings or what I call 'macro frames.' The macro frames, developed and ordered into a logical and coherent narrative structure, were found to be three: 'affective disengagement' (the micro stage), 'ideological disengagement' (the meso stage), and 'political disengagement' (the macro stage). The next three chapters each are to discuss one of these macro frames separately as part of unpacking the process and discourse of disengagement at the level of these three stages classified at the beginning of this introduction.

The frame analysis is treated as part of critical discourse analysis (CDA) which I use generally to analyze the disengagement experiences represented in these interviews and autobiographies. I adopt the conceptualization of Norman Fairclough, one of the pioneers of CDA, who set three levels of analysis. At the first level, 'discourse as a text,'[36] the book addresses both questions of form and questions of meanings appertaining to the semantics of the language of disengagement. For example, the textual features of the disengagement narratives include the movability of the two pronouns 'we' and 'I' as reflections of the shifts in identity

---

[34] Ebaugh, becoming an ex, p. 10.

[35] Entman, R. M. (1993). Framing: Towards clarification of a fractured paradigm. *Journal of Communication, 43*(4), 51–58.

[36] Fairclough, N. (1992). *Discourse and social change* (Vol. 10, pp. 74–78). Cambridge: Polity Press.

from what is collective to what is personal (see Chapter 2). At this level, words, sentences, or paragraphs represent 'surface structures' drawing 'local-level meanings' on disengagement. These 'local-level' meanings are also traced through repetition or frequency, as well as relations of 'synonymy, entailment or presupposition' among them.[37] They have to transform into 'global meanings' as fragmented elements of texts and their meanings (referred to as frames) coalesce into macro frames representing the three broader thematized stages of disengagement mentioned above as 'affective,' 'organizational,' and 'political'. Again, this analysis is part of tracing the process of disengagement as it moves from smaller 'atomized' local units identified in texts through 'titles' and 'keywords' or 'metaphors' into 'global' units which can 'abstract' and 'summarize' the whole 'discourse of ex-hood.'[38]

At the second level of Fairclough's conceptualization, 'discursive practices,' the book's interest expands into the 'production' and 'interpretation' of texts, that is, how certain frames and macro frames gain salience through features as 'force,' 'coherence,' or 'intertextuality.'[39] This level of analysis allows an understanding of the connections between all different texts under study. It also allows moving beyond ex-hood-related texts. For example, via intertextuality, exiting members resorted to texts of existing members as 'resources' which they have drawn from construct their 'cues,' in Fairclough's words,[40] building their own texts. In this process of transforming prior texts and restructuring existing discourses related to the Brotherhood, exiting members can generate a new discourse, which we can call the 'discourse of ex-hood,' through which they can resist, challenge, and counter the hegemony of the Brotherhood and its pre-emptive/punitive measures against disengagements.[41]

---

[37] Van Dijk, T. A. (1988). Semantics of a press panic: The Tamil invasion. *European Journal of Communication, 3*(2), 167–187 (170).

[38] Ibid., p. 10.

[39] Fairclough, N. (1992). *Discourse and social change*, pp. 78–86.

[40] Ibid., p. 80.

[41] In this sense, the framing itself becomes both process and discourse as the individuals and the groups are engaged in what Benford and Snow call an 'active, processual phenomenon that implies agency and contention at the level of reality construction.' Each side seeks to 'locate, perceive, identify, and label' parts of this reality in its own way and for its own purpose; see Benford, R. D., & Snow, D. A. (2000). Framing processes and social movements: An overview and assessment. *Annual Review of Sociology, 26*, 614.

This leads to Fairclough's third level of analysis, 'discourse as social [or political] practice.'[42] From a less abstract and more contextualized semantic analysis, the book investigates frames in relation to ideology and to power in the surrounding environment. It is about how the evolution of the discourse of disengagement in texts is drawn on a process of evolution of power relations, struggle, and resistance related to the Brotherhood and broader social and political structures in which they dis/function. By ideology, I mean the 'thematized meanings'[43] projected on individual members by their leaders and which they have to adhere to. The time limitation in the study is thus justified as the production, consumption, and interpretation of the texts can be explored against specific workings of the socio-politics in 2011 and afterwards.

CAVEAT

Admittedly, the framing, which is the core of this project, remains a 'biased' process despite my attempts to ameliorate this bias through such measures as arriving toward a more representative sampling. Intrinsically, by drawing 'salience' based on 'selection,' the framing is a biased 'schemata of interpretation' by exiting members (the producers of frames and macro frames) and myself as the one who carries, transmits, or also selects frames before grouping them into the shape of another text (this book). Exiting members frame as they intentionally 'locate, perceive, identify, and label' particular events and occurrences, thus 'rendering meaning, organizing experiences, and guiding actions' related to the disengagement.[44] This means that the 'truthfulness' of these frames can never be guaranteed. Any claims of truth thus rest largely on the evidence of linguistic examples constructed by each side as part of the framing process. The task of comparing and contrasting these frames by setting them against each other, and also against the group's 'dominant' frames, seeks to counter cannot fully resolve this problem. This is because each side, including myself as the author of this book, could be seen as seeking to enforce its own frames as part of and its 'biased

---

[42] Fairclough, N. *Discourse and social change*, pp. 86–91.

[43] Van Dijk, T. A. (1998). *Ideology: A multidisciplinary approach*. Sage.

[44] Goffman, E. (1974). *Frame analysis: An essay on the organization of experience* (p. 21). Cambridge: Harvard University Press.

schematic of interpretation' of what is happening. Therefore, the book sets itself the modest task of identifying and analyzing frames which constitute 'alternative' truths long hidden, falsified, and downsized by the dominance of the Brotherhood on a single sanctified version of 'truth.' Taking this 'process tracing' as a matter of central concern, I reject the possibility of reaching an absolute and objective 'truth' and related assumptions on the disengagement phenomenon. If anything, this truth in the accounts under study can be best described as 'experiential' since it is identified in the interactions and interpretations of language and in questions of 'meaningfulness of everyday experience' as practiced and shared by exiting members.[45]

This admission of mine couples with another; that the knowledge of the disengagement from the Brotherhood or knowledge of the group itself cannot be 'generalized' to sprawl across the entire landscape of 'quit literature' in other cases, including disengagement from other Islamist movements. This explicit statement of 'scope conditions,' also limited by the time under study (the unique post-2011 era of 'Arab Spring'), thus constrains any theoretical claims outlined in the analysis. It also makes it harder to apply any of these claims to other cases of disassociation. This is a specific phenomenon occurring within a specific moment of the history of both Egypt and the Brotherhood. The idea of disengagement is only actualized as discourse and process within these limits and without any claims on 'indeterminate fluid generality' that can apply my findings to disengagement from other movements. This does not mean that the scope cannot be expanded or successful tests cannot be completed because of the research. It is the opposite; the narrow scope is an attempt to make the findings 'less falsifiable'[46] and thus create a solid ground leading the way for other researchers, or perhaps myself, in the future to be 'tentatively' guided by them while testing disengagement from a general perspective.

The scope conditions even face another limitation related to the post-2011 time frame specification, that is the selected texts also belong to individuals who left the Brotherhood because of political and ideological disillusionment. Although the coming chapters discuss the 'micro'

---

[45] Lakoff, G., & Johnson, M. (1980). *Metaphors we live by* (p. x). London: University of Chicago Press.

[46] Harris, W. (1997). On "scope conditions" in sociological theories. *Social and Economic Studies, 46*(4), 123–127. Retrieved from http://www.jstor.org/stable/27866154.

levels of psychological and emotional factors as well as the 'meso' levels of organization and ideology, they remain hostage to the level of 'macro' political developments. The latter level is the one which triggers the articulation and materialization of the two other levels. This means that individuals who leave the Brotherhood for a variety of other reasons such as burnout, fatigue or maturation, and all other manners of mundane and traumatic life events are excluded, under-explored, or submerged within the line of enquiry that takes the 2011 events and all related political shifts as the point of departure. It is possible that those individuals who disengage for these politically led reasons are different from those who left the Brotherhood for other reasons, and this means that the sample is still not 'representative' of all members who exited from the Brotherhood since its creation in 1928. This adds to the aforementioned 'biases' still lurking in the issue of case selection and sampling as I am unable to systematically survey the population of Brotherhood members, or even those who have left the group since its foundation in 1928. Thus, and to reiterate, I do have to reemphasize that any arguments or conclusions made on the case under study are not unconstrained 'universal statements.' They are 'conditional statements' adjusted appropriately against all these limitations. To sum up, theoretical propositions gleaned from my research are not abstract and universal. They always have to refer to time and place among other specific circumstances in which these propositions are applicable.

MAPPING THE BOOK: AN OVERVIEW

The book includes four other chapters. Chapter 2 discusses, from a psycho-sociological perspective, the macro frame of 'affective disengagement.' It includes a discussion of challenges such as the detachment of the ex-member from the personal relationships that were involved in her or his participation in the Brotherhood. The exiting member here is conceptualized as socially embedded in loyalties, obligations, and identities that frame her or his engagement in and support for the Brotherhood. Therefore, the disengagement has to include attempts to end this embeddedness from what are described as 'real' and 'imagined' kinships. The chapter details attempts by the individuals to get away from the long process of de-individuation and Brotherhood-limited socialization that gave rise to values and views that correspond to those of the organization. The chapter includes interesting and intimate details of identity-making components related to assimilation and evaluation, such as how individuals act in their face-to-face encounters with existing members of the Brotherhood, which has long been given priority as basic symbolic elements of micromobilization, and sometimes even change their dress and hairstyles.

Chapter 3 deals with the macro frame of 'ideological disengagement,' in which individuals detail their disillusionment with the group's ideology, its current leaders, and most significantly, the legendary presence of its founder. The ideology, which had provided them with a sense of meaning in relation to the world, now conflicted with disaffection from the Brotherhood as involving a mindless authoritarianism. The chapter also investigates organizational barriers related to this ideology such as the 'spiritual contract' that ensured the dominance of the Brotherhood's ideology in the individual's perception of his environment and the religion itself. Along with such spiritual elements, the chapter also discusses physical barriers such as fears of reprisals and loss of protection, especially in terms of financial interaction with the group. Disengagement is associated with values such as respect for the mind and a rational choice process such as comparing costs against benefits.

Chapter 4 explores political disengagement, wherein ex-members linked their exiting to the events of 2011 and after, the period in which the Brotherhood rose and fell from power in a unique and unprecedented interval of change in Egyptian society and politics. During this time, the Brotherhood faced a moment in which it became an ineffective movement that could not achieve the changes it wanted and could no longer mobilize substantial support from its members. The chapter divides political disengagement into three stages: the Brotherhood before taking power, in power, and out of power. The level of continuing commitment is traced across these three stages, with the individuals in the study reviewing the magnitude of the investments they made in the group and the quality of the alternatives they could now see.

Chapter 5 combines *retrospective* and *real* analysis. It considers disengagement to be an entity that exists in the present but is in dialogue with the past. Meanings constructed in the presentist moment of narrating disengagement have a history, or exist in time. The chapter discusses two specific cases of disengagement before 2011. Again, this comparison is not meant to draw any causality or generalization about disengagement from the Brotherhood in general as both individuals cannot represent a sufficient comparison set of people who left the group before 2011. It is rather an attempt to test my hypothesis and validate my findings on describing and explaining disengagement as process and discourse. Both individuals, with whom I held open interview with one of them that continued for 60 hours, cited the same reasons which post-2011 members gave for departing the group, and the same patterns appear in their explanations. Nevertheless, they did not articulate or operationalize their experiences into *discourse* and *process* drawn on constructing it.

CONCLUSION

This chapter underlines that the book sets out the analysis of disengagement from the Muslim Brotherhood on three levels. The micro-level focuses on individual dispositions, which include affects and emotions related to exiting and dis-identification from the group. The meso-level deals with how each individual interacts with people outside the group and develops partly on this basis a meaningful interpretation allowing him to adopt new understanding of the Brotherhood's ideology and his relationships to the figures of its founder and current leaders. The macro-level links what is individual and organizational with what is broadly socio-political, by considering how the post-2011 era presented a window of opportunity for disengagement. Making use of frame analysis and CDA enables me to combine the linguistic with the extra-linguistic, in showing how individuals narrate their experiences and how the resultant meanings shape and are shaped by the context, continuities, and discontinuities in the personal histories.

BIBLIOGRAPHY

'Abdelrahman, M. (2009). 'With the Islamists?—Sometimes. With the state?—Never!' Cooperation between the left and Islamists in Egypt. *British Journal of Middle Eastern Studies, 36*(1), 37–54 (49–52). https://doi.org/10.1080/13530190902749556.

Al-Anani, K. (2016). *Inside the Muslim Brotherhood: Religion, identity, and politics.* Oxford: Oxford University Press.

Altier, M. B., Thoroughgood, C. N., & Horgan, J. G. (2014). Turning away from terrorism: Lessons from psychology, sociology, and criminology. *Journal of Peace Research, 51*(5), 647–661 (651). https://doi.org/10.1177/0022343314535946.

24   M. MENSHAWY

Aziz, M. (2017). Divisions widen between Muslim Brotherhood factions after policy reassessment initiative. Available via Ahramonline: https://bit.ly/2Uo27PI. Accessed 19 September 2018.

Benford, R. D., & Snow, D. A. (2000). Framing processes and social movements: An overview and assessment. *Annual Review of Sociology, 26*(1), 611–639.

Brown, N. J. (2012). *When victory is not an option: Islamist movements in Arab politics*. Ithaca and London: Cornell University Press.

Denoeux, G. (2002). The forgotten swamp: Navigating political Islam. *Middle East Policy, 9*(2), 56–81. https://doi.org/10.1111/1475-4967.00057.

Ebaugh, H. R. F. (1988). *Becoming an ex: The process of role exit*. Chicago: The University of Chicago Press Books.

Ehud, S. (1991). The process of delegitimation: Towards a linkage theory of political terrorism. *Terrorism and Political Violence, 3*, 50–68. https://doi.org/10.1080/09546559108427092.

El-Baquri, A. H. (1988). *Baqayya zekrayat* [Residues of memories]. Cairo: Al-Ahram Centre for Translation and Publishing.

El-Helbawy, K. (2012). *El-Helbawy announces his resignation on air*. Available via: https://bit.ly/2G0KYbE. Accessed 19 September 2018.

Entman, R. M. (1993). Framing: Toward clarification of a fractured paradigm. *Journal of Communication, 43*(4), 51–58.

Goffman, E. (1974). *Frame analysis: An essay on the organization of experience*. Cambridge: Cambridge Harvard University Press.

Hodges, A. (2011). *The "war on terror" narrative: Discourse and intertextuality in the construction and contestation of sociopolitical reality*. Oxford, UK: Oxford University Press.

Horgan, J. (2014). *The psychology of terrorism*. London and New York: Routledge.

Horgan, J. G. (2009). *Walking away from terrorism: Accounts of disengagement from radical and extremist movements*. London: Routledge.

Huddy, L. (2001). From social to political identity: A critical examination of social identity theory. *Political Psychology, 22*(1), 127–156.

Hunt, S. A., Benford, R. D., & Snow, D. A. (1994). Identity fields: Framing processes and the social construction of movement identities. *New social movements: From ideology to identity* (pp. 185–208). Philadelphia: Temple University Press.

Jaspal, R. (2013). Social psychological debates about identity. In R. Jaspal & G. M. Breakwell (Eds.), *Identity process theory: Identity, social action and social change* (pp. 1–19). Cambridge, UK: Cambridge University Press.

Jaspal, R., & Breakwell, G. M. (Eds.). (2014). *Identity process theory: Identity, social action and social change*. Cambridge, UK: Cambridge University Press.

Kandil, H. (2014). *Inside the Brotherhood.* Cambridge, UK: Polity Press.

Kar, M. (2010). *Reformist Islam versus radical Islam in Iran.* Brookings. Working Paper for Saban Center or Project on US Relations with the Islamic World. Washington, DC. Available via Brookings: https://brook. gs/2SQm9Re. Accessed 17 April 2018.

Lia, B. (2006). *The society of the Muslim Brothers in Egypt: The rise of an Islamic mass movement 1928–1942.* Reading, UK: Ithaca Press.

McAdam, D., Sidney, T., & Charles, T. (1996). *Towards an integrated perspective on social movements and revolution.* New York: Lazarsfeld Center at Columbia University.

Mead, G. H. (2015). *Mind, self & society.* Chicago: The University of Chicago Press.

Mellor, N. (2018). *Voice of the Muslim Brotherhood: Da'wa, discourse, and political communication.* London: Routledge.

Melucci, A. (1996). *Challenging codes: Collective action in the information age.* Cambridge: Cambridge University Press.

Melucci, R. (1989). *Nomads of the present: Social movements and individual needs in contemporary society.* Philadelphia: Temple University Press.

Mishler, E. (2006). Narrative and identity: The double arrow of time. In A. De Fina, D. Schiffrin, & M. Bamberg (Eds.), *Discourse and identity* (23rd ed., pp. 30–47). Cambridge, UK: Cambridge University Press.

Munson, Z. (2001). Islamic mobilization: Social movement theory and the Egyptian Muslim Brotherhood. *The Sociological Quarterly, 42*(4), 487–510.

No Author. (2006). *Terrorist recruitment: A commission's communication addressing the factors contributing to violent radicalisation.* European Commission. MEMO/05/329.

Polletta, F., & Jasper, J. M. (2001). Collective identity and social movements. *Annual Review of Sociology, 27*(1), 283–305.

Robinson, G. E. (1997). Can Islamists be democrats? The case of Jordan. *The Middle East Journal, 51*(3), 373–387.

Snow, D., Rochford, B., Jr., Worden, S., & Benford, R. (1986). Frame alignment processes, micromobilization, and movement participation. *American Sociological Review, 51*(4), 464–481.

Tarrow, S. (1996). States and opportunities: The political structuring of social movements. In *Comparative perspectives on social movements: Political opportunities, mobilizing structures, and cultural framings.* New York: Cambridge University Press.

Tarrow, S. (2011). *Power in movement: Social movements and contentious politics.* New York: Cambridge University Press.

Tilly, C. (2017). From mobilization to revolution. In E. Castañeda & C. L. Schneider (Eds.), *Collective violence, contentious politics, and social change.* New York: Routledge.

Trager, E. (2011). *The unbreakable Muslim Brotherhood: Grim prospects for a liberal Egypt*. The Washington Institute. Available via: https://bit.ly/2FZzBR7. Accessed 18 September 2018.

Wickham, C. R. (2004). The path to moderation: Strategy and learning in the formation of Egypt's Wasat Party. *Comparative Politics, 36*(2), 205–228.

Wickham, C. R. (2013). *The Muslim Brotherhood: Evolution of an Islamist movement*. Princeton, NJ: Princeton University Press.

Williams, R. (2016). *Resources of hope: Culture, democracy, socialism* (pp. 3–14). London: Verso.

York, E., Martini, J., & Kaye, D. (2012). *The Muslim Brotherhood, its youth, and implications for U.S. engagement*. Santa Monica: RAND Corporation.

Zimmerman, D. H., & Wieder, D. L. (2017). Ethnomethodology and the problem of order: Comment on Denzin. In J. D. Douglas (Ed.), *Understanding everyday life: Toward the reconstruction of sociological knowledge* (pp. 285–298). Chicago: Aldine Publishing.

Zollner, B. (2009). *The Muslim Brotherhood: Hasan al-Hudaybi and ideology*. New York: Routledge.

INTERVIEWEES (WHO ARE NOT PART
OF THE SAMPLE OF EX-MUSLIM BROTHERHOOD MEMBERS)

Ammar, N., a friend of Zainab El-Mahdy, Over Skype. 2 November 2014 (The destination is kept anonymous at the interviewee's request).

Sha'ban, M., a journalist and researcher on Islamist groups, in Person, Istanbul. 5, 6, 7 June 2016.

CHAPTER 2

Affective Disengagement

INTRODUCTION

The chapter groups, compares, and contrasts individual accounts in the narrative of ex-members of the Muslim Brotherhood, to identify frames tracing disengagement as a trend or aggregate of stages (a process).[1] Specifically, it traces these frames through the presence of 'affects' building one stage leading the final decision of departing from the group and which I call the macro frame of 'affective disengagement.'[2] 'Affect' as

---

[1] Jasper, J. (1998). The emotions of protest: Affective and reactive emotions in and around social movements. *Sociological Forum, 13*, 397–424. https://doi.org/10.102 3/a:1022175308081.

[2] I consider a frame as organizing the way in which each exiting member determines the meaning of her or his disengagement. To do so, they employ a common stock of 'key words, stock phrases, stereotyped images, sources of information and sentences that provide a thematically reinforcing cluster of facts and judgements' (Entman, R. M. [1993]. Framing: Towards a clarification of a fractured paradigm. *Journal of Communication, 43*(4), 51–58 [52]). Therefore, a frame is constructed from and embodied in 'keywords, metaphors, concepts, symbols, and visual images' emphasized or de-emphasized in the narrative. Frames 'can be detected by probing for particular words that consistently appear in the narrative and convey thematically constant meanings' across the texts and time (Entman, R. M. [1991]). Symposium framing US coverage of international news: Contrasts in narratives of the KAL and Iran air incidents. *Journal of Communication, 41*(4), 6–27 (7). By 'providing, repeating, and thereby reinforcing words' that reference some ideas but not others, frames 'work to make some ideas more salient in the text, others less so _and others entirely invisible', ibid. Thus, framing is about what Erving Goffman calls 'schemata of

© The Author(s) 2020   27
M. Menshawy, *Leaving the Muslim Brotherhood*, Middle East Today,
https://doi.org/10.1007/978-3-030-27860-1_2

an 'umbrella term' has the function to *aggregate*, grouping together all emotions, moods, and sentiments. It is an aggregation enough to expand the focus from a finely grained description of each kind of affective state to their overall presence and how they mediate between events and persons as part of the disengagement process.[3]

Following scholars such as Bert Klandermans's analysis of the 'affective' attachment to, and detachment from, social organizations by individuals,[4] the aim of the chapter is to look at how each individual got *affected* after an event has occurred that seems to impact her or his relationship with the Brotherhood, and how can we collectivize all of these 'affects' into related frames impinging upon the process of disengagement. Beyond steps of description and aggregation into frames, considering 'affect' can allow us grasping power dynamics while being negotiated, challenged, and contested by members and the group they seek to disassociate from. In the words of Michal Hardt, 'affect' illuminates 'both our power to affect the world around us and our power to be affected by it, along with the relation between these powers.'[5] In this sense, exiting members are not the only 'affect producers' as other actors, for example, the Brotherhood's leaders, could also join this

interpretation' that enable individuals 'to locate, perceive, identify, and label' occurrences and events within their life space (Goffman, Frame Analysis, p. 21). This means that frames can render occurrences and events 'meaningful' as they can 'organize experience and guide action, whether individual or collective.' Part of the purpose of the frame analysis in this chapter and the book as a whole is to unpack the underexplored 'individual frames' countering the 'collective frames' long entrenched by the group. A frame can be identified by empirically tracking a recurring pattern that realizes any of these functions: 'defining the problem,' 'diagnosing causes,' 'evaluating actions,' and 'prescribing solutions' (as part of what Entman calls 'selection and salience'). A group of frames that are discursively related and share some of these specific functions can be grouped into a 'master frame.'

[3] The aim is to group all of these elements as part of the 'affect' as an 'umbrella term' that is meant to encompass feelings of all sorts rather than to specify any of these feelings; see Dillard, J. P., & Seo, K. (2013). Affect and persuasion. In J. P. Dillard & L. Shen (Eds.), *The Sage handbook of persuasion: Developments in theory and practice* (pp. 150–166). Los Angeles: Sage.

[4] See Klandermans, B. (1997). *The social psychology of protest*. Oxford: Blackwell; Klandermans, B., & Mayer, N., (Eds.). (2006). *Extreme right activists in Europe: Through the magnifying glass.* New York: Routledge.

[5] Hardt, M. (2007). Foreword: What 'affects' are good for. In P. Clough & J. Halley (Eds.), *The affective turn: Theorizing the social* (pp. ix–xiii [ix]). Durham: Duke University Press.

production as part of a game of dominance and resistance.[6] Accordingly, frames building the 'affective' disengagement could be understood against another process in which the Brotherhood seeks to establish and bolster the 'affective engagement' of its members. For example, its founder Hassan El-Banna dedicated the first page of his seminal work, briefly known as *Al-Rasael* [The Epistles], to 'affect' outlined by him as such: The mission of the movement derives from 'hope', 'love', 'self-sacrifice' among other 'dominant emotions which gripped our hearts, unsettled our sleep and brought tears to our ears.'[7] El-Banna even made it clear that the success of his 'Islamic mission' cannot be done without a 'real awakening' in *Masha'ir* [which can be transliterated as emotions, sentiments, and feelings or 'affect' on aggregate].[8] In other words, if the Brotherhood's engagement is a movement into the direction of imposing a 'dominant' discourse centralizing and instrumentalizing 'affect,' disengagement is to be a movement in the opposite direction in which 'affect' is centralized and instrumentalized to challenge and resist.

The chapter employs a qualitative frame analysis of the narratives of ex-members whom I met in Turkey, Egypt, or the UK, and other ex-members whose autobiographies from the same period I analyzed (see Chapter 1). To add further contextualization to the accounts texted in interviews and autobiographies, constructing frames or identities drawn on them (e.g., the identity of an 'independent' narrator of one's own words) depend on 'potentialities' that supply both the 'affective' needs and the resources to realize them and that give individuals the affective ability to construct an autonomous identity. This contextualization allows me to triangulate the frame analysis with the critical discourse analysis (the triangulation is fully detailed and explained in Chapter 1). This means each frame is always situated as part of a text, as a 'discursive

---

[6]This fits in with the broad definition of affect as a 'multifaceted phenomenon' grouping both internal and external representations of disengagement. It can relate to 'changes in ourselves, circulating through our bodies and subjectivities,' at the same time that they are about 'the modulations of the environment' of each individual that have to be taken into account; Fillieule, O. (2015). Disengagement from radical organizations: A process and multilevel model of analysis. In P. G. Klandermans & C. van Stralen (Eds.), *Movements in times of democratic transition* (p. 47). Pennsylvania: Temple University Press.

[7]El-Banna, H. (1990). *Majmu't rasael al-imam al-shahid Hassan El-Banna* [A collection of epistles of the martyr Imam Hassan El-Banna] (p. 18). Alexandria: Da'wa.

[8]Ibid., p. 132. El-Banna even complained that people analyzing *Da'wa* initiatives abandon 'affect-related' elements and 'psychological incentives,' ibid.

practice' relating it with frames from other texts, and as a 'social practice' in which dynamics of power, resistance, and the availability of resources, opportunities are added to the discussion as factors facilitating or inhibiting the 'affective' disassociation from the group.

This analysis comes with the caveat that the chapter is neither about reaching 'truth' of disengagement, nor the cause-and-effect relationships between stories and the disengagement event, so much as the forms of 'meaningful connectedness' as constructed by the participants in their narratives. I treat these narratives broadly as 'sites of reflection, critique, self-making, self-theorizing, and collectivization,'[9] which ultimately construct a whole 'discourse of disengagement' and the process leading to or moving in parallel with it. This signals that the analysis pays a higher attention to many details or 'domains of affect' relating to subjective experience, behavioral actions such as handshake and hairstyle, and motivations at life and work as long as they can all catch what is 'affective' in the narrativization.[10]

The chapter begins with explaining the restrictions imposed by the Brotherhood and its affiliated circles of socialization in order to hinder disengagement from the group. These restrictions induce tools of an 'affective' engagement evolving on ties with the 'real kinship' represented by the wife, parents, and children, and ties with the 'imagined kinship' mainly represented by friends. Both levels of kinship augment engagement with the group as they submerge the individual and his 'personal identity' symbolized by the 'I' into a collective identity best symbolized by the 'we.'[11] The latter is a pronoun of solidarity conducive to engagement with the group and at the same time, a pronoun of dominance restricting the individual's ability to recover a sense of personal autonomy—or in the words of Alberto Melucci to become an 'autonomous subject of actions.'[12] This autonomy, which can equally be

---

[9]Pollock, D. (1999). *Telling bodies performing birth: Everyday narratives of childbirth* (p. 187). New York: Columbia University Press.

[10]See Dillard, J. P., & Seo, K. (2013). Affect and persuasion, pp. 150–166.

[11]This submergence comes as part of the general logic of collective identities which is 'precisely that they are forged through the erasure of internal differences' where the personal identity can be nurtured and expressed. Sayyid, S. (2003). *A fundamental fear: Eurocentrism and the emergence of Islamism* (p. viii). London: Zed Books Ltd. Sayyid argues that 'this is the case of any collective identity [including] Islam,' ibid.

[12]Melucci, A. (2002). Becoming a person: New frontiers for identity and citizenship in a planetary society. In M. Kohli & A. Woodward (Eds.), *Inclusions and exclusions in European societies* (pp. 71–85). London: Routledge.

symbolized by the pronoun 'I,' could provide the individual with the ability to independently select his own social milieu in which the act disengagement can be both induced and nurtured and the Brotherhood's 'affective tools be neutralized.' Therefore, the first section demonstrates how an exiting member has to lose the 'we' as one step leading to the second chapter in which I explain how she or he can gain the 'I.'

LOSING THE 'WE': THE REAL KINSHIP

A 'salient' frame emerges as experiences, anecdotes, and events in the texts of exiting members magnified the role of spouses as a key component of the depicted reality of disengagement. Indeed, if the 'essence of framing is sizing, i.e.; magnifying or shrinking elements of the depicted reality,'[13] this factor is of utmost importance especially among male exiters.

The Wife Factor

The word 'wife' is used repeatedly and together with other words making engagement and disengagement a 'family business.' The wife's influence includes her being a key partner in a 'dyadic' kind of reciprocal interaction based on daily face-to-face exchanges where both individuals feel the 'attention' of the other and also 'co-construct' their experiences.[14] Mohamed 'Affan, who exited the group in 2011 after 14 years of membership, is an example. Meeting him in a café overlooking the hustle and bustle of a square located in the middle of Istanbul, 'Affan, who disengaged mainly for political and ideological reasons (see Chapters 3 and 4) took as his first hurdle to overcome his wife's reaction to his decision to leave. He recounts this as follows:

> It was hard for my wife to accept my decision. She said, 'Our family life was almost based on membership in the group. We even designed our house to accord with our membership, something you can tell by the number of Qur'an copies and prayer beads that we kept for the weekly

---

[13] Entman, Symposium framing US coverage of international news, p. 11

[14] Zahavi, D. (2015). You, me, and we: The sharing of emotional experiences. *Journal of Consciousness Studies*, *22*(1–2), 84–101.

Brotherhood gatherings in it... How can you abandon all of that?' she kept asking me with tearful eyes.[15]

Such wife-related pressures were very much encouraged by the Brotherhood. The group would rely on the wife as the first line of influence and strategy by interconnecting 'reform of the Muslim nation' with the 'reform of the woman.'[16] The group also enhances a 'husband–wife similarity'[17] type of marriage as one of the functions most assigned to female members that was that of marrying a 'Brother.' This fits a notion of an incipient nation imagined as a family and understood to be held together as such by Islam since they both have the mission of creating the 'Muslim house' as the nucleus of the covered 'Muslim nation.'[18]

[15]'Affan, M. (2017). The wife refers to norms under the Brotherhood which requires members to meet every week. Melucci defines norms as 'the point at which operational needs (the allocation of resources) come together with the needs of integration and control (power)' (cited in Al-Anani, K. [2016]. *Inside the Muslim Brotherhood: Religion, identity and politics* [p. 119]. Oxford: Oxford University Press). Therefore, it is symbolically significant that the wife evokes the 'house,' 'praying carpets,' and 'prayer beads' as physical resources through which the group controls the husband's sense of integration and social belonging.

[16]In his seminal work, *Al-Rasayyel*, El-Banna took as one of the *Arkan* [cornerstones or principles] of the oath of allegiance is that a male member of the Brotherhood has to 'pick the right wife, push her towards her rights and duties, ... and direct her towards the principles of Islam.' The wife's role increases by giving priority to raising children 'on the principles of Islam'; El-Banna, Majmu't rasael Al-Imam, p. 394.

[17]The marriage types inside the Brotherhood belong more to the 'husband–wife similarities' theory (hypothesized on 'birds of a feather') rather than 'complementariness' theory (hypothesized on 'opposites attract'). As both share belonging to a more collectivized grouping, husband–wife correlations could be presumed to be higher especially as they share same activities, habits, and even personality traits nurtured by the group as part of identity-making processes. Nias, D. K. B. (1977). Husband–wife similarities. *Social Science*, 52(4), 206–211. Available via: http://0-www.jstor.org.library.qnl.qa/stable/41886198. Accessed 22 October 2018.

[18]El-Banna, Majmu't rasael Al-Imam, p. 394. Kandil, H. (2015). *Inside the Brotherhood* (p. 74). Malden: Polity Press. What comes to mind is the family of El-Banna himself as a representative of this way of thinking. El-Banna married one of his daughters to Said Ramadan, who became as one of the Brotherhood's main leaders in the 1950s. Ramadan re/established branches of the movement in countries such as Jordan, Syria, Lebanon, Saudi Arabia, and Switzerland. One of his two sons is Tariq Ramadan, a prominent Muslim scholar and is a Professor of Contemporary Islamic Studies at St Antony's College, Oxford. His other son, Hani Ramadan, is the director of the Islamic Center of Geneva and the author of several books and newspaper articles on Islam.

The Brotherhood has always encouraged intermarriage among its members,[19] and a leader of the group even warned that for a Brother to marry a non-Brotherhood member would delay reaching the coveted 'victory' of the group and realizing its goal of establishing Islam as a comprehensive order.[20] What intermarriage does is the ability to turn any possible independence of the individual from the Brotherhood, exactly as any objective relation of membership in a political or social group could be, into a full interdependence drawn on the husband–wife relationship or the husband–wife–children ties. Ahmed 'Abdel-Gawwad is a case in point, a 41-year-old Cairene who left the group in 2011. He is the child of parents who have been members of the Brotherhood. 'Abdel-Gawwad 'depended' on the Brotherhood to marry him to another member of the Brotherhood, a young lady whose father was also a leading figure in the group. This marriage, arranged within the group, enhanced the intensity of the social relationships tying him to the Brotherhood and brought 'Abdel-Gawwad closer to it through what Donatella de Porta calls a 'strong emotional position' based on 'absolute human relationships' that can impose 'solidarity even over the little things' and increase 'renunciation' by reducing interaction with people outside either the family or the Brotherhood.[21] With this family expansion and 'emotional sharing' encompassing 'the other as participating, with me, in that experience,'[22] a strong tension seems to have existed for him and many in the Brotherhood between the possibility of an individuated self and the reality of one that was highly assimilated to the expectations of those around them especially spouses.

---

[19]'Essam-Eddin, M. (2012, June 22). *Al-Ikhwan wal Akhawat 'Eila Wahda* [The brothers and sisters: One family], Al-Shabab. Available via: http://shabab.ahram.org.eg/News/4000.aspx. Accessed 26 May 2019. See also Abdel-Hady, F. (2011). *Rihlati ma' al-Akhawat al-Muslemat* [My journey with the female Muslim Brotherhood members]. Cairo: Dar Al-Shorouk.

[20]Subhi Saleh yantaqed zawaj al-Ikhwani min gheir al—Akhawat [Subhi Saleh criticizes a male member marrying a non-member who is not a sister], Youtube. Accessed 10 May 2019.

[21]Della Porta, D. (2008). Leaving underground organizations. In T. Bjorgo & J. Horgan (Eds.), *Leaving terrorism behind: Individual and collective disengagement* (pp. 66–87 [81–82]). London: Routledge.

[22]Hobson, R. P., & Hobson, J. (2014). On empathy: A perspective from developmental psychopathology. In H. Maibom (Ed.), *Empathy and morality* (pp. 172–192 [188]). Oxford: Oxford University Press.

Discipline and Punishment

The policies of the Brotherhood to augment intermarriage and give primacy to the 'wife' factor are not about building this 'affective engagement' per se. The Brotherhood had another incentive in encouraging this endogamy: it would serve as a form of discipline keeping members in line through intimate social control, and this discipline would also forestall the disengagements it always had to fear. In accordance with the teachings and literature of the group itself,[23] wives were even encouraged to keep an eye on their 'Brother' spouses and report disapproved activities and instances of vice.[24] An investigative committee once warned a troublesome member who had objected to his seniors' decision to punish him in a way that turned his domestic life upside down: 'Remember, you have your wife and kids with us.'[25] There are many examples of Brotherhood wives acting to defend, against their husbands if need be, the collective norms of the group.[26]

'Eid came under pressure from his wife, his marital relationship involving 'a whole year of tension,' in the aftermath of his disengagement. The wife, Azza Afify, reported that she suffered from a 'psychological crisis' due to his decision and the group's pressure on her to convince her husband to stay.[27] She said: 'The main pressure came from

[23] The group seeks woman as having a significant role mainly as a wife and a mother. As put by Labiba Ahmed, one of the first female leaders in the 1930s and as applauded by El-Banna himself who cited her speech: 'The basis of reforming the nation is reforming the family, and the basis of reforming the family is reforming the girl. A woman is the master of the world. She rocks the cradle by her right hand and rocks the world by her left hand'; El-Banna, *Muzakerat al-d'awa wal da'ia*, p. 202.

[24] Kandil, *Inside the Brotherhood*, p. 74; The Brotherhood founded the Muslim Sisters as a framework for recruiting and training female activists. According to their first pamphlet published in 1947, the goals of the Sisters 'is to take part in social jihad, or struggle aimed at the establishment of Islamic social justice, and ensuring that families retained values based on Islam'; see Rosen, E. (2008). The Muslim Brotherhood's concept, taken from Zaki, M. S. (1980). *Al-Ikhwan al-Muslimun wa-al-mujtama' al-Misri* [The Muslim Brotherhood and Egyptian society] (pp. 195–198). Cairo: Dar al-Ansar.

[25] 'Eid, S. (2013). *Tajribati fi saradeeb Al-Ikhwan* [My experience in the basements of MB] (p. 42). Cairo: Jazeerat al-Ward.

[26] The Brotherhood encouraged women to 'reform their family' and prevent any 'ethical degradation' at the level of her family, and this mission is described in the literature of the group as one of 'the most sacred missions'; El-Banna, *Muzakerat al-d'awa wal da'ia*, p. 202.

[27] YouTube. (2017). *Shahed...Qissat zawjaeen taaebayen min Al-Ikhwan yakshefan asrar al-tanzeem* [Watch... Story of a couple of two repentants from the Brotherhood revealing

the Brotherhood, which excluded and ostracized us to the extent that I thought I had no option but to divorce my husband.'[28] Tareq Aboul-Sa'd, 50 years old, felt such 'marital' pressures when he disengaged in 2011 after a 26-year membership. 'My wife [who was still a member of the Brotherhood] was really sad and angry with me at the same time. She said that I would not be a good Muslim and would not keep my full commitment to Islam or its practices such as prayers.'[29]

The case of Kamal El-Helbawy, 79 years old, and a leading figure in the group before disengaging from it after more than 60 years of membership, is indicative of the workings of 'wifely' power. I managed to interview both El-Helbawy and his wife, Zainab Mustafa, in their house in London. 'When my husband announced his resignation from the Brotherhood on the air in 2012, many other female members began to ask me to divorce him. "Why do you continue living with him?"' said Mustafa, who is today a leading member of the group's female section in London.[30] Again, this request is not an anomaly as accords with the rules of the Brotherhood pertaining to the organization of family relationships.[31] As she continued her membership in the Brotherhood, and

the secrets of the group]. Al-Arabiya. Available via: https://goo.gl/Dsmdpn. Accessed 21 October 2018.

[28] Ibid.

[29] Aboul-Sa'd, T. (2017). This reaction can also be understood as part of the duties of the wife who is also a member of the Brotherhood. In other words, by making this accusation to her husband, Aboul-Sa'd's wife carries out her duty as a committed member of the group. El-Banna outlined in his memoirs that the Brotherhood's Minhaj [platform] includes calls for every member to apply the 'Aqida [faith] of the group, which he said is fully taken from Islam, 'inside her/his house despite all forms of hardship' which might encompass this step. Even if this would destabilize her relationship with her husband, the wife has to maintain its position and estrangement because he 'does not apply the rules of Islam inside his house' and because this is part of her 'Jihad with a price and sacrifice' as El-Banna called it; see El-Banna, *Muzakerat al-d'awa wal da'ia*, pp. 179, 240.

[30] Mustafa, Z. (2017).

[31] According to the dominant discourse of the Brotherhood, El-Helbawy would be in charge of his family not only as a breadwinner, but also as a keeper of its commitment toward both the Brotherhood and Islam. A proof of this sanctified intractability of relationships is in many documents including the one called *Aqidatena* [Our Faith] written by the Guidance Bureau: 'The Muslim is responsible for his family, and it is his duty to keep its righteousness, its ethics and its faith. I do undertake to do my best to realize this and to spread the teachings of Islam among members of my family…,' El-Banna, *Muzakerat al-d'awa wal da'ia*, p. 214.

still expresses 'sadness and shock' over her husband's decision, she did not stop exercising these pressures, if subtly, including reminding him of the original and long-standing connection between their marriage and the Brotherhood, as other wives also did. Looking to El-Helbawy confidently from the armchair of their house in London after she joined the interview: 'Had the Brotherhood not introduced us, we would not have met or gotten married, since I was living in Egypt and Kamal [her husband] was living in London.'[32] She nonetheless publicly, if reluctantly, supported her husband's disengagement.

Furthermore, the wives have supported their husbands by not objecting when their partners left the movement in a 'highly vocal way'; the couple would then typically show that they shared the same 'affects' of disengagement.[33] The above quote from Afify, 'Eid's wife, is taken from her appearance in an interview with *Al-Arabiya*, one of the most watched pan-Arab news stations. She even used the same language adopted by 'Eid himself, such as describing the disengagement using the same expression, detailed below, of membership as 'being in prison.' The couple in the interview would collaborate in replying, each completing, as they sat together on their sofa in Cairo, sentences started by the other, and using the same forms and figures of speech. El-Helbawy also appeared with his wife (Mustafa) on a flagship Egyptian television show, essentially to offer her personal support by supporting his narrative. Mustafa, sitting next to El-Helbawy, when asked about the pressures on her husband, said simply, 'I respect his decision on disengagement.'[34] The effect was to confirm the definitiveness of his departure. Yet, both with me and in some of his appearances on television with his wife, El-Helbawy would break into tears showing how hard the decision to disengage had been.[35]

---

[32] Ibid.

[33] Klandermans, B. (2015). Disengaging from movements. In J. Goodwin & J. Jasper (Eds.), *The social movements Reader*. Chichester: Wiley-Blackwell.

[34] YouTube. (2013). *Munadhrah nareyah bayn Kamal El-Helbawy wa zawjatuh al-Ekhwaneyah* [A hot debate between Kamal El-Helbawy and his Ikhwani wife]. Available via: https://www.youtube.com/watch?v=obLKZm4dGsU. Accessed 25 November 2018.

[35] YouTube. (2014). *Buka al-dictoor Kamal al-Hilbawi bisbab johood al-Ikhwan* [Crying of Dr. Kamal al-Hilbawi due to the ingratitude of Muslim Brotherhood members]. Available via: https://www.youtube.com/watch?v=QZGcVUWJz4I&t=12s, https://www.youtube.com/watch?v=RNq2x1_uTHE. Accessed 18 October 2018.

All these cases mentioned above are the 'luckier' cases. Disengagement becomes more costly when exiting members are not supported or accompanied by spouses and families. Many ex-members got divorced and found that their 'martial life was almost in ruins' as husbands decided to exit the group against their wives' will.[36] Mustafa, the wife of El-Helbawy, mentioned 'many family relationships which I know collapsed under such pressures.'[37] As the head of the 'Muslim women's society in London,' she said she knew of many such cases from her wide contacts among female Muslim Brotherhood members.

The Mother/Father Factor

The wife exerts pressures not only in her capacity as a marriage partner responsible for guaranteeing the commitment of other members of her 'Muslim' family. These pressures also have to do with her being a 'mother.' Given the importance of the mother in Egyptian society, a woman typically has almost exclusive responsibility for taking care of the children during their formative years.[38] Although this means more work for the wife and mother, it also confers on her more 'affective power.' As Sharon Hays puts it, there is an 'ideology of intensive mothering,'[39] which 'declares that mothering is exclusive, wholly child-centered, emotionally involving, and time-consuming.'[40] This has meant that a woman's disengagement tended to heavily impact her children, who would be most emotionally attached to their mother, though she might in fact be emotionally more attached to the Brotherhood. A departing father might find his children taking the side of his wife in a dispute about exiting, and departing wives would portend saddling the father with childcare tasks that he would find burdensome or for which he was ill-prepared.

[36]'Affan, M. (2017).

[37]Mustafa, Z. (2017).

[38]Bell, S. (2006). Becoming a mother after DES: Intensive mothering in spite of it all. *Discourse and identity* (pp. 233–252 [233]). https://doi.org/10.1017/cbo9780511584459.012.

[39]Hays, S. (1996). *The cultural contradictions of motherhood*. New Haven: Yale University Press.

[40]Arendell, T. (2000). Conceiving and investigating otherhood: The decade's scholarship. *Journal of Marriage and Family, 62,* 1192–1207 (1194). https://doi.org/10.1111/j.1741-3737.2000.01192.x.

This is how 'Affan remembers part of his wife's argument to dissuade him from the exit: 'She reminded me how our children were part of the Brotherhood junior groups and they always played with other children with the same affiliation.'[41] There is no wonder that some exiting members, as I understood during my research over four years, were estranged from their wives and children as well. Practically, many members prefer to remain in the Brotherhood to avoid these pressures and associated 'goal conflict,'[42] that is, the goal of losing the group would negatively impact on the goal of keeping relations with the wife and children intact. As Tareq El-Beshbeshy, a 53-year-old who had been a member for 20 years, said: 'I could not risk my exit without the acceptance of my wife and my children.'[43]

All these pressures create what Dan Zahavi calls 'constitutive interdependence'[44] through which the wife, the husband, and the children share their belonging to the Brotherhood through affective bonds also linking each of them together. However, this bonding of 'interdependence' is not fully based on 'communicative dialogue' where the 'I' and 'we' can be reciprocated and exchanged as part of mutual engagement. It is a relation more of dominance than of reciprocity as the Brotherhood, and all attached tools of socialization including the biological family, seek to impose unification and *interlocked* identification of the 'I' as a subservient part of the 'we.'[45]

[41] 'Affan, M. (2017).

[42] 'Goal conflict' arises when the 'personal goal' that has a 'special individual character' such as the desire to disengage from the Brotherhood gets in tension with the 'activating potential' of situations and relations with others dictating competing goals such as to maintain relations with his wife and children, Staub, E. (1978). Predicting prosocial behavior: A model for specifying the nature of personality–situation interaction. *Perspectives in interactional psychology* (pp. 87–110 [90–93]). Boston, MA: Springer. Lexically, the word 'goal' itself carries this 'internal–external' interaction. A 'goal' implies a 'preference for certain outcomes or end states' (e.g., breaking the engagement with the Brotherhood) and at the same time it implies 'an aversion for certain outcomes or the desire to avoid them (e.g., the outcome of breaking the marital engagement), ibid.

[43] El-Beshbeshy, T. (2017).

[44] Zahavi, D. (2015). You, me, and we, pp. 84–101.

[45] As evidence of this unification and interlocked identification, many of the interviewees identified the date of their engagement with the group at the moment of their birth, 'I was born a Muslim Brotherhood member like my parents and siblings' is a repeated

Remarkably, individuals exiting the group are fully aware of this inter-locking, and some of them take the 'sense of togetherness' caused by it with them in the process of disengagement. In other words, they *disengage* together exactly as they once *engaged* together. In many cases, to be sure, the wife of a man who had recently disengaged would follow him in this. The reasons were sometimes simply practical, involving various inconveniences including pressure from the group. A. Z., 51 years old, joined the group when invited by her elder brother, and left 20 years later in 2012 following her husband. Although 'he gave me the freedom to continue,' she reports, 'he kept talking to me about problems and contradictions inside the Brotherhood, which made me rethink and led me to disengage.'[46] Aboul-Sa'd's wife reproached and ridiculed him for leaving at first, but eventually left herself after realizing that, as he says, 'I had been right.' S.E., 28 years old, still living in Egypt, followed his father in disengaging in 2011; his mother, 'who attempted to dissuade both of us from such a step, followed suit two years later.'[47]

Still, these cases of cordial or coordinated disengagement do not represent the whole picture. There are cases where pressures from family members turn into severe physical punitive measures to abort any potential desires for exiting the group. I.'O., 24 years old at the time he exited the group in May 2015, said that his father had blocked all of his previous attempts to exit the group. On one occasion, I.'O. decided to leave a meeting with a Brotherhood member because of his objection to the orders he was being given. 'My father was really aggressive and also kicked me out of the house for one night. He warned me that he would do that permanently if I did not listen to the orders of my prefect.'[48] The father had always controlled his son's network of friends, and would 'ask me to talk to this individual and not to talk to other individuals.'[49] I.'O. said, 'I kept pleading with my father, saying that I could not continue to be a member of a group led by corrupt people. My father got

---

phrase. Other researchers found the same pattern such as Al-Anani, K., *Inside the Muslim Brotherhood*, p. 80.

[46] A.Z. (2017).

[47] S.E. (2017).

[48] I.'O. (2017).

[49] Ibid.

angry, and told me that I should show respect to what he called 'your brothers.'[50] I.'O. left the Brotherhood when his father was imprisoned, and said that he moved to Turkey because 'otherwise [without such distance] it would have been harder to disobey my father.'[51]

The Whole Family Factor: Status and Role

As families generally were expected to and did consider their identification with the organization as central to the identities of their members, many ex-members share fears that exiting the Brotherhood would destabilize the 'role and status' of the family both inside and outside the group.[52] In my two interviews with him conducted over a total of six hours, 40-year-old Ahmed Nazily, who exited the group in 2011 after 35 years of membership, more than once paused in his scathing diatribe against the Brotherhood to mention the role both his parents had played at critical junctures of the Brotherhood's history. He recommended that, to know more about him, I read a book that referred to the 'great' activities performed by his mother that led her to detention under Nasser. He also made similar 'role and status' references to his wife: 'My father-in-law was a big name in the Brotherhood as he was a senior figure in Cairo at the end of Hassan El-Banna's era.'[53] He reported that during his childhood, he would make use of his family's 'role and status' to 'prestigiously and boastfully identify myself'[54] in conversations with Brotherhood members and the leaders, and with people on the outside. 'I still remember this sense of admiration and respect in the eyes of other

---

[50] Ibid.

[51] Ibid.

[52] See Parsons, T., & Bryan, S. T. (2005). *The social system.* London: Taylor & Francis. I adopt this term from Talcott Parsons, who argued that the basic unit of the social system was the 'status-role' bundle. A status is a structural position within the social system, and a role is what the individual who has that status does. For example, 'brother' or 'sister' could refer to a status, and there are certain roles that are generally associated with these statuses. Further, to bring Parsons' conceptualizations into relevance, individuals in this system are weaker actors, as they have to fulfill certain system functions and take on various roles in order to maintain order in the system. The system has its own social control 'mechanisms' which are 'forestalling and reversing the deep-lying tendencies for deviance'; see ibid., pp. 319–320.

[53] Nazily, A. (2017).

[54] Ibid.

members or leaders once I mentioned my full name. That really made me happy and proud of my family connection at the time.'[55]

Again, all these emotions cannot be separated from the organizational dynamics of recruitment and mobilization inside the Brotherhood. The group had long entangled the 'religious' with the 'traditional' as it focused its recruitment campaigns partly on building networks of patronage via, for instance, inviting local elites as guests at the group's events, as it sought the support of dignitaries who wielded influence and patronage.[56] El-Banna, the Brotherhood's founder, would encourage sons of *'Ayyan* [prominent families] with 'traditional social standing' to join the society, expecting that then the family or the clan would be linked to the Brotherhood.[57] This would in turn tend to make the family's internal ties more restrictive on its members. Mohamed Aboul-Gheit, whom I met in London, where he has worked as a journalist since exiting the group in 2011, described his father as a distinguished figure in the group and a well-respected and famous medical doctor of 'high social standing' in the Governorate of Asyut where he lives. He said boastfully that his grandfather was the chairperson of the engineers syndicate branch in the town and at the same time was one of the first two individuals who were selected to join the Brotherhood after its foundation.[58]

Against this background, the pressures drawn on claims of defending societal role and status and drawn on such 'family tree' connections to the Brotherhood open the door to more family members other than parents, spouses, or siblings. The pressures could come from extended family members such as uncles. For example, in the case of A.S.R., a 31-year-old who exited the group in 2012 after 14 years of membership, pressure came from his uncle, who was 'one of the hawks' or traditionalists of the movement. A.S.R. was blamed by other family members for 'shaming' his uncle and being a 'disgrace' in the face of the uncle's record of commitment.[59]

Social pressures such as divorce or estrangement threats, or accusations of undermining the family's role and status inside and outside the Brotherhood could be translated into 'affective' pressures. One form of

[55] Ibid.

[56] Banna, *Muzakerat al-d'awa wal da'ia.* pp. 80–81.

[57] Lia, *Society of Muslim Brothers in Egypt*, p. 135.

[58] Aboul-Gheit, M. (2017).

[59] A.S.R. (2017).

this 'affect' relates to the inculcation of shame.[60] Shame can be defined as 'seeing [the] self negatively through the eyes of others, such as feeling rejected, unworthy and inadequate.'[61] Shame may be treated as a 'class name' for a family of emotions and feelings wherein the self is viewed negatively through the eyes of others; these can include fear, embarrassment, humiliation, or rejection.[62] Shame can thus impede or fully abort the potentiality of disengagement in two ways. First, it has the power of enforcing a 'destructive conformity' where an individual has to conceal her or his objections and suspicions as well as the desire to depart the group in order to avoid any sense of 'otherness' or exclusion.[63] Secondly, as a 'social emotion,' shame associates with the group's principles and policies based on 'blind obedience' (see Chapter 3) as the shamed individual has to 'court favour with their superiors and avoid being rejected for not complying with requests or orders.'[64] Nazily is a case in point. His father had been a leading figure on the Brotherhood's *Shura Council.* 'My father,' Nazily recalled, 'was really psychologically traumatized.'[65] He may even have had to give up some of his duties inside the Brotherhood 'as a consequence of my behavior, which led to the disengagement from the group.' He was aware of the embarrassment that his departure had caused his father. He said that he had caused his father 'humiliation,' as his father had to announce the group's decision to sack his son to the media: 'That was really harsh and I do believe that it was part of a psychological warfare launched by the group against me,'[66] he added. This serves one main function of shame, which is to signal trouble in one's personal relationships. Nazily said that his relationship with his father became especially strained 'when the group's leaders launched a smear campaign tarnishing

[60]Sabini, J., Garvey, B., & Hall, A. L. (2001). Shame and embarrassment revisited. *Personality and Social Psychology Bulletin, 27,* 104–117.

[61]Scheff, T. (2003). Shame in self and society. *Symbolic Interaction 26,* 239–262 (254). https://doi.org/10.1525/si.2003.26.2.239.

[62]Ibid., pp. 239, 245.

[63]Deonna, J. A., Rodogno, R., & Teroni, F. (2012). *In defense of shame: The faces of an emotion* (p. 22).Oxford: Oxford University Press.

[64]Gilbert, P. (2003). Evolution, social roles, and the differences in Shame and Guilt. *Social Research,* 1205–1230 (1225).

[65]Nazily, A. (2017). See also Scheff, Shame in self and society, pp. 239, 251.

[66]Nazily, A. (2017).

my image.'[67] He described one of the confrontations he had then with his father:

> My father came to me after exiting the group, saying, "Is it true that you got hundreds of thousands of dollars from an organization which is based abroad?" I told him: 'My father, you know me, your son; can you believe such a rumor?'.[68]

It is a case where both the father and the son shared feelings of shame as they were both involved in the disengagement decision, one disengaging and the other announcing the disengagement.

LOSING THE 'WE': IMAGINED KINSHIP

Kinship for Brotherhood members tended to have an imaginary dimension that could equate with the 'biological' kinship relationship in terms of order, intensity, or even affective attachment. It meant that relationships with other members might be treated like familial ones. One can argue that a prefect (the person in direct authority over each member and his first point of contact) is more important and influential than a parent. A prefect might provide 'protection, social insurance, and a warm and relaxing environment; in short, a haven from the larger world.'[69] He might be able to access the individual's 'stock of meanings,' making him and other leaders more capable of controlling and exploiting members.[70] A prefect would conduct a personal interview with his 'brother' on a weekly and even daily basis, in an intimate and ongoing relationship that could be compared in its intensity and force to psychiatric interviews in semi-clinical conditions,[71] with the prefect asking the member for a detailed account of his thoughts and feelings, desires and doubts.

[67] Ibid.

[68] Nazily, A. (2017).

[69] Ibid., pp. 9–10.

[70] This control of the prefect through friendship begins even at the early stages of recruitment marked with 'chasing the prey.' Al-Anani explains his description as that the recruiter (the hunter) 'infiltrates' the potential member (the prey)'s 'private life and initiate a persistent but gradual psychological and ideological change that leads him to join the movement,' Al-Anani, *Inside the Muslim Brotherhood*, p. 70.

[71] Lasswell, H. (1927). The theory of political propaganda. *American Political Science Review, 21*(3), 627–631 (628). https://doi.org/10.2307/1945515.

Ahmed Ban, a 50-year-old man who had been a member for 22 years until his resignation in October 2011 put it thus: 'Your prefect in the Brotherhood dominates the member's life. He is the one who is closer to you than your mother or father and whom you consult on everything related to your life decisions such as whom to marry, what to study, where to work, and even where to travel.'[72]

Membership in the Brotherhood could thus be more inclusive and emotionally engaging than 'real kinship.' The prefect, who sometimes was also a member of the person's real family, as one outcome of the recruitment dynamics inside the Brotherhood as indicated above, would play a key role in both interpersonal and collective identity, affecting the individual as member of both a family-like relationship and the group as a whole. This could mean that the private and public life of the member are undistinguished. As most members are also recruited at younger ages, their parents also give up their ability to *role model* particular 'lifestyles' if they want to. Prefects are the ones who take up the role as well as 'parental' obligations.[73] The 'prefect' and other leaders of the group now role model on 'how to be a Brother.' Organizationally, much was also done to inculcate a sense of belonging to and sharing the group identity drawn on this 'imagined kinship.' For example, the *jawalla* or 'Rover Scouts' created in the 1930s, which would aim to strengthen these in-group sentiments by 'embarking on tours, reviving thereby the Islamic tradition of mutual visits [*Sunnat Al-Tazawur*]'[74]; they served as 'a fundamental factor in moulding a strong sense of community and group cohesion within the Society'[75] and in enhancing the Brotherhood's tools of control.[76]

---

[72] Ban, A. (2013). *Al-Ikhwan Al-Muslimoon wa mehnat al-watan wal deen* [The Muslim Brotherhood and the predicament of nation and religion]. Cairo: Al-Neel Centre for Strategic Studies.

[73] Purgin, E. (2012). Hey, how did I become a role model? Privacy and the extent of role-model obligations. *Journal of Applied Philosophy, 29*(2), 118–132 (122).

[74] Lia, *Society of Muslim Brothers in Egypt*, p. 102.

[75] Ibid.

[76] Al-Anani noted that these visits, among other social activities such as giving gifts and making regular phone calls, are one of the main tools of the Brotherhood's recruitment strategy based on building a 'personal relationship with the potential member.' It is a tool of control as the recruiter also 'permeates the individual's private sphere,' Al-Anani, Inside the Muslim Brotherhood, p. 75.

The intensity of the group's 'imagined kinship' and other claims on the member's identity could leave departing members feeling an affective vacuum.' To the question, 'What are the things you have most missed since exiting the Brotherhood?' the answer invariably was, 'My [Brotherhood] friends' including the prefect. The answer similarly was invariably 'my friends' when ex-members were asked, 'In one sentence describe to me your membership in the group.'[77] Ahmed Ramzy said that the hardest feeling that he experienced in the exiting process was losing his Brotherhood friends, who 'had always been closer to me than my [biological] family members.'[78] M.'A.Z., who exited after a ten-year membership, said that what he missed most was the 'sense of Brotherhood' he shared with his Brotherhood friends.[79]

Furthermore, the 'imagined kinship' as represented in friendships serves as a hindrance to disengagement also because the relationship is sanctified. As the first founding members suggested to call the group a 'society,' 'a syndicate,' or a 'club,' El-Banna, the founder, told them at their first meeting in March 1928: 'We are brothers serving Islam, so we have to be "the Muslim Brothers".'[80] Indeed, El-Banna made the 'real kinship' less important than the 'imagined kinship' when he sanctified the latter as drawn on what he called '*Al-Ukhwa Al-Imaniyya*' [the faith brotherhood].[81] Members are made 'thematically aware' of this importance when they are instructed to 'spread the Islamic mission (*Da'wa*),' which means that friendship is not

---

[77] Anan, M. I. (2017).

[78] Ramzy, A. (2013). *Dawlat al-murshid wa Sanam Al-Ikhwan* [The state of the guide and the statue of Muslim Brotherhood] (p. 36). Cairo: Rodiy.

[79] M.'A.Z. (2017).

[80] El-Banna, *Muzakerat al-d'awa wal da'ia*, p. 85. This story was cited in El-Banna's autobiography only five lines after another mention emphasizing this 'Brotherhood in Islam' foundational principle. He said as the six companions made their oath of fealty to El-Banna, the latter said describing it as such: 'It was an oath to live as brothers working for Islam and striving for its sake', ibid., p. 84.

[81] El-Banna, Majmu't rasael al-imam, p. 60. El-Banna also adopted variations of the term in Arabic by describing the Brotherhood's smallest unit as Usra [grouping close family members a father and a mother] and bigger units such as ''Aila' [grouping distant relatives]. In a 1938 conference, he described as the gathering as a 'Mu'tamar 'Aili [a family conference] grouping the usra of the Muslim Brotherhood,' El-Banna, Majmu't rasael al-imam, p. 181. This intensive functional use of language at an all-inclusive of what is a 'family' brings an intertextual emphasis to the concept.

only an affect-laden value of solidarity, but an instrument of mobilization and recruitment. El-Banna instructed his followers to apply 'friendship and gentleness' in seeking to recruit new members through personal contacts.[82] Leaders would warn members not to make friends with those whom were perceived as less 'religious,' as members would feel the incongruity between Islamic morality and secular decadence, and resolve this tension once and for all by thrusting themselves into the Brotherhood's arms. Many ex-members recounted how during the recruitment and indoctrination process into the group they felt forced to make a choice between their old friends and new 'Islamic' friends. 'Eid, who recounted his disengagement from the group in an autobiography along with other books on his experience published after 2011, recalled how the Brotherhood had pushed him toward cutting off links with his non-Brotherhood friends when he joined the group at age 10.[83] 'Eid even lamented that he had earlier recruited many of his friends and family members, including his brother and two sisters, ironically the same individuals by whom he felt pressured when he disengaged from the group.[84]

This process can be linked to identity-making as it relates to two principles of Brotherhood doctrine: renunciation and communion. Renunciation refers to the member's withdrawal from all of her or his social relationships outside the group, with the goal of ensuring a maximum of internal cohesion.[85] Communion indicates belonging to the 'we' feeling. It involved an assumed unanimity and a will to exclusion. This was meant to ensure the full conformity of individuals to the group and to avoid any of the 'free-riding' that was thought implicit in any significant assertion of individual autonomy.[86] Sameh Fayez, 33 years old, who had been a member for 11 years until he left in 2011, reflects on the

---

[82] Lia, *Society of Muslim Brothers in Egypt*, p. 107.

[83] 'Eid, Tajribati fi saradeeb Al-Ikhwan, p. 34.

[84] The testimony is verified by the stages of the 'Brotherhood's recruitment strategy' including 'individual call' and 'general connectivity.' Al-Anani wrote it is an indication of how the Brotherhood's recruiters 'invest heavily in kinship and friendship to recruit new members,' Al-Anani, *Inside the Muslim Brotherhood*, p. 73. On another page, he reiterated, 'The Brotherhood also capitalizes on family connections to recruit new members,' ibid., p. 80.

[85] Bittner, E. (1963). Radicalism and the organization of radical movements. *American Sociological Review, 28*(6), 928–940; Coser, L. (1974). *Greedy institutions: Patterns of undivided commitment*. New York: Free Press.

[86] Filliele, *Disengagement from radical organizations*, p. 47.

significance of renunciation and communion. He writes in his autobiography, aptly titled 'The Paradise of Brotherhood':

> You read Brotherhood literature, written by Brothers on Brothers. You pray in Brotherhood mosques, built and run by Brothers. You marry a Sister [a female member of the Brotherhood] nurtured in a family according to Brotherhood guidelines. Even on recreational trips, you meet Brothers, ride buses owned by Brothers, and stay at a place administered by Brothers.[87]

All these acts of solidarity and high levels of socialization create an undifferentiated 'we' which captures more than simply the fact that there was a common goal of being members of the same group. It is unification and a feeling of togetherness dominant enough that individuals as subjects of the same experience can no longer decompose the 'we' into 'I' and 'you.' Therefore, members wanting to exit would be thus treated like outsiders, deprived of all these activities at once and threatened with the loss of their friendship connections in the group. To oversimplify, a member leaves the group and his friends leave him. Islam Lutfy, exiting the group in 2011, noted that many of his Brotherhood friends joined the group's 'character assassination and smear campaigns, which included accusations against myself as serious as abdicating Islam, [and engaging in] moral decadence and financial corruption.'[88] 'I know those friends since birth,' he added. 'We lived, ate, played, and worked together within the fold of the Brotherhood. It really pains me that they

[87] Fayez, S. (2011). *Janat Al-Ikhwan: Rehlat al-khuroug min al-gam'a* [The MB paradise: The journey of getting out of the group] (p. 15). Cairo: Al-Tanweer. The late Hossam Tammam, one of the leading authorities on the Brotherhood, made a remark similar to Fayez, arguing that the Brotherhood 'creates its own community within society'; El-Hennawy, N. (2011, April 17). A split in the Muslim Brotherhood? Not so easy. *Egypt Independent*. Available via: http://www.egyptindependent.com//news/split-muslim-brotherhood-not-so-easy. Accessed 15 May 2019. Al-Anani calls this intensive and exclusive level of communication 'a society within a greater society' that has its own distinctive 'subculture,' Al-Anani, *Inside the Muslim Brotherhood*, p. 81.

[88] Islam Lutfy. (2017). These accusations are substantiated by the literature of the Brotherhood which makes the relation between Islam and the Brotherhood intractable. He made it clear in his memoirs that the path of the Brotherhood is 'all drawn from Islam, and any gaps in this path are gaps in the righteous Islamic concept itself'; El-Banna, *Muzakerat al-d'awa wal da'ia*, p. 240.

spread these false rumors.'[89] A.S.R. repeated much the same sentiments, saying, 'My prefect began propagating the idea that I am a source of trouble and suspicions, which sent the message to my friends that they should stay away.'[90] M.'A.Z. also felt that the disengagement left him 'isolated,' as many Brotherhood friends not only cut their ties with him, but 'added me to the list of enemies.'[91] 'What really hurt me the most was to feel that I am outcast and that my history of membership is fully erased and that this personal amiability all evaporates as my once closest friends now consider me their enemy.'[92]

In such ways, rewarding and punishment on behalf of the group were done by members themselves, including friends. S.E. said that the moment of his wedding and marriage preparations was when he most felt the affective consequences of disengagement. He said: 'When I got married after exiting the group, not one single friend of mine came to the wedding or helped me. I was really saddened and shocked.'[93] The 'affective' loss of imagined kinship could include greetings, such as the 'Salamu 'aleykum' [peace be upon you] greeting usually expressed among Muslims. S.E. said, 'It is really embarrassing that the persons whom I was friends with all my life for thirty years meet me in the street without greeting.' The sociologist Erving Goffman said that, in such cases of embarrassment, 'equilibrium or self-control can be lost, balance can be overthrown.'[94] S.E. said that interaction with 'no greetings in the street' left him 'shaken' and led to 'hesitance' in building new friendships. Expressing his sadness, he said, 'I really suffer from this vacuum and the pain of boycott and ostracism imposed by the Brotherhood friends.'[95] As these friendships extend for years and even decades, given the recruitment tactics of the Brotherhood which target potential

---

[89] Islam Lutfy. (2017).

[90] A.S.R. (2017).

[91] M.'A.Z. (2017).

[92] Ibid.

[93] S.E. (2017).

[94] Goffman, E. (1956). Embarrassment and social organization. *American Journal of Sociology, 62*, 206. https://doi.org/10.1086/222003.

[95] Ibid.

members at young age and from the same families,[96] exiting members lose more than friendships. They are 'relationships for life.'[97]

From a utility maximization perspective, for all of the reasons mentioned above, losing family members and friends can tip the balance of costs against benefits, as other case studies of social movement disengagement have found.[98] However, there are options to re-trip this balance in favour of benefits. Ex-members felt driven to search for ways to obtain forms of social support that could outweigh the costly loss of real and imagined kinships that were tightly bound to membership. Focusing on discourses of identity, the next section describes how some ex-members developed coping strategies that benefitted from today's rapidly interconnecting world to minimize the impact of the loss.

GAINING THE 'I'

My argument here is that the 'affective' losses incurred by the exiting member at the level of real and imagined kinships were compensated by 'affective' gains that involved taking the individual and not the group as the point of reference. This always involved a search for personal identity or what can be called the 'gaining of the I' against the 'losing of the we.' It is possible to speak of a division in a person's sense of self between an 'I' and a 'we,' the self as spoken of or acted upon (which symbolic interactionism refers to as the 'me') and the self as an assumed identity with agency.

My argument, that is losing the 'we' has to be compensated with the gaining of the 'I' for the process of disengagement to happen, is based on patterns in texts of exiting members. A repeatedly invoked frame among people I interviewed involved how a new 'I' is created, affirmed, or transformed. 'I wanted to regain myself,' said M.E., a 23-year-old man who left the Brotherhood in 2014 and whom I interviewed in

[96]'For example, in each district there is a "buddy" (bara'im) committee that is responsible for attracting and recruiting young members.' There is a 'children's activities committee,' Al-Anani, Inside the Muslim Brotherhood, p. 79.

[97] Della Porta, Leaving underground organisations, pp. 66–87 (81–82).

[98] Hwang, Panggabean and Fauzi concluded their findings of interviews with 23 ex-Jihadi members: 'Twelve of those interviewed cited new friendships and relationships developed with individuals outside the Jihadi circle as fostering or reinforcing a decision to disengage,' pp. 765–767.

Istanbul. 'I wanted to be the one who takes decisions, not others who dictate to me how and when to move right or left according to their own wishes.'[99] 'I wanted to be I,' said Mohamed Aboul-Gheit simply, in an interview conducted in London.[100] 'It is a search for my I', said Ahmed Nazily, whom I interviewed in Doha.[101] Nazily said that he preferred to be called Ahmed El-Sayed, as using his middle name 'would allow me to be myself, to live my own experience, and to build my own social ties away from these links with my family.'[102] The repetition and frequency of the 'I' is evident in accounts of all exiting members: 'I gained a respect for myself, my ideas, my beliefs,'[103] 'I now have become myself. I can convince myself of what I want and I can act on what I am convinced of'[104]; 'I won myself by exiting the group.'[105]

The same patterning of the frame can also be identified in autobiographies. Intissar 'Abdel-Mon'im says at the beginning of her autobiography that by writing about her exit experience, she wants 'to prove that I have [my own] identity.'[106] Sameh Fayez made it clear that his decision to leave the Brotherhood was mainly about regaining the basic right of individual freedom of choice.[107] 'I ["me" in our conceptualization] wanted to be an I,' he writes in his autobiography.[108]

Again, this salience of the 'I' as a frame, judged by the repetition in both interviews and autobiographies, is significant once we compare language of the present with language of the past. For example, earlier interviews conducted with members of the group more often started with 'we,' emphasizing the group against the individual.[109] Nathan Brown, a specialist on the Brotherhood who is the author of some illuminating studies of it, takes this transformation as 'revolutionary.' Brown

[99] M.E. (2017).

[100] Aboul-Gheit, M. (2017).

[101] Nazily, A. (2017).

[102] Ibid.

[103] S.E. (2017).

[104] A.S.R. (2017).

[105] El-Qaddoum, A. (2017).

[106] 'Abdel-Mon'im, I. (2011). *Hekayati ma' Al-Ikhwan* [My story with the Muslim Brotherhood] (pp. 12–20). Cairo: General Egyptian Book Organization.

[107] Fayez, Janat Al-Ikhwan, pp. 17–18.

[108] Ibid.

[109] Brown, N. (2018).

said that he had long recognized during the many interviews he had conducted over the years that when a member of the Brotherhood began speaking, 'The first word or answer to any question would start with "we," not the "I".'[110] In interviews with some of the same people in 2015, he noted the transformation: 'What comes first from the mouth in answering my question now begins with "I".'[111]

In addition, the salience of the 'I' is not only about its linguistic predominance in texts. It is also about power. In recounting their disengagement, the interview subjects and autobiographers would use 'I' to indicate that they are the ones who take decisions and weigh the costs and benefits of disengagement. Language thus empowers an individual to be 'an object of himself.' 'He acts toward himself and guides himself' in a process that involves 'addressing himself as a person and responding thereto.'[112] The self-story accounts of ex-members are all direct speech, either in talking to me directly or as voiced in their autobiographies, while their accounts of the Brotherhood and its collective identity and values were invariably rendered in 'indirect speech.' The latter were in general only mentioned in the narratives in order to be refuted, ridiculed, or refused as I will elaborate on below. In other words, members, long treated as 'silent' or 'obedient' addressees taken for guaranteed as part of the collective 'we,' are now present in texts of their own making and are enjoying the power of full representation and symbolic power drawn on moving from the plural to the singular. This empowerment is also about autonomy, since the 'we' was always used by the Brotherhood leaders functionally to merge themselves in their speeches and writings as speakers and authors with members; the obedient addressees, as extensions of them in an 'undefined territory'[113] based on obfuscating gaps between what is personal and what is collective.

---

[110] Ibid.

[111] Ibid.

[112] Blumer, H. (1969). *Symbolic interactionism: Perspectives and method* (p. 13). Chicago: Chicago University Press.

[113] Abdul-Latif, E. (2011). Interdiscursivity between political and religious discourses in a speech by Sadat, p. 63. The fact that the plural pronoun, *nahnu* (we) can also be ambiguously used to express a single speaker, such as the case with majesty and which is also common in Quraan to refer to God, adds to this functionality of the pronoun to serve meanings and interests of the Brotherhood. As such, the shift in language not only 'emancipates' the pronouns related to the 'I,' but also disambiguates its functionality by making it to end this 'disambiguation.'

However, the balance in favour of the 'I' was neither a journey of smooth sailing nor was it complete. The 'I' of the present is always entangled and attached to the 'we' of the past. Fayez said that he still remembers the moment his Brotherhood recruiter, who had been a friend for 20 years, turned his face away when he saw him in the street, in the same small village where they both lived, seven years ago.[114] This simple but symbolically weighted and painful act led Fayez to seek the help of a psychiatrist.[115] Mohamed 'Affan said that he needed more time, as he still felt disoriented six years after exiting the group: 'I am at a loss. I do not know what is right from what is wrong.'[116] Ahmed Nazily, resisting tears, when I asked him how hard it had been to exit the group, said: 'It was like cutting off one of your fingers. And this is not an exaggeration.'[117] M.'A.Z. also admitted: 'I still suffer from this loss... I feel isolated and lonely...I feel conflict inside me.'[118]

Exiting members have overcome these conflicts and 'affective' pressures through two forms of identity-making, as defined by identity process theory (IPT).[119] According to IPT, identity has two main features: 'assimilation/accommodation' and 'evaluation.' Assimilation/accommodation refers to the absorption of new information or development (i.e., being an 'ex-') as part of one's identity and the adjustment that makes this identity seem to fit one's surrounding environment. It is within such assimilation and accommodation that each individual can identify himself as an 'I' (no longer a member of the group) rather than just a 'we' (drawn on her or his role and duties as a member of the real-kinship and imagined-kinship groups) in terms of her or his membership in the Brotherhood. This separateness of pronouns is drawn on a separateness of experiences bringing to an end the 'dependency' of the individual on the Brotherhood. 'Evaluation' is the process of viewing one's new identity against an earlier one and seeing it in comparison as negative or positive, powerful or weak, active or passive.

---

[114] Fayez, Janat Al-Ikhwan, p. 17.

[115] Fayez, S. (2018). I made a phone conversation with Fayez to ask for some clarifications mentioned in his autobiography.

[116] 'Affan, M. (2017).

[117] Nazily, A. (2017).

[118] M.'A.Z. (2017).

[119] See Jaspal, R. & Breakwell, G. M. (Eds.). (2014). *Identity process theory: Identity, social action and social change.* Cambridge, UK: Cambridge University Press.

Evaluation would often come first and be followed by the self-adjustment, the former helping to articulate a language of ex-hood, and processes of assimilation and accommodation would translate it into certain attitudes, behaviors, or actions that would justify disengagement or help embolden the person to engage in it. So I shall first detail the evaluation part of identity-formation, and then explore assimilation efforts, tracing both in the narratives of ex-members through language-drawn framing, that is, how individuals adopted a 'frame re-alignment process'[120] in order to draw evaluations supporting their disengagement. In the re-alignment process, including features or stages such as 'amplification,' 'transformation,' and 'bridging,' the dominant frames of the Brotherhood are reconstructed to serve as frames of resistance serving the broader process of disengagement.

GAINING THE 'I': EXITING BY EVALUATION

The evaluation through frame re-alignment is evidenced in how many ex-members described the past inside the Brotherhood as being for them a 'prison' or 'slave camp,' and their current departure and assumption of a new identity as a form of 'emancipation.' These metaphorical constructions bolster 'affective disengagement' by constituting it through a 'bipolar valence,' that is one way of conceptualizing emotions or feelings as located on the extreme ends of a continuum ranging from 'good to bad.'[121] In this case, and on basis of conceiving one thing in terms of another, the 'metaphorical' continuum of expressing emotions moves from one extreme, that is, imprisonment or slavery, to another, that

---

[120]The frame alignment process is used by David Snow and Robert Benford among others to refer to 'the linkage of individual and SMO [social movement organisation] interpretive orientations, such that some set of individual interests, values and beliefs and SMO activities, goals, and ideology are congruent and complementary' (Snow, D., Rochford, E., Worden, S., & Benford, R. [1986]. Frame alignment processes, micromobilization, and movement participation. *American Sociological Review, 51*(4), 464–481 (467). Available via: http://www.jstor.org/stable/2095581). The authors use the term in a limited manner by linking it with movement participation. I employ the 'frame re-alignment' to indicate a counter-process in which this re-alignment is a necessary condition for ending this linkage or conjunction between individual and Brotherhood interpretive frameworks (see also Benford, R. [1993]. Frame disputes within the nuclear disarmament movement. *Social Forces, 71*(3), 677–701. https://doi.org/10.2307/2579890).

[121]Dillard, J. P., & Seo, K. (2013), p. 150.

is, emancipation. Strikingly, the metaphorical contradictions in both extremes mix well with no ill effect as they all cohere. This coherence perhaps has to do with the fact that these metaphors are already there in the literature of the Brotherhood. What exiting members have done, as I will also elaborate below, is transforming their meanings into the opposite directions while they also use them to bridge between their past and their present.

First, I can prove through language and patterns in texts the salience of the metaphors of slavery and imprisonment by their presence in texts as an evidence of negative evaluation of engagement with the Brotherhood. Fayez evaluated his membership in the group as a form of slavery: 'I was a slave to the religion of Brotherhood,'[122] a frame he also associated with imprisonment: when asked why he left the Brotherhood, he said, 'Because I climbed over this wall that the group surrounded me with.'[123] Tharwat El-Khirbawy, 61 years old, described his 20-year membership as a 'human chain of slavery,' which he said was worse even than the real slavery in the US, since it 'chained my body and soul.'[124] On other occasions, he invoked the idea of slavery more concretely by speaking of Shawshank prison and Kunta Kinte, the fictional African who became an American slave in Alex Haley's book *Roots* and the 1977 American television mini-series based upon it.[125] 'Eid said simply of his feeling after leaving the Brotherhood: 'I was freed from slavery.'[126] These are descriptions from other ex-members: 'I was tied to chains.'[127] It was a 'cage chaining man into yes/no, halal/non-halal texts and restrictive or arbitrary interpretations of them.'[128] It is striking to what extent ex-members who did not know each other and were different in

---

[122] Fayez, Janat Al-Ikhwan, p. 46.

[123] Ibid., p. 16.

[124] El-Khirbawy, T. (2012). *Ser Al-M'abad: Al-Asrar al-khafiya li gama't Al-Ikhwan Al-Muslemeen* [The temple's secret: The hidden secrets of the Muslim Brotherhood] (p. 16). Cairo: Nahdet Masr. Although El-Khirbawy disengaged in 2002, he wrote his autobiography, published in 2010, a few months before the 2011 events that are taken as the designated time frame for this study. As of 2011, he also wrote more books carrying autobiographical accounts of his membership.

[125] El-Khirbawy, Sir al-ma'bad, pp. 16, 18.

[126] 'Eid, Sameh, Tajribati fi saradeeb Al-Ikhwan, p. 73.

[127] Ibid., p. 157.

[128] Ban, A. (2017). *Ikhwan wa Salafiyyon wa Dawa'ish* [Brothers, Salafists and ISIS Loyalists] (p. 255). Cairo: Al-Mahrousa.

age, role, status, or geographic location would use similar metaphors and ways of speaking of their experience.

The frames of slavery and imprisonment are not only symbolic or metaphorically structured as a matter of language or mere words; they are metaphorically structured as a 'concept' and an 'activity.'[129] They were illustrative of actual physical practices such as being placed under house arrest on the orders of his leaders in the Brotherhood following an enquiry into his non-obedience of the rules of the group, being asked to work without being paid or rewarded, calling this forced labor, causing a sexual deprivation by the group that was used to limit a member's ability to talk to girls, being forced to walk for ten kilometers. Ahmed Nazily remembered how his seniors in the group objected to his lifestyle of 'sitting in a local café to drink tea or coffee; even the friends I sat with were also members of the Muslim Brotherhood.'[130] They told him that 'a good Muslim must not sit in a local café.' Other restrictions also included implicit rules regulating dress and hairstyle, which brought to some members memories of detention in prisons where they were forced to follow much the same rules. Mohamed El-Qassas remembered that he had had to take off his sunglasses before getting out of his car, 'as the Brotherhood found it distasteful for its members to wear them in public.' Restrictions, synonymized with imprisonment and slavery, can be virtual, including limits on the use of social media, which was subjected to the scrutiny of the group. A.Y. remembers that when he published a Facebook post warning against a potential 'military coup' against the Brotherhood on July 2, 2013, he received a phone call from his prefect. 'I had to take it out.'[131]

On the opposite side, the frame of emancipation is widely invoked as part of the positive evaluation. El-Khirbawy said in his autobiography that he decided to leave the group in 2002 because he wanted the 'emancipation I had coveted all my life,'[132] the journey toward which gave him a 'new birth certificate.'[133] 'Eid, who wrote in his autobiography that leaving the Brotherhood, also after 20 years, meant that

[129] Lakoff, G., & Johnson, M. (1980). *Metaphors we live by* (p. 4). London: University of Chicago Press.

[130] Nazily, A. (2017).

[131] A.Y. (2017).

[132] El-Khirbawy, Ser al-m'abad, pp. 17–60.

[133] Ibid., p. 34.

'I breathed freedom and felt that I restored my soul, which had been earlier peeled off me.'[134] When I asked 32-year-old 'A.G. what he gained most after exiting the Brotherhood in 2014, to which he had belonged since birth due to the membership of both of his parents, he said: 'It is mostly the freedom to take my own decisions.'[135] Emancipation, which fits in with the rise of the 'I,' was generally spoken of in terms that were not obviously political, but more personal. Emancipation tended to be spoken of with mention to affective states such as happiness or joy, and life, as well as with individual rights and responsibilities.[136] On the other hand, personal identity could be 'emancipated' or realized through such things as sitting in a café, changing one's hairstyle, or even wearing sunglasses in public.

The presence of these metaphors is heavily concentrated through reiteration in each text and across the whole different texts produced by exiting members across years. This supports the metaphors with, to adopt the jargon of the frame re-alignment process, a 'frame amplification.' The latter is defined as the 'clarification and invigoration of an interpretive frame that bears on a particular issue, problem, or set of events.'[137] Take the metaphor of breathing as indicative of the 'emancipation' frame. These are quotes from two separate texts: 'Outside the Brotherhood, I can breathe air. The air is polluted, but I have the freedom to breathe it or not,'[138] it is about 'feeling that I breathe a fresh air.'[139] These are quotes from one single text, which is a single page of El-Khirbawy's book, *The Temple's Secret*: 'I have felt for a long time that this group is a prison for me'; 'I am a prisoner who cannot move towards his freedom'; 'Heavy are my chains. I hope that I have not gotten addicted to the prison and its staff.'[140] He also titled the first chapter of his book 'The Voice of Emancipation.'[141] Ahmed Ban titled one

---

[134] Ibid., p. 73.

[135] 'A.G. (2017).

[136] Tiriandis, H. C., & Vassiliou, V. (1967). *A comparative analysis of subjective culture* (p. 48). Group Effectiveness Research Laboratory, University of Illinois.

[137] Snow, Frame alignment, micromobilization and movement participation, p. 469. The definition makes amplification closer to what Robert Entman calls 'salience' of a frame.

[138] A.S.R. (2017).

[139] S.E. (2017).

[140] El-Khirbawy, Al-Asrar al-khafiya li gama't Al-Ikhwan Al-Muslemeen, p. 19.

[141] Ibid., p. 9.

of the chapters of his autobiography 'Emancipation Comes First, before Belief.'[142] Adding interdiscursivity (by which critical discourse analysis theorists mean relationships connecting or 'chaining' different texts[143]) to the framing of the metaphor, its reiteration is also witnessed in interviews. Tareq Aboul-Sa'd told me this quote:

> Exiting the Brotherhood, you feel emancipated from the group and its duties... emancipated from all social relations...At times I felt in this process of emancipation that I imagined myself jumping up and holding the sky in a moment of happiness because I got rid of all this slavery.[144]

The frame re-alignment process happens as the identity-making through evaluation is not a discursive construction of new frames drawn on juxtaposing slavery/imprisonment with emancipation as two salient frames in texts. It is a reconstruction as exiting members transform already existing meanings of these two exact frames which are part of the hegemonic discourse of the Brotherhood and through which the group has long pitted the collective identity against the personal identity. The group has widely necessitated the need for all members to be 'slaves' as a condition for their commitment within its utopian pursuit of the 'Islamic project.'[145] However, while a member has to limit her or his servitude to God, the leaders of the group *re-aligned* the frame commitment to their orders as part of this 'godly' servitude (see Chapter 3). This means the relationship that ties the leaders with members would be regarded as one of 'ownership and servitude.'[146] The frame re-alignment relates to identity

---

[142] Ban, Al-Ikhwan Al-Muslimoon wa mehnat al-watan wal deen, p. 207.

[143] Fairclough, N. (1992). Intertextuality in critical discourse analysis. *Linguistics and Education*, 4(3), 269–293.

[144] Aboul-Sa'd, T. (2017).

[145] El-Banna drove home this intertextual transformation in his speeches, statements, and writings. In his seminal work, he repeated 'slave' and words which derive from or associate with it more than 200 times as roughly counted in one of his texts. The examples include supplications in which a member has to perform and in which announces to God that 'I am your slave' or in which he shows full obedience through a 'true servitude between your hands'; see El-Banna, Majmu't rasael al-imam.

[146] For example, this is the content of a letter sent by Zaynab El-Ghazali, one of the leading female figures in the Brotherhood, to El-Banna: 'Zaynab al-Ghazali approaches you today as a slave... you are the one who can sell this slave at the price he wishes for the cause of God the Exalted. Waiting for your orders and instructions, my lord the imam,' Euben, R. L., &

as the leaders of the Brotherhood have long amplified the 'we' as part of
a spiritual sanctified contract in which the 'I' is slaved. If liberated, the 'I'
is reserved for those facing excommunication or expulsion from the flock
of the faithful 'we.' In other words, the 'I' is a punishment rather than a
reward since it connotes aberration from the sanctified collective identity
and also associates with negative evaluations that require isolation, shame,
guilt, and stigmatization from the other 'we'-committed members. The
individual would not celebrate his 'I-ness' in this case as she or he would
'feel left out and unhappy if he were given much personal freedom,' or
if 'in-group members left him in peace by now allowing him to be concerned with his own problems.'[147]

On the other hand, the Brotherhood has also re-aligned 'emancipation' in its dominant discourse to carry out similar purposes of empowering the group identity against the individual identity. El-Banna made
the group's 'conceptual system' metaphorically structured and defined
around 'emancipation.' He said membership in the Brotherhood is about
each individual's ability to 'emancipate' her or his 'psychological needs'
and 'biological luxuries,' synonymized with 'lust' and corrupt souls all
for the sake of giving primacy to the 'renaissance of the nation.'[148] In
his memoirs, El-Banna made it clear that the 'self' has to make sacrifices
and abandon itself to the collective identity in order to reach this emancipation. In the memoirs, the 39 mentions of the 'self' are always meant
to stress the need to 'sacrifice it' or to 'resist it for the sake of God' in
order to emancipate the self by associating it with the 'Islamic' collectiv-
ity.[149] Although he always emphasized the 'personal freedom,' he kept
it qualified and conditioned by necessitating that it should be based on
the rules of Islam and based on the rules of the group which prioritizes
unity and consensus.[150] In other words, the Brotherhood's version is an

Zaman, M. Q. (Eds.). (2009). *Princeton readings in Islamist thought: Texts and contexts from El-Banna to Bin Laden* (chapter II, pp. 288–301 [289]). Princeton University Press.

[147] Tiriandis, A. *Comparative analysis of subjective culture*, p. 48.

[148] El-Banna, *Muzakerat al-d'awa wal da'ia*, pp. 172–173.

[149] See El-Banna, *Muzakerat al-d'awa wal da'ia*, p. 307.

[150] See El-Banna, Majmu't rasael al-imam. In the book, El-Banna articulated the meanings of 'emancipation' in a contradictory, ambiguous, and confusing manner. While he portrays the 'freedom of belief' and 'personal freedom,' at the same time he warns against
'partisanship,' 'disunity,' 'differences,' or 'divisions' among members of his group.

'emancipation' realized by de-emancipation. What exiting members do is to re-align this re-aligned correlation the other way round. In the case of 'slavery' and emancipation, it is an interdiscursivity in reverse, as individuals disassociate these terms from the meanings projected by their Brotherhood leaders, and associate them with new meanings which bolster their journey of disengagement. They have been able to do this shift in meanings as the process of constructing metaphors, and the 'conceptual system' drawn on them works on the principle of 'highlighting and hiding'[151] (a similar one to the principle of 'salience' and 'selectiveness' involved in the framing process). Individuals 'hide' the sublime meanings of slavery contained in the literature of the Brotherhood as part of submission to God, and they 'highlight' new meanings that pejoratively define it as a submission to the group and its leaders.

GAINING THE 'I': EXITING THROUGH ACCOMMODATION AND ASSIMILATION

The process of assimilation and accommodation, the other side of identity-making, includes that ex-members have to deal with a number of principles guiding their self-identification. Glynis Marie Breakwell has identified one of these principles: uniqueness, or distinction from others. The focus on social ties is what has made the Brotherhood distinctive and unique among ideological movements, political parties, and even religious sects.[152] Many of them found that a sense of distinction was achieved within the Brotherhood through real and imagined kinships mentioned above. Therefore, what exiting members have to do is to abandon earlier forms of distinction and acquire new ones by replacing social ties.

Accordingly, new forms of distinction were formed through the adoption of new friendship networks, which was possible in an environment as changed as the one after 2011 in Egypt (see Chapter 4). Intissar 'Abdel-Mon'im built a new circle of friends by promoting her career as a novelist, which started with publishing her autobiography after she left the group. Her Facebook page shows her attending many literary events and making friends with fellow novelists, literary critics, and journalists

---

[151] Lakeoff, G., & Johnson, M. *Metaphors we live by*, pp. 11–13.
[152] Kandil, *Inside the Brotherhood*, p. 71.

from all over the world. She posted a picture of herself with a friend from China who wrote her master's thesis on her, 'Abdel-Mon'im's, writings. She keeps posting images of new friendships made as she travels to new countries including Spain and as she engages into more activities related to her career shift. In general, 'alternative' networks bring distinction to members in ex-hood, because they frame friendships in the same manner as employed by the Brotherhood: they are a tool of power, or at least of empowerment. One example is from the experience of Nazily: He said that his own 'emancipation' grew as he founded or joined several social and political groups, all of which 'allowed me to avoid all restrictions on my movement that were long imposed by the Brotherhood.' After the removal of Mubarak from the presidency in February 2011, Nazily, along with several other friends who were Brotherhood members who exited a bit later, founded a social group by the name of *Al-Ahrar*, which means 'the Emancipated Ones.' It was in this context that Nazily was able to rid himself of the 'ghetto mentality' of the Brotherhood that had once engulfed him for the 'broader society' in which he was able to build new friendships.[153]

Still, the alternative circles also had some 'homogeneity' which can counterbalance the homogeneity enforced by the Brotherhood-attached circles. In fact, exiting members often maintained many of the same social ties, and many members followed friends or family in exiting, or kept the same work or professional life relationships. For example, in 2015, at *Al-Araby* TV, based in London, Islam Lutfy, the Chairman of its Board of Directors, was working with Mohamed Shams, Mohamed Aboul-Gheit (who exited the Brotherhood after 2011), and 'Abdel-Moneim Mahmoud (who exited before 2011). In Qatar, I was intro-duced to Ali El-Mashad, who exited the group in 2011, and was working as a producer at Al-Araby's office in Doha. After a few minutes of chat-ting by coincidence during one conference in Doha that Ali was covering for the channel, I realized that El-Mashad is a friend of someone whom

---

[153] El-Sherif, A. (2014). *The Egyptian Muslim Brotherhood's failures* (p. 20). New York: Carnegie. However, it is fair to counter-argue that the re-assimilation is also made easier by the Brotherhood itself. The Brotherhood does isolate its member through such tools as emphasizing tight personal bonds. Yet, Nathan Brown argues, it avoids 'turning inward on itself' as part of its goals is to 'change the broader society' through such tools as 'advocacy, activism, teaching, organizing, and preaching,' Brown, N. J. (2012). *When victory is not an option: Islamist movements in Arab politics* (p. 69). Ithaca and London: Cornell University Press.

I met a few weeks earlier in Istanbul: 'Affan, who is also El-Mashad's brother-in-law. Thus, just one workplace linked five ex-members, who shared a sense of what he can call career solidarity. This work-friendship solidarity, also seen among other ex-members I encountered and interviewed in Turkey, served as an alternative to the more hierarchized (and formalized) collective solidarity once offered to them in the Brotherhood. Judging by psychology, this solidarity acts as an incentive or external reward stimulating individuals to continue the process of their disengagement.[154] S.M., who had close friends who had exited the Brotherhood before him, said that this 'meant that I can keep my network of friends.'[155] Again, this solidarity is not only about the practicalities of replacing jobs or friends. It is also about replacing the restricted 'emotional sharing' once enjoyed by belonging to the brotherhood. This time, the emotional sharing with other ex-members respects a 'preservation of plurality and a certain self-other differentiation.'[156] On the basis of my random observation of exiting members during interviews conducted in Egypt, Turkey, the UK, or Qatar, I can identify the differences in frames used by exiting members even if they share the same meanings of articulating and operationalizing their disassociation from the Brotherhood. Again, this is a sign of accommodation and assimilation in the process of disengagement since exiting members can strike the 'right balance between difference and similarity' as they keep their 'own ordinary, but exclusive, first-personal self-experience' while joining and participating in a 'we-experience.'[157]

The role of friendships and work solidarity in identity-(re)formation can be influential, creating and consolidating the stage of 'affective disengagement.' As Klandermans put it, 'People might be puzzled by some aspects of reality and try to understand what is going on. They look for others with similar experiences' and who can provide an environment 'to exchange experiences, to tell their stories and to express their feelings.'[158] Ex-hood itself acted like a social counter-movement offering

---

[154] Jessen, J. T. (2015). Job satisfaction and social rewards in the social services. *Journal of Comparative Social Work, 5*(1).

[155] S.M. (2017).

[156] See Zahavi, D. You, Me, and We.

[157] Ibid.

[158] Klandermans, B. (2004). The demand and supply of participation: Social-psychological correlates of participation in social movements. In Snow, D. A., Soule, S. A., &

both practical and emotional support, just as the prefect to which each of these individuals had been assigned once had done. Tareq Aboul-Sa'd said that he found it easier to network with other 'ex-members' who shared their Brotherhood experiences, a process he called 'therapeutic.' He explained:

We share the same destiny and understand each other's circumstances. The 'other' in society is always suspicious of us, considering us as vicious, inferior, and even traitors, especially as the group has obtained this sense of victimization since being outlawed in 2013 [as to be detailed in Chapter 4].[159]

Self-Efficacy and Self-Esteem

Two other elements of personal identity that are important to, and serve as indicators of, assimilation and accommodation, are self-efficacy and self-esteem. Breakwell defines self-efficacy as 'feeling confident and in control of one's life,' and 'self-esteem' as consisting of feelings of 'personal worth.'[160] Related to these, other researchers identified as indicators of personal identity 'belonging,' which refers to the need to maintain feelings of closeness to others and be accepted by them, and 'meaning,' which refers to the need to find significance and purpose in one's life.[161]

Ahmed Ban found his self-efficacy, self-worth, belonging, and meaning in his career after he exited the Brotherhood. He has become a regular TV guest. He now writes for several widely circulating newspapers, such as the pan-Arab *Al-Hayat*, the Lebanese newspaper *Al-Safeer*, the Egyptian newspaper *Al-Watan*, and widely read websites such as dot. Misr and *Al-Youm Al-Sabei*. Introducing himself as 'a researcher and a specialist writer on Islamic movements,' Ban even wrote the scripts of a

Kriesi, H. (Eds.). (2007). *The Blackwell companion to social movements* (pp. 360–379). Malden: Blackwell.

[159]Aboul-Sa'd, T. (2017).

[160]Breakwell, G. M. (1986). *Coping with threatened identities*. London: Methuen.

[161]Vignoles, V. L., Regalia, C., Manzi, C., Golledge, J., & Scabini, E. (2006). Beyond self-esteem: Influence of multiple motives on identity construction. *Journal of Personality and Social Psychology, 90*, 308–333.

number of documentaries for Arabic and foreign-language channels.[162] All of these writings are mainly dedicated to explaining the behavior and attitudes of the Brotherhood. This means that Ban's experience became an asset since it made him wield what Walter Lippman called the 'power of the expert.'[163] His recognition was such that ordinary Egyptians could partly depend on him and other ex-members for their knowledge of the Brotherhood. As a knowing subject, Ban reveals his private information (including about himself, or his experiences) and a public information based on 'truths' concealed by the Brotherhood. In 'telling all,' he would expose the Brotherhood's culture to the public light and not just government interrogators, disclosing not only what was demanded but what might be of interest to many Egyptians. As the state crackdown on the Brotherhood continued as of 2013, often involving imprisonment or torture, other ex-members also opted for a strategy of maximal public disclosure of both their past engagement on the group and of what they knew about the Brotherhood. This activity relates to identity as it shows how Ban draws new meanings of his past and shifted his belonging in the present.

'Abdel-Mon'im is another example showing these key elements long subsumed by the collective identity of the Brotherhood.[164] She signed contracts to publish several novels that she was writing, while refusing to be identified as 'a former member of the Brotherhood.' After writing an autobiography on her experience inside the Brotherhood, she now felt that she was independent enough to reject requests for interviews as a former member of the movement, preferring instead to just cultivate her career as a novelist. Her successes in her career as a novelist, to be detailed below, are important for the motivational purpose as it makes full disengagement from the Brotherhood as a 'goal' that

[162] Ban, Ikhwan wa Salafiyyon wa Daawaish, p. 339.

[163] Lippmann, W. (1997). *Public opinion* (p. 384). New York: Free Press Paperbacks.

[164] Again, this runs counter to the Brotherhood's dominant discourse. El-Banna has always abhorred those who 'live for their selves only and who dedicate their talents, time and efforts to serve their personal selfish [desires] and do nothing to serve their [Islamic] nation.' He also emphasized that the self has to be sacrificed for the sake of satisfying God and that any feelings of self-worth or self-efficacy have to be part of 'the goal which God set for us not the one which we set for ourselves,' El-Banna, Majmu't rasael al-imam, pp. 103, 105. 'Abdel-Mon'im said that she attempted repeatedly to show her skills in novel writing to her leaders in the group but she got suppressed due to 'favoritism' and 'corruption.'

needs to be set and resumed as well as to succeed. In other words, if fully departing from the Brotherhood is a goal for 'Abdel-Mon'im, it is now worth living as exiting members can now change and develop her or his self to becoming a 'better human being.'[165] As evidenced by her Facebook posts and interviews, 'Abdel-Mon'im keeps feeling best about herself when she is proud of her achievement in doing something which the Brotherhood or 'activating environment' long made it difficult to realize (in her autobiography, she kept focusing how the Brotherhood had long suppressed her desire to be an author). This is further satisfying as 'Abdel-Mon'im *achieved* the goal of fully disengaging from the Brotherhood and at the same time *achieved* other associative goals related to her desire to 'perform' and 'master' the task of writing as a professional at full competence and ability.[166]

Self-efficacy, self-esteem, belonging, and meaning also emanate from new forms of assimilation and accommodation, bolstering the act of disengagement and the rise of personal identity such as 'role modeling.' Aboul-Sa'd, who found his self-efficacy in regularly taking part in TV programs in which he analyzed political events, was introduced into this 'media' world by another ex-member, the well-connected and well-known El-Khirbawy. El-Khirbawy also wrote the introduction to autobiographies of younger exiting members such as Sameh Fayez, who is half his age. El-Khirbawy also led social gatherings of ex-members. Judging by his popularity, wide access and well connectedness within media circles after disengagement, he successfully traveled the path of exiting the Brotherhood upon which newer exiting members are following in his footsteps. It is a role modeling by precedence. This means that individuals, repeating a task which had been achieved before, can be better prepared to manage or overcome the difficulties that they are experiencing in this journey of disengagement.[167] This 'repeatability'

[165] Prsaud, R. (2005). *The motivated mind: How to get what you want from life* (p. 38). London: Bantam Press.

[166] This relates to the 'goal orientation theory' in psychology and its dimensions such as 'Mastery/Approach Goal' and 'Performance/Approach Goal'; Wolters, C. A. (2004). Advancing achievement goal theory: Using Goal structures and goal orientations to predict students' motivation, cognition, and achievement. *Journal of Educational Psychology, 96*(2), 236. See also Senko, C., & Tropiano, K. L. (2016). Comparing three models of achievement goals: Goal orientations, goal standards, and goal complexes. *Journal of Educational Psychology, 108*(8), 1178.

[167] Prsaud, *The motivated mind*, p. 36.

in action, and indeed in discourse of ex-hood itself as this chapter has shown, manifests in an 'unembarrassability,'[168] which is to say that exiting members feel more assertive and less embarrassed as they 'can ask advice from those who have attained the goal they now seek,' as Aboul-Sa'd did when he engaged in long conversations with El-Khirbawy who convinced him of the validity of his decision to disengage from the group. To oversimplify, what exiting members would feel can be translated in the emphatic hypothesis: 'If El-Khirbawy did it, we can do it.'

Rituals

The shifting identity and understanding of ex-members as refashioned through processes of assimilation and accommodation were also shaped partly through new sets of rituals and forms of stylizing appearance such as manner of dress, hairstyles, and even ways of talking. On the basis of these rituals, the Brotherhood has long claimed distinction,[169] one principle of identity-making as cited above. It is a unique code of identity that Al-Anani coined for the term '*ikhwanism*' [derived from the Arabic name of the Brotherhood and it literally means 'Being a Brother']. Al-Anani noted that ikhwanism is not a mere slogan or ideology but a 'way of life': 'To be an ikhwani is to think, live and behave as a committed and obedient member.'[170]

Members of the Brotherhood are expected to speak in 'a distinctive way' that makes them recognizable to other members and even the larger society. 'The society of the Brothers is one where collective virtue overwhelms individual sins,' declared General Guide Omar El-Telmessany proudly, adding: 'You never hear a swear word or a curse, but only praise of God, innocent amusement, and unsullied chat.'[171]

---

[168] Ibid.

[169] According to Mahmoud 'Abdel Halim, one of its founders, the Brotherhood was keen from its inceptions to set certain rituals as part of gaining a 'distinctive section of the Egyptian society.' 'Abdel Halim mentioned that El-Banna and his close circle met in order to approve the creation of insignia pins that a member can wear to show belonging to the group. The marks also include a ring on which the phrase 'the Muslim Brothers' is engraved; see 'Abdel-Halim, M. (1994). *Al-Ikhwan al-Muslimoon: ahdath san't al-tarikh, ru'ya min al-dakhil* [The Muslim Brotherhood: Events that made history, an inside perspective] (p. 111). Alexandria: Da'wa.

[170] Al-Anani, *Inside the Muslim Brotherhood*, p. 119.

[171] Kandil, *Inside the Brotherhood*, p. 72.

Indeed, many members had been attracted to the organization as a 'sacred society,' a notion that was given meaning and enforced through separation from the larger society 'outside.' It had almost the character of speaking a different language. Newly joined members also were, according to many of the ex-members I spoke with, expected to choose between their old and new friends, the latter being their 'brothers' in the organization. Calling members of the group 'brothers' expressed what William A. Gamson calls 'adversarial framing'[172] and other scholars 'boundary framing'[173]: a way of delineating boundaries between insiders and outsiders considered, respectively, as 'protagonists' and 'antagonists' (which relates the two abovementioned principles of 'communion' and 'renunciation'). It is no wonder then, that exiting members stopped calling any member of the movement a 'Brother.' They would feel the need to reframe their language and thinking about other matters. All of the ex-members whom I met developed, ad hoc, new sets of rules for social interactions to replace the old ones that for them were now in disuse. These rules included expressing gratitude with a simple *shukran* (thank you), where Brothers had insisted on using the more formal and less common *jazak Allah khair* (May God reward you with good).[174] None of the dozens of ex-members interviewed for the book mentioned the latter phrase during the hours of our conversations. On a perhaps less trivial level, the transcripts of the interviews are full of swear words that the Brotherhood society had long boasted of avoiding. R.S. referred to the leaders as *walaad weskha* (a common slang expression or curse that literally means 'sons of a dirty woman,' akin to the English 'son of a b***h' or the Spanish *hijo de puta* or 'son of a whore'), an expression that one interviewee, M.I.'A., used in referring to the post-Morsi regime. This was far from the language authorized by the Brotherhood, Article 7 of whose General Law states, 'Bluntness, crudeness, and abuses in words or by hints must be avoided at all cost.'[175]

---

[172] Gamson, W. A. (1995). Constructing social protest. In H. Johnston & B. Klandermans (Eds.), *Social movements and culture: Social movements, protest, and contention* (vol. 4, pp. 85–106). Minnesota: University of Minnesota.

[173] Hunt, S. A., Benford, R. D., & Snow, D. A. (1994). Identity fields: Framing processes and the social construction of movement identities. In E. Laraña, J. R. Gusfield, & H. Johnston (Eds.), *New social movements: From ideology to identity* (pp. 185–208 [194]).

[174] Kandil, *Inside the Brotherhood*, p. 73.

[175] Lia, *Society of Muslim Brothers in Egypt*, p. 110.

It may have been partly a rebellion against Brotherhood norms of purity, civility, or simply linguistic correctness as such; it was in any case quite plainly a refusal of its prescribed way of speaking, and in favour of one, less regulated for its propriety. To sum up this point, changes in emotions correspond with changes in 'linguistic expressions.'

Abandoning the role of Brotherhood as an affective act is not only a matter of texturing; among other domains in which 'affect' is observable are 'alternations' in external aspects of behavior with regard to codes of dress and hairstyle. When I met M.S. in a café near Istanbul, he recounted his pursuit of emancipation by disengaging from the Brotherhood: 'The brotherhood restricts your freedom, even literally to the extent of asking you to comb your hair to the side instead of combing it to the back.'[176] Indeed, he appeared with his hair slicked back, a hairstyle that in Brotherhood circles is considered unmanly and perhaps gay (a taboo, to be sure). When I asked, 'What do you call such an act?,' he answered sarcastically, *hureiyeeeee* [freeeeedom] (that is, using the Arabic word with an elongated vowel for emphasis). These are all performances of identity through, or against the background of, shifting linguistic and behavioral codes. Other members made a point of mixing with women, a previously proscribed behavior that their new spatial position encouraged. They are performances of the kind that can permit or require representing oneself in a way that is at odds with certain visible signs or expectations which the Brotherhood's identity always dictates. When I confronted him with the semiotics of the hairband in the dominant narratives in Egypt and inside the Brotherhood, M.E. answered: 'I do not care. I am still a good Muslim. I pray and practice religion, but in my own way, not the way of others.'[177]

Along with such re-codifications of appearance, the behavior of exiting members also tended to involve changes in manners. M.E. described how he now 'has many female friends, with whom he can go out and sit in cafes.' He considered it appropriate to have female friends 'as long as it is not a full relationship,' a partial deregulation that contrasts with the Brotherhood, which restricts communications between males and females.[178] M.E. told me that many of his friends who also had exited

---

[176] M.S. (2017).
[177] M.E. (2017).
[178] Kandil, *Inside the Brotherhood*, p. 73.

the Brotherhood and were in their early 20s 'drink alcoholic drinks and sleep with girls in the same houses that were provided by the group after they came to Turkey before they announce their disengagement.'[179] K. F., who had been a prefect himself, confirmed the commonality of such cases and also attributed these new modes of social life were partly a consequence of geographic re-spatialization.

'AFFECTIVE DISENGAGEMENT' CONTEXTUALIZED: OPPORTUNITIES AND RESOURCES

The argument made above can give a sense of causality in explaining 'affective' disengagement. Individuals lose the 'we' of the group's collective identity and its dominant discourse and this causes them to gain the 'I' as a symbol of autonomy, personal identity, and a discourse of resistance. The argument can also give the sense that this causality extends to language; frames construct disengagement into a consistent and coherent discourse drawn on repetition and resonant usage of similar keywords, phrases, or even sentences inside and across texts of exiting members. Nevertheless, any such sense of causality has to be ruled out as we have no cases of existing Brotherhood members through whom we can compare engagement with disengagement, the 'we' with the 'I' or even the past with the present. Furthermore, language is significant enough to create disengagement, but it is also created by other elements outside the texts and which can provide resources and opportunities for its articulation and materialization. Some of these elements can be *structural*, related to the state; *temporal*, related to the revolutionary moment that began in 2011; *processual*, as they are a presentist stage extending from similar attempts of disengagement in the past; *spatial*, as they can relate the geographically physical or relocation of members of the Brotherhood to countries other than Egypt. Furthermore, elements contributing resources and opportunities to disengagement could be more virtual and symbolic as part of globalized meanings recognizing no borders in formulation, circulation, and communication. To keep the analysis focused, I will portray the spatial and element while the other elements are to be thrown into analysis in next chapters.

---

[179] M.E. (2017).

Geographic re-spatialization has served as an affective resource creating opportunities even after the Brotherhood's dramatic fall from power in 2013, as thousands of members left Egypt due to different reasons. The change of place brought new opportunities, including careers and social circles. For some, it meant a voluntary 'positive isolation,' including from restrictive circles of family and Brotherhood-specific friends. All of the ex-members I interviewed who were living in the UK or Turkey cited an 'emancipation' (the same frame identified across texts as cited above) from family restrictions that they had found easier due to their distance from Egypt. The new spaces also made available coping strategies to counter the affect-related 'costs' of exiting and the 'threats' felt from within membership to an identity developing outside it. As I mentioned, El-Qaddoum said that moving to Turkey made it easier for him to disengage from the group, as in Egypt his father used to punish him severely for expressing the desire to leave. M.E., who in 2014 exited the Brotherhood, in which his father is a leading figure, 'carved out' a space for an independent career and lifestyle once he moved to Istanbul, and it was there that he finalized his decision to exit the group.[180] He found a job as an employee at an Istanbul hotel, and also enrolled in the engineering faculty of the city's Technical University, one of its premier higher education institutions. In Turkey, M.E. also developed a network of Turkish friends, both male and female. He learned the language, and after two years spoke it fluently. He said that he avoids communicating with members of the Brotherhood, who are densely concentrated in certain areas of Istanbul. 'I want to be dependent only on myself,'[181] he said, noting that he particularly avoided visiting districts where many members of the Brotherhood live. The negotiation of space based on identities was crucial for him in affirming his own more independent sense of self.

The ex-members I interviewed who lived in the UK also noted that their adaptation to a new place was 'emancipating.' Living in the West, with its advanced educational systems, liberal family values, broad personal rights, and, in some cities, many cultural opportunities, could facilitate the construction of a more modern, and 'entitled' self, far the Brotherhood's 'collective identity.' An ex-member living in the UK

---

[180] M.E. (2017).
[181] Ibid.

described how his wife ended up 'taking off her hijab [headscarf] when she came to the country after their exit from the Brotherhood.' He added, 'It is her personal freedom which I have to respect. Although her family stopped talking to her, she is coping well here without the head-scarf.' If he were still in Egypt, I wondered aloud, would his wife take such a step, and would he support her as such? The ex-member answered emphatically: 'Of course not. It is different here.' At the time of the interview, in 2017, the husband preferred not to be named, and he also kept his participation a secret from his family and friends. Less than one year later, as I was drafting this book, they both were emboldened to publish her picture without the hijab, taken while they were celebrating her birthday in London.

Changes in spaces mean changes in frames and the power they hold. In these new spaces, the frames of the Brotherhood no longer have power to induce members to filter perceptions of the world in a particular way, nor essentially making some aspects of our 'multi-dimensional reality' more noticeable than other aspects. In Turkey, as an example, there are many cases of disgruntled members of the Brotherhood who decided to live far from the Brotherhood-concentrated areas where most of their fellows live. This dislocation 'is purposeful as it made it harder for the Brotherhood to contact group members for weekly meetings (part of the duties of each member) in a city as big as Istanbul, or even for leaders to monitor or punish their behaviour as has been the case in Egypt.'[182] K.F., a former Brotherhood junior official, admitted that fewer than 10% of members living abroad attended meetings of their Brotherhood family (the smaller unit in the structure of the group) in Turkey, and that these meetings had been a must-attend back in Egypt. 'It is a different environment,' he noted. For members in exile, the Brotherhood lost what Scott Atran called the overlapping of society and space: When 'spatial and social constraints coincide or strongly overlap, as with a village of tribal lineage…then defection becomes relatively easy to spot and weed out.'[183] The Brotherhood can no longer create this coincidence or overlapping of constraints. While it had earlier been able to exclude the ex-members as 'dissidents' or spatially isolate them

[182] Sha'ban, M. (2018).
[183] Atran, *Talking to the enemy: Violent extremism*, p. 311.

by warning members against approaching or interacting with them, such punishments were impractical in countries like Turkey or the UK. Perhaps the opportunities emanating from geographic re-spatialization can also be evident where it is absent, that is, the cases of exiting members who did not relocate outside Egypt. The ex-members I interviewed who were living in Egypt tended to express emotional pain due to what we call 'negative isolation' from family and former friends, as contrasted with the 'positive isolation' experienced by those living in countries such as Turkey or the UK. The 'negative isolation' was actively expressed, as attempts at explicit norm-enforcement that included refusing to shake hands and not being invited to weddings and other events. The fact that actors and subjects of this isolation live in the same geographical place provides a 'context dimension'[184] eliciting conditions of such negative emotions as shame. In addition, space comes with, as part of these conditions, the 'presence of audience,'[185] who engage in interactions with the exiting member and create circumstances which will call for his feeling of shame. Tareq El-Beshbeshy, a member of the Shura Council of the Brotherhood in the Governorate of El-Beheira, said the 'fear of isolation' was one of the things that 'scared him in the exiting process.' He also had earlier witnessed cases of isolation of members after they had exited the group to show how this fear is linked to geographic proximity as 'most of my family members and friends live near each other in the same area. All my brothers, who are members of the group and live nearby, cut their links with me. They took me as their enemy and started spreading rumors.'[186] The fact that many individuals referred to incidents in which a former close friend from the Brotherhood would meet an exiting member without a greeting—nor even so much as a facial expression of acknowledgment normally due to a friend—as the hardest and most painful moments after disengagement substantiate this correlation linking disengagement and re-spatialization. It is a correlation which can prevent individuals from one of their basic 'psychological' needs and components of achievement: 'Affiliation.'[187] The latter

[184] Deonna, J. A., Rodogno, R., & Teroni, F. (2012). *In defense of shame*, p. 24.

[185] Ibid.

[186] El Beshbeshy, T. (2017).

[187] Buechner, V. L., Stahn, V., & Murayama, K. (2018). The power and affiliation component of achievement pride: Antecedents of achievement pride and effects on academic performance. In *Frontiers in education* (Vol. 3, p. 107). Frontiers.

can also trigger all these emotions of acceptance and approval of others, be it friends, neighbors, or co-members in the same group (and in the case of the Brotherhood and as alluded to above, the list of 'others' can include all of those categories). At the same time, the limitation also prevents individuals from another basic 'psychological' need: power (of movement).[188] El-Beshbeshy ameliorated the consequences of this isolation by 'virtual' and internal re-spatialization. His Facebook page was full of pictures of him meeting friends, mostly ex-members, in cafés, seminars, or prayer services led by other exited members. In other words, and by adopting a broader definition of space beyond geography, exiting members inside Egypt created their own form of 'internal' or virtual re-spatialization even when they did not move abroad. It is not just being in a different country but being in a different space that can make the difference. This is really important from the motivational perspective, as each exiting member is ultimately not completely alone; that is to say, disengagement is not a 'lonely business' as each exiting member can find others who share each other's vision and they can link up with them through rituals of being an ex-.[189] This means, each exiting member has a better chance of completing his disengagement as she or he can find others living in the same time and space who share the same desires and are willing to communicate.[190]

CONCLUSION

Exiting the Muslim Brotherhood was a process of identity-making, as analysis of the written and verbal narratives of exiting individuals reveals. This process includes a work of assimilation/accommodation and evaluation. Through their means, new developments in the structure of an identity were achieved, by defining oneself as an ex-member, adjusting to a new social context, and evaluating one's experience as positive, powerful, and active. Also involved was a patterned re-alignment of frames reflecting the new identity. Frames such as slavery and emancipation or expressions of an 'I' against a mere 'we' were amplified, transformed, extended, and bridged to reflect the affective meanings pertaining to disengagement.

[188] Ibid.
[189] Prsaud, *The motivated mind*, p. 36.
[190] Ibid.

This process of building a new identity was not always straight-forward or without risks. It was not easy to get rid of closely-knit net-works of family that had always provided members of the Brotherhood with a sense of continuity across time, place, and situation. The loss of friendships, which functioned as imagined kinship, was painful as exit-ing members could be subjected to efforts of isolation or 'smear cam-paigns' launched against them. The impact of these losses could be severe because family and friends were central inside the Brotherhood. They tended to serve as a 'social looking-glass,' a mirror reflecting to each ex-member how others were reacting to her or his doings and feel-ings. This could be used to invoke shame or guilt, particularly in, or in relation to, exiting members.[191] More significantly, and relevantly to our debate, these losses directly hamper any desire for disengagement, as they lead to 'silence,' and those with critical views would prefer not to express their ideas in fear of becoming isolated from their limited and closed environment which is fully controlled by the Brotherhood.[192]

This meant that the new identifications of the 'self' in a more indi-vidual and less collectively prescribed manner were far from being clear-cut, straightforward, or even causally driven. It is a process of struggle and hesitation. Ahmed Ramzy describes in the preface to his autobi-ography how he feared the 'anger' of his father, a loyal member of the Brotherhood, who might misunderstand his telling of his story as 'act of disobedience.'[193] 'Abdel-Mon'im said that she feared that in pub-lishing her autobiography, she might lose more friends and even have poorer chances of marriage, based on the principle that 'a member of the Brotherhood marries another member of the Brotherhood.'[194]

As part of this struggle in the process leading to the disassociation from the group, exiting members seek to 'cope' with these social and psychological pressures. They would pray in different mosques than those frequented by Brotherhood members, and networked with each

---

[191] Smith said, 'This is the only looking-glass by which we can, in some measure, with the eyes of other people, scrutinize the propriety of our own conduct.' Smith, A. (2011). *The theory of moral sentiments*. Gutenberg Publishers.

[192] This argument is informed by the theory of 'Spiral of Silence'; see Noelle-Neumann, E. (1977). Turbulences in the climate of opinion: Methodological applications of the spiral of silence theory. *Public Opinion Quarterly, 41*(2), 143–158.

[193] Ramzy, A. (2013). Dawlat al-murshid wa sanam al-ikhwan, p. 7.

[194] 'Abdel-Mon'im, I. (2011). pp. 19, 39.

other to form a 'society of ex-members.' They changed their dress, speech, and gender separation practices. Re-spatialization, whether geographical, by physically moving to new countries such as the UK or Turkey, or by consolidating their virtual communications, also helped greatly to sustain their disengagement discourse.

BIBLIOGRAPHY

Abdel-Hady, F. (2011). *Rihlati ma' al-Akhawat al-Muslemat* [My journey with the female Muslim Brotherhood members]. Cairo: Dar Al-Shorouk.

Abdel-Halim, M. (1994). *Al-Ikhwan al-Muslimoon: ahdath san't al-tarikh, ru'ya min al-dakhil* [The Muslim Brotherhood: Events that made history, an inside perspective]. Alexandria: Da'wa.

Abdul-Latif, E. (2011). Interdiscursivity between political and religious discourses in a speech by Sadat: Combining CDA and addressee rhetoric. *Journal of Language and Politics, 10*(1), 50–67.

Al-Anani, K. (2016). *Inside the Muslim Brotherhood: Religion, identity and politics.* Oxford: Oxford University Press.

Arendell, T. (2000). Conceiving and investigating motherhood: The Decade's scholarship. *Journal of Marriage and Family* (1194). https://doi.org/10.1111/j.1741-3737.2000.01192.x.

Atran, S. (2010). *Talking to the enemy: Violent extremism, sacred values, and what it means to be human.* London, UK: Penguin.

Bell, S. (2006). Becoming a mother after DES: Intensive mothering in spite of it all. In *Discourse and identity.* https://doi.org/10.1017/cbo9780511584459.012.

Benford, R. (1993). Frame disputes within the nuclear disarmament movement. *Social Forces, 71*(3). https://doi.org/10.2307/2579890.

Bittner, E. (1963). Radicalifsm and the organization of radical movements. *American Sociological Review, 28*(6), 928–940.

Blumer, H. (1969). *Symbolic interactionism: Perspectives and method.* Chicago: Chicago University Press.

Brown, N. J. (2012). *When victory is not an option: Islamist movements in Arab politics.* Ithaca and London: Cornell University Press.

Breakwell, G. M. (1986). *Coping with threatened identities.* London: Methuen.

Clough, P., & Halley, J. (2007). *The affective turn: Theorizing the social.* Durham: Duke University Press. James Jasper argues that 'there would be no social movements' if we did not have 'affective' responses to developments near or far: Jasper, *Sociological Forum, 13*, 397–424.

Coser, L. (1974). *Greedy institutions: Patterns of undivided commitment.* New York: Free Press.

Della Porta, D. (2008). *Leaving underground organizations, leaving terrorism behind: Individual and collective disengagement*. New York: Routledge.

Dillard, J. P., & Seo, K. (2013). Affect and persuasion. In J. P. Dillard & L. Shen (Eds.), *The Sage handbook of persuasion: Developments in theory and practice*. Los Angeles: Sage.

Deonna, J. A., Rodogno, R., & Teroni, F. (2012). *In defense of shame: The faces of an emotion*. Oxford: Oxford University Press.

El-Banna, H. (1990). *Majmu't rasael al-imam el-Shahid Hassan El-Banna* [A collection of epistles of the martyr imam Hassan El-Banna]. Alexandria: Da'wa.

El-Sherif, A. (2014). *The Egyptian Muslim Brotherhood's failures*. New York: Carnegie.

Entman, R. M. (1991). Symposium framing US coverage of international news: Contrasts in narratives of the KAL and Iran air incidents. *Journal of Communication, 41*(4), 6–27.

Entman, R. M. (1993). Framing: Towards a clarification of a fractured paradigm. *Journal of Communication, 43*(4), 51–58.

Fairclough, N. (1992). Intertextuality in critical discourse analysis. *Linguistics and Education, 4*(3), 269–293.

Fillieule, O. (2015). Disengagement from radical organizations: A process and multilevel model of analysis. In P. G. Klandermans & C. van Stralen (Eds.), *Movements in times of democratic transition*. Pennsylvania: Temple University Press.

Gamson, W. A. (1995). Constructing social protest. In H. Johnston & B. Klandermans (Eds.), *Social movements and culture: Social movements, protest, and contention*. (Vol. 4). Minnesota: University of Minnesota.

Gilbert, P. (2003). Evolution, social roles, and the differences in Shame and Guilt. *Social Research, 70*(4), 1205–1230.

Goffman, E. (1956). Embarrassment and social organization. *American Journal of Sociology, 62*, 206. https://doi.org/10.1086/222003.

Hays, S. (1996). *The cultural contradictions of motherhood*. New Haven: Yale University Press.

Hobson, R. P., & Hobson, J. (2014). On empathy: A perspective from developmental psychopathology. In H. Maibom (Ed.), *Empathy and morality* (pp. 172–192). Oxford: Oxford University Press.

Hunt, S. A., Benford, R. D., & Snow, D. A. (1994). Identity fields: Framing processes and the social construction of movement identities. In E. Laraña, J. R. Gusfield, & H. Johnston (Eds.), *New social movements: From ideology to identity* (p. 194). Philadelphia: Temple University Press.

Jasper, J. (1998). The emotions of protest: Affective and reactive emotions in and around social movements. *Sociological Forum, 13*, 397–424. https://doi.org/10.1023/a:1022175308081.

Jessen, J. T. (2015). Job satisfaction and social rewards in the social services. *Journal of Comparative Social Work*, 5(1), 1–18.

Kandil, H. (2015). *Inside the Brotherhood*. Malden: Polity Press.

Klandermans, B. (1997). *The social psychology of protest*. Oxford: Blackwell.

Klandermans, B. (2004). The demand and supply of participation: Social-psychological correlates of participation in social movements. In D. A. Snow, S. A. Soule, & H. Kriesi (Eds.), *The Blackwell companion to social movements*. Malden: Blackwell.

Klandermans, B. (2015). Disengaging from movements. In J. Goodwin & J. Jasper (Eds.), *The Social movements Reader*. Chichester: Wiley-Blackwell.

Klandermans, B., & Mayer, N. (Eds.). (2006). *Extreme right activists in Europe: Through the magnifying glass*. New York: Routledge.

Kriesi, H. (Ed.). (2007). *The Blackwell companion to social movements*. Malden: Blackwell Pub.

Lasswell, H. (1927). The theory of political propaganda. *American Political Science Review*, 21, 628. https://doi.org/10.2307/1945515.

Lia, B. (1998). *The society of Muslim Brothers in Egypt: The rise of an Islamic mass movement, 1928–1942*. Reading: Ithaca Press.

Lippmann, W. (1997). *Public opinion*. New York: Free Press Paperbacks.

Melucci, A. (2002). Becoming a person: New frontiers for identity and citizenship in a planetary society. In M. Kohli & A. Woodward (Eds.), *Inclusions and exclusions in European Societies*. London: Routledge.

Nias, D. K. B. (1977). Husband-Wife similarities. *Social Science*, 52(4), 206–211. Available via: http://0-www.jstor.org.library.qnl.qa/stable/41886198. Accessed 22 October 2018.

Parsons, T., & Bryan, S. T. (2005). *The social system*. London: Taylor & Francis.

Pollock, D. (1999). *Telling bodies performing birth: Everyday narratives of childbirth*. New York: Columbia University Press.

Purgin, E. (2012). Hey, How did I become a role model? Privacy and the extent of role-model obligations. *Journal of Applied Philosophy*, 29(2), 118–132.

Sabini, J., Garvey, B., & Hall, A. L. (2001). Shame and embarrassment revisited. *Personality and Social Psychology Bulletin*, 27(1), 104–117.

Scheff, T. (2003). Shame in self and society. *Symbolic Interaction*, 26, 239–262. https://doi.org/10.1525/si.2003.26.2.239.

Smith, A. (2011). *The theory of moral sentiments*. London: Gutenberg Publishers.

Senko, C., & Tropiano, K. L. (2016). Comparing three models of achievement goals: Goal orientations, goal standards, and goal complexes. *Journal of Educational Psychology*, 108(8), 1178.

Snow, D., Rochford, E., Worden, S., & Benford, R. (1986). Frame alignment processes, micromobilization, and movement participation. *American Sociological Review*, 51(4), 464–481 (467). Available via: http://www.jstor.org/stable/2095581.

Staub, E. (1978). Predicting prosocial behavior: A model for specifying the nature of personality-situation interaction. *Perspectives in interactional psychology*. Boston: Springer.

Tiriandis, H. C., & Vassiliou, V. (1967). *A comparative analysis of subjective culture*. Group Effectiveness Research Laboratory, University of Illinois.

Vignoles, V. L., Regalia, C., Manzi, C., Golledge, J., & Scabini, E. (2006). Beyond self-esteem: Influence of multiple motives on identity construction. *Journal of Personality and Social Psychology, 90*, 308–333.

Wolters, C. A. (2004). Advancing achievement goal theory: Using goal structures and goal orientations to predict students' motivation, cognition, and achievement. *Journal of Educational Psychology, 96*(2), 236–250.

Zahavi, D. (2015). You, me, and we: The sharing of emotional experiences. *Journal of Consciousness Studies, 22*(1–2), 84–101.

Zaki, M. S. (1980). *Al-Ikhwan al-Muslimun wa-al-mujtama' al-Misri* [The Muslim Brotherhood and Egyptian society] (pp. 195–198). Cairo: Dar al-Ansar.

AUTOBIOGRAPHIES

'Abdel-Mon'im, I. (2011). *Hekayati ma' Al-Ikhwan* [My story with the Muslim Brotherhood]. Cairo: Al-Hayaa Al-Misriyya Al-'ama leil Kitab.

Ban, A. (2013). *Al-Ikhwan Al-Muslimoon wa mehnat al-watan wal deen* [The Muslim Brotherhood and the predicament of nation and religion]. Cairo: Al-Neel Centre for Strategic Studies.

Ban, A. (2017). *Ikhwan wa Salafiyyon wa Dawa'ish* [Brothers, Salafists and ISIS Loyalists]. Cairo: Al-Mahrousa.

'Eid, S. (2013). *Tajribati fi saradeeb Al-Ikhwan* [My experience in the basements of MB]. Cairo: Jazeerat al-Ward.

'Eid, S. (2014). *Qissati ma' Al-Ikhwan* [My story with the Muslim Brotherhood]. Cairo: Mahrousa.

'Eid, S. (2014). *Al-Ikhwan Al-Muslimoon, al-hader wal mustaqbal: Awraq fil Naqd Al-Zati* [The Muslim Brotherhood, the present and the future: Papers from self-criticism]. Cairo: Al-Mahroussa.

El-'Agouz, A. (2012). *Ikhwani out of the box* [A Muslim brother out of the box]. Cairo: Dewan.

El-Khirbawy, T. (2012). *Ser al-m'abad: Al-Asrar al-khafiya li gama't Al-Ikhwan Al-Muslemeen* [The temple's secret: The hidden secrets of the Muslim Brotherhood]. Cairo: Nahdet Masr.

Fayez, S. (2011). *Janat Al-Ikhwan: Rehlat al-khuroug min al-gam'a* [The MB paradise: The journey of getting out of the group]. Cairo: Al-Tanweer.

Ramzy, A. (2013). *Dawlat al-murshid wa sanam Al-Ikhwan* [The state of the guide and the statue of Muslim Brotherhood]. Cairo: Rodiy.

OTHER INTERVIEWEES

Brown, N., an American scholar of Middle Eastern law and politics at George Washington University, in Person, 4 March 2018.

Mustafa, Z., the wife of former Brotherhood leader Kamal El-Helbawy, London, 5 June 2017.

Sha'ban, M., a journalist and a researcher on Political Islam, in Person, Istanbul, 5 June 2017.

*For additional Interviewees who are ex-members of the Brotherhood see the appendix Table A.1.

**For Age groups at the time of joining the Muslim Brotherhood (divided by ages and stages of development from children to youth and beyond) see the appendix Table A.5.

CHAPTER 3

Ideological Disengagement

INTRODUCTION

This chapter is about how some individual members acted against some of the ideas that were central to the Muslim Brotherhood's ideological character and influence, as part of the process of their disengagement. The concept of ideology can be broadly understood as indicating relationships of power creating 'distortions' in the way members understand the social world and their role in it, that keep them from developing a true or adequate understanding of the circumstances in which they find themselves, or that entangle them in an imaginary relationship of hegemony and domination with their real conditions of existence. But beyond questions of power and systematic 'distortions' in thoughts, it is also possible to consider ideology as sets of 'thematized meanings'[1] to 'think about' along with being 'an interpretive code' to 'think from.'[2] In this sense, the Brotherhood's leaders and members could be both managers of meaning. This chapter analyzes how exiting members activate their own interpretive codes by invoking ideas and meanings attached to

---

[1] Holloway, I., & Todres, L. (2003). The status of method: Flexibility, consistency and coherence. *Qualitative Research, 3*, 345–357 (347). https://doi.org/10.1177/1468794103033004.

[2] Ricoeur, P. (1981). *Hermeneutics and the human sciences: Essays on language, action and interpretation* (J. Thompson Ed., and Trans.) (p. 227). Cambridge: Cambridge University Press; Porter, R. (2006). *Ideology: Contemporary social, political and cultural theory* (p. 6). Cardiff: University of Wales Press.

© The Author(s) 2020
M. Menshawy, *Leaving the Muslim Brotherhood*, Middle East Today,
https://doi.org/10.1007/978-3-030-27860-1_3

them and that may have been long suppressed, hidden, or falsified by the dominant ideas and meanings in the group, including those attributed to the group's leaders. As the case study involves autobiographies and interviews in which exiting members narrate their experiences inside and outside the Brotherhood, my argument is that these individuals have begun a process of ideological disengagement in their minds. As disengagement was essentially a product of their own thinking (or was experienced as such), the relevant ideas could be both *personal* and *cognitive* at the same time of being *collective* and *social*.[3] Still, this process of meaning-making is also based on happenings and mechanisms outside their mind and which allow us to understand the phenomenon both as process and discourse (see Chapter 1). Thus, it is important to consider, as I do in this chapter, not just persons, but also actions, interactions, interpretations, situations, groups, societies, and even the state, as playing a role in the process of constructing an 'ideology of resistance,' that being essentially to describe and explain their disengagement.

The previous chapter investigated how each individual disengaged from her or his social 'relation of belonging,' having earlier been thrown into a particular social tradition that shaped most of their thinking, through a counter-framing of the self, and real and imagined kinship. This chapter explores the same process at the level of ideology: How each individual shifted his or her ideological 'relation of belonging' through a frame re-alignment process. This is a process whereby specific meanings related to the Brotherhood's ideology are negotiated and contested in relation to new frames and frames. A frame, manifesting in linguistic formats represented by certain words, metaphors, or expressions, is explored 'in motion'; it can interact with relevant frames one broader frame conveying joint meanings or it can reconstruct, reinterpret, or counter other frames mostly used by the Brotherhood itself to build and process its own hegemonic 'engagement' discourse.

---

[3] By 'cognition,' I mean the general mental processes allowing individuals to 'perceive and act upon objects.' According to the standard view in cognitive psychology, individuals use perceptual processes to 'analyze input into coherent units.' It is also said that they do this through processes of 'grouping' (putting elements together into 'perceptual wholes') and 'segregating' (i.e., parsing these wholes into 'separate objects'). See Reisberg, D. (2013). *The Oxford handbook of cognitive psychology* (pp. 9–10). Oxford: Oxford University Press. This provides another way of understanding the processes of grouping and segregating of discursive themes by exiting individuals in the process of ideological engagement and disengagement.

IDEOLOGY OF THE BROTHERHOOD: A CASE OF 'ANTI-INTELLECTUALISM'

Ex-members put an emphasis in their narrative on disillusionment with one key aspect of the Brotherhood's ideology: Its anti-intellectualism. Anti-intellectualism is difficult to define, as it is a discrete phenomenon that eschews spatial or temporal boundaries. Consequently, it would little avail to have a simple definition based on singling out one trait among a complex of traits.[4] I therefore treat it as a continuum with intellectualism at the opposite end, and as including both cognitive and affective features.[5] On this continuum, anti-intellectualism may be a result of a style of obtaining 'knowledge' intuitionally, through instincts, character, moral sensibilities, and emotions. Intellectualism, on the other side, can be a 'rational complexity associated with intellectual pursuits.'[6] Here exiting individuals' perceptions can be analyzed in terms of their rejection or embrace of intellectual values in the Brotherhood's dominant ideology.[7] In analyzing the texts of exiting members, I will search for all frames related to anti-intellectualism as a scale/frame comprising frames such as 'cognitive inflexibility,' 'the need to structure,' 'authoritarianism,' and 'dogmatism.'

THE 'NO MIND' FRAME

One frame is drawn on recurring expression in the narratives of exiting members is, 'The Brotherhood has no mind.' Intissar 'Abdel-Mon'im in her autobiography says that she became 'so indoctrinated in the group, enough to lose the functionality of our mind.' She specifically mentions misogynistic practices, such as not allowing women to question 'plans

[4]Hofstadter, R. (1962). *Anti-intellectualism in American life* (p. 7). London: Jonathan Cape.

[5]Eigenberger, M., Critchley, C., & Sealander, K. (2007). Individual differences in epistemic style: A dual-process perspective. *Journal of Research in Personality, 41*, 3–24. https://doi.org/10.1016/j.jrp.2006.01.003.

[6]Shogan, C. (2007). Anti-intellectualism in the modern presidency: A republican populism. *Perspectives on Politics, 5*, 295–303. https://doi.org/10.1017/s153759270707079x.

[7]Marques, M., Elphinstone, B., Critchley C., & Eigenberger, M. E. (2017). A brief scale for measuring anti-intellectualism. *Personality and Individual Differences, 114*, 167–174. https://doi.org/10.1016/j.paid.2017.04.001.

laid out by male members.'[8] Ahmed Ramzy writes in his autobiography that 'the Brotherhood is a group without a mind,' mentioning that in the group obeying an order 'comes before thinking of it' and that it had created members who are 'without mind and always share a herd mentality.'[9] Ahmed El-'Agouz says in his autobiography that the group wanted him to live 'with body and without mind,' and 'to paralyse the mind.'[10] Sameh 'Eid highlighted his disillusionment with the group's failure to contain his attempt to 'raise debate and open minds.'[11] This frame was so salient that several individuals causally attributed to it their choosing to 'texture' their experiences in an autobiography. These are examples from different autobiographies: The book is an attempt to 'take my mind out of any attempts to freeze it'[12]; the book is a 'search for my critical mind'[13]; the book is 'the by-product of half my mind, as the group destroyed the other half.'[14] On some occasions, the attribution is causal and direct. Ahmed Ban included in his autobiography his full resignation letter, from February 2012, which mentions how 'the group fixated in

---

[8] 'Abdel-Mon'im, I. (2011). *Hekayatii ma' Al-Ikhwan* [My story with the MB] (p. 2). Cairo: Al-Hayaa Al-Misriyya Al-'Ama leil Kitab. This 'misogynist' attitude can be justified by the writings of the leaders of the Brotherhood including those of El-Banna. Due to physical features and rules of Islam, a man has the upper hand as he is in charge of 'reforming,' 'sponsoring,' and 'disciplining' a woman, said El-Banna in one of his main writings. A woman, he added, should be educated 'the basics of her mission' as a mother including 'reading, writing, maths, religion….., house running and raising children…' For a woman to learn any other sciences is 'a waste of time' and 'nonsense' as 'Islam sees that a woman's main mission is her house and children'; El-Banna, H. (1990). *Majmu't rasael al-imam el-shahid Hassan El-Banna* [A collection of epistles of the martyr imam Hassan El-Banna] (pp. 298–305). Alexandria, Egypt: Da'wa.

[9] Ramzy, A. (2013). *Dawlat al-murshid wa sanam Al-Ikhwan* [The state of the guide and the statue of Muslim Brotherhood] (p. 42). Cairo: Rodiy.

[10] El-'Agouz, A. (2011). *Ikhwani out of the box* [A Muslim Brother out of the box] (pp. 24, 21). Cairo: Dawen.

[11] Eid, S. (2014). *Al-Ikhwan Al-Muslimoon: Al-hader wal mustaqbal, awraq fil naqd al-zati* [The Muslim Brotherhood: The present and the future: Papers from self-criticism] (p. 27). Cairo: Al-Mahroussa.

[12] El-'Agouz, *Ikhwani out of the box*, p. 8.

[13] 'Abdel-Mon'im, *Hekayatii ma' Al-Ikhwan*, p. 210.

[14] Ban, A. (2013). *Al-Ikhwan Al-Muslimoon wa mehnat al-watan wal deen* [The Muslim Brotherhood and the predicament of nation and religion] (p. 7). Cairo: Al-Neel Centre for Strategic Studies.

my mind some unreasonable and justified facts which we have to abide by for the sake of promotion into its ranks.'[15]

The frame repeatedly and frequently mentioned in autobiographies was also found in interviews.[16] For instance, when I asked interviewees, 'Why did you leave the Brotherhood?,' many spoke of gaining or regaining an independence of mind. Thus, responses included: that disengagement was a 'journey into regaining my mind'[17]; 'I had a different way of thinking from the dogmatic traditionalists inside the group'[18]; 'I gained my mind. The Brotherhood wants you to shut down your mind'[19]; 'I gained a respect for myself and my mind'[20]; and 'They wanted me to cancel my mind by not questioning any orders which I had to obey. Simply, the mind should be turned off.'[21] This expression was common across differences of age, geographical location, rank within the group when they were members, or manner of leaving (some exited the group at a time (2011–2012) when they held a high profile and the group was in power, and others (during the 2013–2015 period) after being imprisoned and/or tortured after the group lost its power).

The significance of the frame lies in its 'metonymical nature.' In texts, many exiting members use the mind and the brain not as separate entities but indistinctively and interchangeably (e.g., one recurring description in autobiographies is 'the group is a body without the brain part of it'). This signals that the mind is only a 'part' standing for the whole of the Brotherhood's 'body,' or what George Lakoff and Mark Johnsen refer to as 'the part for the whole.'[22] The metonymy serves the framing process by adding 'salience' based on 'selectiveness' of particular characteristics of the group as highlighted by exiting members. In other words, as eloquently put by Lakoff and Johnsen, 'which part we pick out determines which

[15] Ban, *Al-Ikhwan Al-Muslimoon wa Mehnat al-watan*, p. 284.

[16] See Fairclough, N. (2003). *Analyzing discourse—Textual research for social research.* New York: Routledge.

[17] M.E. (2017).

[18] M.S.M. (2017).

[19] Nazily, A. (2017).

[20] S.E. (2017).

[21] S.M. (2017).

[22] Lakoff, G., & Johnson, M. (1980). *Metaphors we live by* (pp. 37–38). London: University of Chicago press.

aspect of the whole we are focusing on.'[23] As examples mentioned above indicate, ex-members highlight certain aspects of what is being referred to in the ideological disengagement. When they think of the Brotherhood's 'mind,' ex-members are not thinking of it, in and of itself. They think of it in terms of its relation with the group's power of imagination, recognition, appreciation, the ability to process different views or new ideas.

The metonymical use of the mind and body to refer to the Brotherhood as an ideology creates another element supporting the ideological disillusionment: Personification. Viewing something as abstract and theoretical as ideology in human terms thus has an 'explanatory power' of the sort that makes sense to most people. This not only gives a 'specific way of thinking' about ideology, now being a person with a body and a brain/mind, but also a way of 'acting toward it.'[24] In individual disengagements from the Brotherhood, exiting members can see the whole group or its ideology as another 'person' that can be attacked, hurt, or even destroyed as an adversary. Strikingly, as ideology is personified, sections below show how the texts include an unprecedented phenomenon of directing criticism at one specific person, El-Banna, the long revered founder of the group and a self-proclaimed 'personifier' of its ideology.

Ex-members, by stripping the Brotherhood of the 'mind' and attached faculties, make us understand that their disengagement is based on and processed by the 'mind.' Most of them attribute their disengagement to a process of 'conscious' thinking and cognitively driven meanings resulting in the decision to get out of the group (as evidenced in the practice of cumulative independent reading, literature review, and argument-based debating that are explained below). Having said that, the metonymical concept allowing us to perceive the group in terms of its mind is not merely a matter of language. They cannot be even treated as isolated instances of random or arbitrary occurrences. They are systematic in the sense of responding to the Brotherhood's dominant frames also based on systematically claiming full respect to the 'mind' in its ideology. The group organize thoughts and actions on these claims. The 'group has no mind' frame is thus connected by interdiscursive opposition with the Brotherhood's ideology emphasizing that the 'group

[23] Ibid., p. 36
[24] Ibid., pp. 33–34.

has a mind.'[25] The First Pillar of the Oath of Allegiance, which members had to take before being admitted as full members of the group, is 'Comprehension.' El-Banna also stressed it by showing how the group's ideology 'liberates the mind' and 'respects' different views.[26] The claim has always been qualified by rules and principles paradoxically calling for the opposite: Blind obedience to unquestioned orders. Therefore, the texts of exiting members draw this construction and as they counter another frame in the group's ideology and which relates to one of its main rules and principles: *Al-Sam' wal T'a* [hearing and obedience].

The 'Hearing and Obedience' Frame

Al-Sam' wal T'a [hearing and obedience] is drawn on the Sixth Pillar of the Brotherhood's Oath of Allegiance, and which is named as 'Obedience.' It might seem to contradict with the principle of 'Comprehension' mentioned above. However, the latter is always based on the former. A member should blindly obey the Quraanic interpretations and other opinions issued by her or his leaders with no space for comprehension.[27] El-Banna, the founder, warned members not to get involved in debating 'meanings of the Quraan' or discussing subjects that are controversial in Islam, such as the historical disagreements between disciples of Prophet Muhammad.[28] This is also evidenced in the 'cultivation' curriculum used by the leaders of the group: when introducing the pillar of 'Comprehension,' they were to emphasize 'the necessity of bringing Muslims together around a single interpretation of Islam' and 'turn[ing] away from debate and arguments.'[29]

Almost all of the exiting members mentioned struggling against this principle. Nazily said that his exit, announced in 2011, was a set of gradual steps toward dissociating mainly from the 'hearing and obedience'

[25] In one of his writings, El-Banna repeatedly highlighted that 'Islam liberates mind,' El-Banna, *majmu't rasayyel al-imam*, pp. 416, 393.

[26] El-Banna, *Majmu't rasayyel al-imam*, p. 391

[27] Ibid., p. 391.

[28] Ibid., pp. 391–392. The position has always been justified inside the Brotherhood by evoking certain verses in Quraan which convey the same meaning such as 'O you who have believed, do not ask about things which, if they are shown to you, will distress you' (Quraan 5:101).

[29] Cited by Kandil, H. (2014). *Inside the Brotherhood* (p. 30). Cambridge: Polity Press.

requirements. Born into the group in 1978 (to a father and a mother who were leaders in it), Nazily said he had 'always been rebellious,' questioning all of the decisions issued by his prefect, who expected full obedience. He explained: 'I always wanted to understand any request or order before obeying it. Asking me to execute these orders as they are was really like chaining me to a wheel around which I should turn blindfolded.'[30] Nazily remembered one occasion 15 years earlier, when he had to act independently in the absence of this prefect 'On one occasion, I worked my mind and suggested to other members of the group to hold the meeting, share tasks and deputize the duties of the absent prefect [the leader of the Brotherhood family which is the smallest unit inside the group].'[31] A typical Brotherhood member would not do this act on basis of adhering to the hearing and obedience rule applied by the absent prefect.

The insistence on 'hearing and obedience' challenged here is part of the 'anti-intellectualism' frame as it shows on main feature of identifying it on the intellectualism/anti-intellectualism continuum agreed in the introduction above, that is 'cognitive inflexibility.' This is defined as the lack of 'awareness of options and alternatives in a situation, or the willingness and adaptability to be flexible.'[32] As exiting members found the group less flexible or considerate of options and alternatives, their perceptions and meanings thus draw its ideology as anti-intellectualistic.

One area in which this 'cognitive inflexibility' tended to be demonstrated was education. On one occasion, Nazily lamented that every member had to study a 'standard curriculum' of writings selected from a limited number of edited books that were printed out and distributed to the members.[33] 'Retrospectively,' Nazily added, 'I found it an

---

[30] Nazily, A. (2017).

[31] Nazily, A. (2017). The reaction to Nazily's behavior also runs against other Pillars of the Oath, that is, 'trust' as a member has to show 'full loyalty' to her or his leader. El-Banna even set a number of questions for a member to test the degree of putting her/his trust in the leaders: 'Are you ready to take the orders of the leaders as absolute, categorical and not open to debate, hesitation, criticism or modifications?,' El-Banna, H. (1990). *Majmu't rasayyel al-imam el-shahid*, p. 400.

[32] Martin, M., & Rubin, R. (1995). A new measure of cognitive flexibility. *Psychological Reports, 76,* 623–626. https://doi.org/10.2466/pr0.1995.76.2.623.

[33] According to the cultivation curriculum, composed of these edited volumes, a typical lesson of a weekly family meeting comprised 'carefully selected extracts from the Qur'an, Hadith, and the lives of the Prophet and his companions, followed by excerpts from the writings of El-Banna, and sometimes Qutb.' Kandil, H. (2015). *Inside the Brotherhood* (p. 9). Malden: Polity Press.

attempt to control our minds and keep them closed and exposed only to whatever limited material to offer it.'[34] The criteria used to determine the curriculum of study and other approved books was that they had to be 'action-driven,' that is, supplying Brotherhood members with the amount of knowledge 'needed for practice' so as to bring them closer to God and to nurture a 'new generation of Muslims committed to reviving and implementing Islam in all realms of human activity.'[35] This frame can be traced as patterns on the basis of the repetition and frequency. For instance, similar views to that of the 40-year-old Nazily in Qatar were expressed by the 28-year-old Mohamed Aboul-Gheit, who now lives in London. Nazily used to live in Cairo, the capital, while Aboul-Gheit is from the conservative town of Assuit in the south of Egypt. Both mentioned incidents indicating these frames. They even mentioned similar incidents. Aboul-Gheit objected to the censored curriculum of the Brotherhood, much as Nazily did. Aboul-Gheit was labeled 'Mohamed the troublemaker' because he often would question the orders of his seniors in the group instead of applying them, under the 'hearing and obedience' rule. He narrated this dialogue with his prefect: 'I asked: Why must we go to the camp? … How many days we will stay? … What we will do there?…' The prefect responded to all these questions in same sentence: 'We will tell you later.'[36]

This conversation reveals a marked cognitive inflexibility and closure. All of the questions Aboul-Gheit asked in this exchange were seeking informational answers. But the answers only were vague declarations of promises with no specific content, whose repetition underscores that they are not answers at all, but only attempts at evasion, patronizingly invoking an expected blind faith in the leaders. Even when, at the camp,

[34] Nazily, A. (2017).

[35] Kandil, H. (2015). *Inside the Brotherhood*, p. 17. Malden: Polity Press; Rosen, E. (2008). The Muslim Brotherhood's concept of education. *Current Trends in Islamist Ideology*, 7(85), 115–129, available via:https://www.hudson.org/research/9881-the-muslim-brotherhood-s-concept-of-education. Accessed 20 May 2019.

[36] Aboul-Gheit, M. (2017). The Brotherhood's 'Rover Scouts' unit which organizes such camps has a 'militaristic' nature enough not to allow raising such questions. El-Banna who established the unit was impressed with militaristic youth groups established in fascist Italy and Nazi Germany, and he wanted to create an Islamic version of these groups, so members of the Brotherhood can be better trained and qualified to spread da'wa and take part in 'Jihad'; see Brynjar, L. (1998). *The society of the Muslim Brothers in Egypt*. Reading: Ithaca Press, p. 167.

they started to participate in the activities, Aboul-Gheit and other members were told to carry out activities without questioning them. It was, of course, a practice of control. New members were told not to burden the teacher with questions, debate with, or interrupt him.[37] Aboul-Gheit described some of the physical activities that this involved, including 'sleeping for four hours in five days or running in the desert for long hours.' Yet, the activities that mostly triggered his disillusionment were mental ones. He described 'mind games' based on withholding information from members, and *disinformation*, presenting wrong or manipulated information to deceive members and control them. He recounted for me examples of training activities such as blindfolding him and other members and then telling them that one of them has to be chosen to carry out a 'martyrdom' attack: 'Some of us started shivering and others crying, since we all knew this would be an order which we could not refuse.'[38]

The 'Brotherhood Is Army' Frame

Another frame conveying the anti-intellectualism as found in the narratives of many ex-members is the notion: the Brotherhood's militarism. In order to draw meanings on this notion, exiting members would engage in a frame re-alignment process whose one feature is 'bridging.' This is when two distinct frames or concepts, such as the Brotherhood and the army, are treated as ideologically congruent and structurally connected. The effect can be to strengthen sentiments related to belonging (or disengaging) through an effect of multiplication.

Several ex-members would repeat the expression, 'the Brotherhood is an army,' in their autobiographies and interviews. Sameh 'Eid cited a 'quasi-military' educational system propagating 'loyalty, obedience, organisational discipline, secrecy.'[39] Ban said that the group kept treating its members as 'soldiers' controlled by 'army-like commanders' working under the principle of *al-Sam' wal T'a* ('hearing and obedience')

[37] Quoted in Kandil, *Inside the Brotherhood*, p. 23.
[38] Aboul-Gheit, M. (2017). This practice would fit in with the criteria set by the Brotherhood to measure almost all of the Pillars of the Oath of Allegiance such as obedience, devotion, loyalty, steadfastness, Jihad, Sacrifice, Brotherhood, Work, Faithfulness; see El-Banna, *majmu't rasayyel al-Imam*.
[39] 'Eid, *Al-Ikhwan Al-Muslimoon: Al-Hader wal mustaqbal*, p. 29.

in all cases.[40] El-'Agouz drew on the same analogy: 'It is the *gundia* (militarism) which turned us into obedient and loyal members.'[41] This 'militant nature,' Ramzy concurred, obstructed any freedom of speech, since 'trust would override dialogue.'[42] He gave examples of 'militant' orders that led to his ideological disillusionment. On one occasion, he was asked by his prefect in 2008 to take part in protests in support of the Lebanese group Hezbollah against Israel, while at the same time, he was instructed not to take part in the simultaneous protests against the Mubarak regime.[43] Mohamed El-Qassas, who exited in 2011, noted the group's use of militaristic terminology. He said:

> The group names a *Katiba* (battalion) to refer merely [to] a meeting for people to read Qur'an and pray. It calls a *Muaskar* [a military camp whose origin in Arabic means to militarize] what may just be merely a gathering for games of sport. Some leaders even name camps and activities after military battles in Islam.[44]

Again, judging by the level of emphasis, the frame cut across the experiences of ex-members, independently of age, geographical destination after leaving the group, gender, and type of narration (i.e., verbal or written account). This brings in-text 'interdiscursivity' where all texts of exiting members got related by using the same frame. In one of his books, 'Eid repeatedly describes Brotherhood members as 'soldiers' and its prefects as 'army commanders.'[45] It also mentions the words 'army,' 'militarisation,' 'military work,' and 'army titles' in a space of just two pages.[46] Later in the book, he slams the executive leaders of Brotherhood as 'army commanders' and 'army generals.'[47] Frames can seem 'amplified' by such dense or heavy repetition across texts. Ban's

---

[40] Ban, A. (2017). *Ikhwan wa Salafiyyon wa Daawaish* [Brothers, salafists and members of ISIS], p. 285.

[41] El-'Agouz, *Ikhwani out of the box*, p. 107.

[42] Ramzy, *Dawlat al-murshid wa sanam Al-Ikhwan*, p. 49.

[43] Ibid., p. 155.

[44] El-Qassas, M. (2017).

[45] 'Eid, *Al-Ikhwan Al-Muslimoon: Al-hader wal mustaqbal*, pp. 27, 28, 29, 54, 90.

[46] Ibid., pp. 114–115.

[47] Ibid., pp. 120–121.

book on one page speaks of the Brotherhood's 'military environment,'[48] its being 'plagued with militarism,' and indoctrinating members to be 'army-like soldiers' for a war-like 'battles.'[49]

Relatedly, the meanings drawn in texts of exiting members are counter-constructions of the dominant discourse of the Brotherhood. It is like an interdiscursivity *in reverse*, where meanings in one text are directed at undermining or countering meanings in the other text. In his main book, *Al-Rasael* [The Epistles], El-Banna uses, amplified the same frame bridging the army and his group. He mentioned words 'soldiers,' 'army,' and 'militarism' 71 times across the text. In his other seminal piece of writing, *Muzakerat Al-Da'wa* [Memoirs of Da'wa], he uses these words 68 times. The emphasis appears in the titles and headings of his manuscripts. He adds resonance to the frames by sanctifying them as part of Islam. He mentions verses from Quraan to convey the same meanings.[50] It could be argued the frames of El-Banna and counter-frames of exiting members could not be related since part of the reasoning for the 'army-like' status at the time of El-Banna is externalized, that is the need to face the 'British' occupation when he founded the Brotherhood in 1928. However, this status has always been internalized to direct the relationship between members and their leaders. In the texts of El-Banna, principles of 'military life' should be 'unity,' 'obedience,' and 'self-sacrifice,' and they should be adopted by each member and should be applied inside the group.[51] Therefore, this connectivity serves the broader frame of 'anti-intellectualism' as exiting members cite the group's militarism as evidence of instruments for the internal suppression of intellectual curiosity and of the right to raise questions or to criticize the group.

Disengagement by Intellectualism

As mentioned above, the group's anti-intellectualism exists on a continuum that includes a process of interpreting the group's ideology as

---

[48] Ban, *Al-Ikhwan Al-Muslimoon wa mehnat*, p. 231.

[49] Ibid., p. 289.

[50] El-Banna, H. (1990). *Majmu't rasayyel al-imam*, p. 76.

[51] Ibid. On other sections of the book, he highlighted the two values as 'cornerstones' of the whole concept of the Brotherhood, ibid., p. 37.

moving toward the direction of 'cognitive inflexibility.'[52] If so, this means that disengagement is a process in the other end of the continuum, that is, an exit by intellectualism. One of the activities that would later trigger a certain intellectualism was the reading. Exiting individuals would often engage in solitary reading not bound by either the texts given to them, which they had to read in a censored or excerpted form, nor those read together in supervised weekly family sessions. The independent reading set those who practiced it apart from the other group members who remained obedient to the group's approved contents and strict reading habits. Aboul-Gheit causally attributed his journey of disillusionment with the Brotherhood to just this activity of independent reading of books not assigned by his prefect. Though he acquired his reading habits while within the Brotherhood, he expanded his practice reading on account of the urge to read what was missing from the group's bookshelves. This included the writings of independent thinkers who had been associated with the Brotherhood, such as Mohamed El-Ghazaly and Youssef El-Qaradawy. 'I found them open-minded. I began to ask myself: "Why do they [the leaders of the Brotherhood] not allow us to study these pioneers who are still part of the group?"'[53] His reading expanded, taking him to the writings of the Egyptian Nobel laureate Naguib Mahfouz, and this further stimulated his quest for knowledge from outside the orbit of the Brotherhood, and increased his disillusionment with the group's 'anti-intellectualism.' He said: 'The leaders kept telling us he won the Nobel Prize simply because he was against Islam. I found this is a lie when I read his works.'[54]

Aboul-Gheit's journey into the world of reading points to the social aspects of forms of intellectual engagement. It introduced him to a different 'multitude of social beliefs about what is the case, good or bad,

---

[52] This frame is strikingly different from the frames made in some parts of the scholarly literature arguing that organizational and ideological features of the Muslim Brotherhood include 'responsiveness and flexibility.' The movement, Nathan Brown for one, can often 'squeeze' itself 'into any opening that conditions allow'; Brown added that this can take the form 'registering as a charitable association, chartering a political party, or opening an orphanage'; Brown, N. J. (2012). *When victory is not an option: Islamist movements in Arab politics* (p. 69). Ithaca and London: Cornell University Press.

[53] Aboul-Gheit, M. (2017).

[54] Aboul-Gheit, M. (2017).

right or wrong, for them, and to act accordingly.'[55] Reading dissolved the in-group/out-group division maintained by intellectually closed groups like the Brotherhood (see the Brotherhood's policies of 'communion' and 'renunciation' as detailed in Chapter 2). Aboul-Gheit articulated the impact of his reading as such: 'That was first time I realized there is the *other* through reading.' By interacting with the 'out-group' through readings and discussions, Aboul-Gheit disavowed any need to structure the world into the Brotherhood's more 'simplified' and 'manageable' forms ('the need to structure' is another element on the anti-intellectualism continuum).[56] In contrast, moving in the opposite direction involved both increasing complexity and the formation of another 'we' that was less unitary and exclusionary than the Brotherhood's leaders would have liked it to be. This is evidently clear when he took his passion online forums on reading. He said:

> The readers in the forum falsified all my beliefs in a constructive way. They simply asked me to read the 'other point of view. I really loved this mind-opening practice. I was even awarded the 'best participation' prize because of my passionate involvement in the activities of the forum.[57]

Aboul-Gheit's practice of reading moved away from the confines of the Brotherhood as he developed different patterns of thinking as well as he broke further restrictive rules of the Brotherhood such as those related to socialization and geographic spatialization. Aboul-Gheit now found his movements to be no longer restricted by the need for the approval of his Brotherhood prefect, who would dictate where he could go. The control of his freedom of movement had regularly been used as a punishment. On one occasion, his prefect asked Aboul-Gheit to walk across Cairo on foot for six kilometers, marking a restrictive spatial control of a large terrain that his desire to read finally led to his breaking with. A few years before his exit, he had attended courses in Civilizational Development at Cairo University, organized by independent Islamist thinkers who were not Brotherhood members. The

[55] Dijk, T. (1998). *Ideology: A multidisciplinary approach* (p. 8). London: Sage.

[56] Neuberg, S., & Newsom, J. (1993). Personal need for structure: Individual differences in the desire for simpler structure. *Journal of Personality and Social Psychology, 65,* 113–131 (113). https://doi.org/10.1037/0022-3514.65.1.113.

[57] Aboul-Gheit, M. (2017).

courses included recommended debates, readings, and referenced ideas with which Aboul-Gheit had not been familiar as a member of the Brotherhood.[58] These included discussions of how to reconcile Islam and modernity, and they also opened a door for Aboul-Gheit and other disgruntled members to gather and share concerns about the anti-intellectual practices of the Brotherhood. Strikingly, many members who attended these courses, without the approval of their prefects, who would definitely have objected to them, ended up disengaging from the Brotherhood. This included Mustafa El-Najjar and Abdel-Rahman Ayyash. During the interview, Aboul-Gheit identified himself with other exiters, commenting, 'We [each] have a mind that should be respected, and our gatherings were a journey in search and in respect for this mind.'[59] All this brought about what might also be called a process of re-ideologization. This involved changes in the 'languages, the concepts, categories, imagery of thought, and the systems of representation' that exiters began to deploy in order to make sense of the world around them.[60] Based on open discussions and debates, the independent readings and courses appeared starkly different from the style of education within the Brotherhood, which was based on a 'mechanical uniformity of studies and methods' that creates a kind of 'uniform immobility.'[61]

Relatedly, all this process of intellectualizing relates to identity-making which is a key part of disengagement (see Chapter 1). By gathering in new reading-related events, reading Mahfouz at home, or chatting online with non-Brotherhood members, these rebellious members began to realize aspects of themselves that had once operated only in hidden, irregular, and more or less forbidden ways.[62] This individuation came with a certain empowerment gained through positive evaluation as

---

[58] For example, the fact that the events include debates put it in the opposite direction of the education program inside the Brotherhood. For example, part of the program includes lectures on 'hearing and obeying,' Landau-Tasseron, E. (2010, December). *Leadership and allegiance in the society of the Muslim Brothers.* Series 2, paper 5, p. 4. Hudson Institute.

[59] Aboul-Gheit, M. (2017).

[60] Hall, S. (1996). *The problem of ideology: Marxism without guarantees.* In D. Morley, & K. Chen (Eds.), *Stuart Hall: Critical dialogues in cultural studies* (pp. 25–46 [26]). London: Routledge.

[61] Dewey, J. (1938). *Experience and education* (p. 62). New York: Touchstone.

[62] Ibid.

another component of the process of identity-making (see Chapter 2). To put it in the words of John Dewey, the independent reading and new learning practices in this re-socialization can endow exited or soon to exit members with the power to 'frame purposes, to judge wisely, to evaluate desires by the consequences which will result from acting upon them.'[63] The individuals now found that they could 'stop and think,' and this 'mental process' helped empower them to disengage from the group and to frame this disengagement as an option to be considered.

On the opposite part of this identity-making process, there is negative evaluation of the experience of being a member of the Brotherhood.[64] For example, Ban said that critically re-reading the literature allowed or approved by his seniors in the group made him realize how it had all been dogma, with its tendency to promote a 'relatively unchangeable, unjustified certainty.'[65] 'They taught us dogmatic texts and rigid interpretations of them, which separated the halal from the haram with no middle ground,' said Ban, referencing the Islamic terms for pure and holy or impure and unholy.[66] Tareq Aboul-S'ad, who exited the group after 27 years of membership, remembered how his readings contributed to his reevaluation of the 'mythical stories' cited by his leaders as part of the dogmatic ideology which 'does not respect my mind' and which he had earlier taken for granted as true and unquestionable. Aboul-S'ad remembered a story that the Brotherhood had used to rationalize its relationship with the regime of former President Gamal Abdel-Nasser:

> I remember the story of 'diarrhea as a sign of God's victory.' The story runs that Gamal Abdel-Nasser gave the order to kill all members of the Muslim Brotherhood detained in a specific prison by firing rockets and machine guns on their cells. The prison officer suffered all of a sudden from diarrhea five minutes before executing the order. Every time he wants to fire the artillery, he goes to the toilet due to this diarrhea. I asked my prefect who told this story how he knew about it, especially as I had not read it before. Logically, if the story holds true, the officer could have

[63] Ibid., pp. 63–64.

[64] Ibid, p. 64.

[65] Altemeyer, B. (2002). Dogmatic behavior among students: Testing a new measure of dogmatism. *The Journal of Social Psychology, 142,* 713–721. https://doi.org/10.1080/00224540209603931.

[66] Ban, *Ikhwan wa Salafiyyon wa Daawaish,* p. 330.

easily given the order to fire while he was still in the toilet. The prefect got angry and punished me for this way of thinking.[67]

IDEOLOGY OF THE FOUNDER: *ON* AND *OF* CHALLENGES

In the framed and thematized meanings of exiting members, there are two levels of disillusionment with the ideology of the founder of Muslim Brotherhood El-Banna, that is, challenging ideas *on* him and ideas *of* him.

Ideas on *El-Banna*

Applying theories of 'leadership identity construction process,'[68] El-Banna's leadership had not necessarily been 'co-constructed' as a product of 'socio-historical and collective meaning-making, and negotiated on an ongoing basis through a complex interplay among leadership actors...and/or followers.'[69] This meant that each member of the Brotherhood was not expected to act as an 'an active participant' cooperating with the leaders in constructing the leadership image. As the image of the 'leader' has always been there, the role of followers in this leadership-making was always passive and limited. One reason for this situation is that the leader of the group is *selected* not *elected*. Another reason has to do with the endurance and sustainability of this image although El-Banna got assassinated some 70 years ago: Sanctification.

The sanctification, such that to criticize him was understood to mean criticizing Islam itself, was made a salient frame by El-Banna himself.

---

[67] Aboul-sa'd, T. (2017).

[68] DeRue, D., & Ashford, S. (2010). Who will lead and who will follow? A social process of leadership identity construction in organizations. *Academy of Management Review, 35,* 627–647 (629). https://doi.org/10.5465/amr.2010.53503267.

[69] Humphreys, J., Novicevic, M., Smothers, J. et al. (2013). The collective endorsement of James Meredith: Initiating a leader identity construction process. *Academy of Management Proceedings,* 10021–10021. https://doi.org/10.5465/ambpp.2013.10021abstract; see also Collinson, D. (2005). Dialectics of leadership. *Human Relations, 58,* 1419–1442. https://doi.org/10.1177/0018726705060902; Grint, K. (2000). *The arts of leadership.* Oxford: Oxford University Press; Gronn, P. (2000). Distributed Properties. *Educational Management & Administration, 28,* 317–338. https://doi.org/10.1177/0263211x000283006; Meindl, J. (1995). The romance of leadership as a follower-centric theory: A social constructionist approach. *The Leadership Quarterly, 6,* 329–341. https://doi.org/10.1016/1048-9843(95)90012-8.

In his memoir, El-Banna portrays himself as a 'God-inspired' leader whose main goal is 'obtaining the satisfaction of God,' 'swearing allegiance to God to be a soldier for the Da'wa of Islam,'[70] and 'seeking to serve Islam.'[71] Part of this leadership has to do with the big decisions which El-Banna took about some of the complex and confusing situations of his time, and the social influence he gained from this role. It can also be attributed to his 'charisma', that is, if we adopt the Weberian definition of charisma and leadership.[72] Still, his leadership depended significantly on his personality, but it was framed as part of the reality that he expected his constituents to accept as 'godly' or 'sacramental.'

Drawing on leadership literature, as Gail Fairhurst and Robert Sarr aptly put it, 'We assume a leadership role, indeed we become leaders, through our ability to decipher and communicate meaning' and the 'ability to frame.'[73] This is an 'art' that El-Banna fully mastered and exploited. The Brotherhood's Oath of Allegiance, which members were required to take either before El-Banna,[74] is historically reserved for caliphs and was used by El-Banna as provisional leader 'of the community of the faithful until a new caliphate is established.'[75] His followers began to believe that God had bestowed a divine mission on him and that he was chosen to 'bring the renewal of religion to people,' an idea that was associated with

---

[70] El-Banna, H. (2012). *Muzakerat al-d'awa wal da'ia* [The memoirs of the preaching and the preacher] (p. 227). Kuwait: Afaq.

[71] Ibid.

[72] Lia, B. (1998). *The society of Muslim Brothers* (p. 114). Reading: Ithaca Press, see Weber, M. (1984). Legitimacy, politics and the state. In W. Connolly (Ed.), *Legitimacy and the state* (pp. 50–56). Oxford: Basil Blackwell; see also Weber, M. (1966). *The theory of economic and social organization* (p. 360). New York: The Free Press.

[73] Fairhurst, G. T., & Sarr, R. A. (1996). *The art of framing: Managing the language of leadership* (pp. 2–3). San Francisco: Jossey-bass.

[74] As Al-Anani put it: El-Banna 'linked bay'a [the oath] to himself as a leader,' established it as a 'compulsory procedure for joining the movement' and linked it with 'other values and norms such as obedience and commitment,' Al-Anani, K. (2016). *Inside the Muslim Brotherhood*, p. 121.

The text of the oath reads: 'In the name of Allah and Allah's charter, I offer my fealty to be a loyal committed soldier of the Muslim Brotherhood group.' It also adds, 'I have to listen and obey on all occasions except for those matters going against Allah ... and to sacrifice my effort, my money, and my blood for the sake of Allah.' see Ramzy, *dawlat al-murshid wa sanam Al-Ikhwan*, p. 51.

[75] Kandil, *Inside the Brotherhood*, p. 6.

'the veneration of El-Banna as the Prophet Muhammad.'[76] Although he did not approve of this comparison, El-Banna was a skilled manager of framing adopted meanings that could lead to such interpretations through analogies based on Quraanic verses or claiming the sole mission as 'implementing the words of God and applying the teachings of Prophet [Muhammad].'[77] Members have to read the literature of El-Banna along with the selected extracts from the Qur'an and *hadith* that members of each Brotherhood family are expected to read together at weekly gatherings. 'This deliberate pairing of revelation and movement literature' contributed to El-Banna's sanctification, as it 'conflates the divine and the temporal.'[78]

El-Banna's sanctified leadership reinforced some of the group's ideology-related principles mentioned above such as 'hearing and obedience,' the leader's directives.[79] As Brynjar Lia puts it, 'El-Banna appeared also to have solved the problem of obedience and authority in the Brotherhood. He saw the relationship between himself and his followers in spiritual terms, and he used these spiritual bonds to command obedience.'[80] He assumed the title of *Murshid* (the guide), 'eschewing other titles that he associated with the role of a leader seeking power.'[81] The fact that this title comes from Sufism adds further to El-Banna's sanctified leadership and the requirement to obey him.[82]

[76] Lia. (2006). *The society of Muslim Brothers*, p. 117. The literature of the Brotherhood on El-Banna justifies and normalizes a 'personality cult' evolving around the figure of El-Banna. He is described by some members and leaders as having a 'superhuman capacity,' making people in his presence 'dead bodies in the hands of someone washing their corpses,' and mastering over his followers in an inclusive and complete manner approaching 'sorcery'; see Pargeter, A. (2013). *The Muslim Brotherhood: From opposition to power* (p. 19). London: Saqi.

[77] El-Banna, *Muzakerat al-d'awa wal da'ia*, p. 90.

[78] Kandil, *Inside the Brotherhood*, p. 9

[79] Pondy, L. (1989). Leadership as a language game. In H. J. Leavitt, L. R. Pondy, & D. M. Boje (Eds.), *Readings in managerial psychology* (p. 229). Chicago and London: University of Chicago Press.

[80] Lia, *The society of Muslim brothers*, p. 116.

[81] Ibid.

[82] In Sufism, 'dozens participate in rituals, but only a limited few struggle for real spiritual purification (tazkia), and a handful are eventually selected for divine grace and become saints (awliya),' Kandil, *Inside the Brotherhood*, p. 20.

This sanctification of El-Banna's leadership has to do with questions of both identity as well as ideology. The path of the 'return of Islam' had to go through El-Banna himself; as the one who first envisioned and promoted the sacrifice of the personal identity, the 'I' for the sake of the collective identity, the 'we' (see Chapter 2).[83] In one of his statements, El-Banna spoke of himself as a 'human searching for the meaning of humanity...under the shade of Islam,' and as 'a man aware of the purpose of his existence and who proclaims: "Truly, my prayer and my sacrifice, my living and my dying are all for Allah".' Personal identity was considered by El-Banna as synonymous with 'lust,' unnecessary 'psychological needs' and 'biological luxuries,' which members should rid themselves of, prioritizing the 'spirit of Jihad and sacrifice.'[84] Therefore, some scholars concluded that El-Banna himself became an essential part of the *jama'a* (group) identity. He instilled 'a collective identity within its ideology, structure, and objectives.'[85] Paradoxically, by sacrificing his own personal identity, El-Banna made himself a constituent part of the group identity.

All of this meant that members could not exit the Brotherhood without making El-Banna central in framing their own disengagement. First of all, the exiters in their counter-frames removed from El-Banna's religious sanctity and humanized him as no different from any other leader, of this group or others. From being a semi-deity, he became an ordinary human being who could commit mistakes and thus be responsible for 'erroneous' ideas that led to their disengagement.[86] As Karl Jaspers put it, when persons are ordinary human beings who can be blamed for having caused a problem or threat, 'outrage is the common response.'[87] This outrage took the form of disillusionment with the whole idea of

---

[83] In several writings, El-Banna intended this collective identity that he had envisioned to overtake any 'individualistic' ones. A role in this was played by competing collective identities such as Communism. On one occasion, in discussing this 'comprehensive' Islamic identity, he wondered aloud to his audience: 'Who are you? What are the aims of your life? Do you truly understand Islam? Do you follow the Islamic teachings in everyday life?' quoted by Al-Anani, p. 55. Al-Anani, K. (2016). *Inside the Muslim Brotherhood* (p. 55). Oxford: Oxford University Press.

[84] El-Banna, *Muzakerat al-d'awa wal da'ia*, p. 54.

[85] Al-Anani, *Inside the Muslim Brotherhood*, p. 58.

[86] Some scholars adopted leader-centric approaches to investigate these attributes; see Rost, J. (1993). *Leadership for the twenty-first century*. Westport, CT: Praeger.

[87] Jasper, J. (1998). The emotions of protest: Affective and reactive emotions in and around social movements. *Sociological Forum, 13*, 397–424 (410).

El-Banna's leadership of the Brotherhood. Many examples in the autobiographies and interviews illustrate this. Sameh Fayez reported that he had felt a 'slave to El-Banna' and to 'his own religion, which set up El-Banna as a prophet.'[88] S.M., 31 years old, who exited in 2014, said part of his disillusionment was about the way El-Banna and his followers 'placed themselves as more than prophets of whom we should blindly trust their words which are not said by them but revealed by God.'[89] Islam Lutfy said he still had a lot of admiration for El-Banna due to his 'passion about his religion and due to his role in founding the large Islamic group when he was 20 years old.' However, Lutfy also said he should be regarded merely as a 'studious primary school teacher with a weak intellectual background' and a 'simple way of thinking.'[90] The 52-year-old 'A.E., who exited the group in April 2011 after three decades of membership, said the process of his disengagement included a stage of calling El-Banna 'vicious.'[91] Ban attributed some of the group's failures to mistakes committed by El-Banna, including his 'engagement in a power struggle,' 'approving the use of force,' and 'destabilizing the nation-state.'[92]

The Ideas of El-Banna

However, the legacy of El-Banna should not be reduced to leadership attributes as described above. His ideas were well-integrated into the group's overall ideology, organization, and modes of action that El-Bahy El-Kholy, one of El-Banna's disciples, had put it, 'an idea living in a man.'[93] Therefore, El-Banna's ideas over eight decades have almost been 'untouchable' and altering any of them 'unthinkable.'[94] In light of this, exiters found it challenging yet necessary to strip El-Banna in their own minds of the attributes of leadership and sanctity serving the group's interests as well as of his ideas. Disengagement involved a process based on reading and raising questions about this man's once-venerated deeds

[88] Fayez, S. (2011). *Janat Al-Ikhwan: Rehlat al-khuroug min al-aama'* [The MB paradise: The journey of getting out of the group] (p. 18). Cairo: Al-Tanweer.

[89] S.M. (2017).

[90] Lutfy, I. (2017).

[91] 'A.E. (2017).

[92] Ban, *Al-Ikhwan Al-Muslimoon wa mehnat Al-Watan*, pp. 38–52.

[93] Quoted in El-Banna, *Majmu't rasayyel al-imam*, p. 12.

[94] See Pargeter, A. (2013). *The Muslim Brotherhood*, pp. 22–23.

and ideas as well as his own character. During his exit, 'A.E. said that he
began re-reading El-Banna's books, beyond the excerpts that had been
made available in the Brotherhood's cultivation curriculum. 'I have
always kept a different understanding of the *Epistles*,' he said, 'from the
current one, in which I now realize that the book of El-Banna is merely
a call for violence and a cover to serve his own self-interests that have
nothing to do with Islam.'[95] 'Abdel-Mon'im said that her 'turning point'
in the exit journey was when she found herself questioning El-Banna's
teachings through a full reading of some of his works. She wound up concluding that 'these teachings contradicted the theological teachings of the
prophet Muhammad and his caliphs.'[96]Aboul-Sa'd also said that his journey of disengagement from the group included re-reading the writings
and looking at the beliefs of El-Banna. 'I re-read the seminal and classi-
cal work of El-Banna, *Al-Rasael* [The Epistles]. I found many mistakes
that El-Banna committed in the statements made in the book.'[97] Aboul-
Sa'd also began to question the validity of many principles mentioned by
El-Banna, such as fealty and the insistence on an exclusive 'Islamic identity.' As he took his questions to his prefect, 'the reaction was a fury that
extended to almost accusing me of [being] a *kafir* (apostate) who had left
Islam.'[98] His seniors to mete out a number of punitive measures. They
delayed his promotion to a higher level in the group's hierarchy, and also
warned the younger persons in the family sessions over which he presided
to ignore his instructions. 'In a word,' as he put it, 'I got blacklisted.'

Having determined the ideology and identity of the Brotherhood and
its members until his assassination in 1949, El-Banna is said by scholars to continue to do so, as a result of the ability he had to 'connect
subsequent generations' to both of these things.[99] Exiting members
countered this persistence by considering him a 'man of his own age,'
and his ideas as obsolete and 'outdated' when taken out of their time
of occurrence. Mohamed El-Qassas put it thus: 'El-Banna should be the
man of his age, not of all ages.'[100] I measured the salience of this frame
based on observed repetitions and frequencies and found the salience of

[95]'A.E. (2017).
[96]'Abdel-Mon'im, *Hekayatii ma' Al-Ikhwan*, p. 39.
[97]Aboul-Sa'd, T. (2017).
[98]Ibid.
[99]Al-Anani, *Inside the Muslim Brotherhood*, p. 66.
[100]El-Qassas, M. (2017).

El-Banna's outdatedness as a leading frame.[101] El-'Agouz dedicates the first chapter of his book to an imaginary dialogue with El-Banna. He says that if El-Banna lived 'among us now,' he would not have 'created the Brotherhood in the first place.'[102] A.S.R. said a part of his disengagement process involved a certain practice of reading. Returning to the ideas of El-Banna made him realize that the group's founder was only a man of his age and his generation. 'These ideas are only fitting for a special time and space, and they should be limited in applicability to the past and not to the different present,'[103] said A.S.R., the 31-year-old who exited the group in 2011 after a membership of 14 years. A.S.R. also said that part of his exit journey was 'revising the views of El-Banna, which I found obsolete as they were the byproduct of his time.'[104] He found it striking that 'there are no thinkers in the Brotherhood who have appeared after El-Banna to fill the time or space gap or revise his concepts.'[105]

The consistent appearance of this frame of 'a man of his own age' was evident even among those who expressed an affective attachment to the figure of El-Banna, such as K. F who found that incidents in the post-2011 period exposed the ideas of El-Banna as impractical and inapplicable. K.F., describing himself as ideologically committed to El-Banna and the Brotherhood while organizationally out of it, cited El-Banna's ideas of *shura* (consultation) and the Islamic state as vague and ambiguous enough to lead him to give up on putting these ideas into practice 'especially as they failed to be tested against the post-2011 imperatives of reality'[106] (see Chapter 4 on 'political disengagement').

---

[101] As Entman put it: 'The essence of framing is sizing _ magnifying or shrinking elements of the depicted reality to make them more or less salient.' Aside from words or images used to depict the event, Entman also referred to elements such as 'how much material on the event is available and how prominently is it displayed'; Entman. (1991). Symposium framing US coverage of international news: Contrasts in narratives of the KAL and Iran air incidents. *Journal of Communication*, 9. https://doi.org/10.1111/j.1460-2466.1991.tb02328.x.

[102] El-'agouz, A. (2011). *Ikhwani out of the box* (pp. 44–45). Cairo: Dawen.

[103] A.S.R. (2017).

[104] Ibid.

[105] Ibid.

[106] K.F. (2017).

THE IDEOLOGY OF THE CURRENT LEADERS:
DISCONNECTING THE CONNECTED

In this section, I focus on the ideology that the group's leaders propagated and that ex-members sought to counter in the process of disengagement. Again, the framing focuses on the attributes of leaders based on their sanctification, as was the case with El-Banna, as well as on their ideas, which exiting members would engage with partly to reinterpret.

The 'Unlike El-Banna' Leaders

For many exiting members, the first level of ideological disengagement from the current leadership of the Brotherhood was to separate current leaders from El-Banna. If counter-frames displayed El-Banna as other than the sanctified leader solely representing Islam, they also showed that the current leaders solely represented neither El-Banna himself nor Islam. This double disassociation was a reaction to a long historical process of the transformation of ideas inside the Brotherhood. This transformation was based on this main formula: El-Banna imparted sacredness to his leadership and ideology, and the leaders who followed him transformed the frame to impart sacredness to their own leadership and ideology on the basis of his legacy. To this day, Al-Anani writes, 'it is common practice for the Brotherhood's leaders to invoke El-Banna's thoughts and statements to legitimize and enhance their positions within the movement.'[107] Those leaders also made his epistles and statements constituted as the main source of 'socialization and indoctrination' within the Brotherhood.'[108] They also imposed a 'reward and punishment' mechanism through which each member has to obey El-Banna's teachings and commands, and those who violate these rules are subject to criticism and censure.

Furthermore, the connection with El-Banna was based on a process through which the leaders sought to construct specific meanings of El-Banna's leadership and teachings. For example, when Fayez, who had been recruited when he was seven, visited the only bookstore in his village and brought a book recounting the life of El-Banna, he thought that this would impress his prefect. What happened was the opposite.

---

[107] Al-Anani, *Inside the Muslim Brotherhood*, p. 66.
[108] Ibid.

'The Sheikh got angry and rebuked me. He asked me to return the book and never read this sort of literature. He was talking to me so harshly that I thought El-Banna was his enemy.'[109] As he refused to return the book, and even made the occasion the beginning of his rebellion, based on a personal 'secretive world' paralleling that of the Brotherhood, Fayez said that he realized that the recruiter wanted to align him with the same selective and strictly edited content to which he was being exposed.[110] This drew upon a policy of the Brotherhood that was enunciated as, 'Hear from us. Do not read about us.' The leaders also used their powers against any attempt to distance themselves from El-Banna or to present different interpretations supporting these attempts. On one occasion in 2011, El-Helbawy wrote a piece attempting to warn current leaders of their 'tilting away from El-Banna.' He reported that the article was banned from the Brotherhood's website, due to what he believed to be their 'aversion to directing any criticism to them, including their alleged connection with El-Banna.'[111]

The control was made easier because El-Banna had left behind a few short writings. This was useful for the current leaders who were in a position to make or control dozens of interpretations of El-Banna's short. Furthermore, those leaders could canonize these texts, as limited and brief as they are, as those that members had to read again and again, exactly as with the Qur'an.[112] It was within these interpretations that the leaders could confer favorable meanings on their positioning, based on their claiming of direct descent to El-Banna, regardless of how close they were or were not to his original ideas. As I mentioned above, those leaders also took every measure to keep intact the image of El-Banna as 'the most important component of the group's branding,'[113] and they, as disciples of the founder, can thus confer some of his powers and entitlements on themselves.

Thus, exiting members challenged the framing process through another process countering it. They engaged in a re-alignment that included a reverse frame transformation indicating that the current

---

[109] Fayez, S. (2013). *Janat Al-Ikhwan* (p. 27). Cairo: Al-Tanweer.

[110] Ibid., p. 28.

[111] El-Helbawy, K. (2017).

[112] Kandil, *Inside the Brotherhood*, p. 18.

[113] Mellor, N. (2018). *Voice of the Muslim Brotherhood: Da'wa, discourse, and political communication* (p. 34). London: Routledge.

leaders were not representatives of El-Banna. For example, 'Eid slammed his leaders for the 'illusion of sacredness' bestowed upon them, saying that they had merely 'the ulterior motive of stifling any internal criticism against them' by members of the group.[114] 'Abdel-Mon'im also debunked the 'El-Banna myth' within the group, by arguing that reprinting El-Banna's books, which were bestsellers since they were essential reading within the curriculum of the Brotherhood, was only meant to consolidate a 'clientelist' system maximizing profits for Brotherhood-owned publishing houses.[115] 'A.E. remembers how he had always been 'deceived' into the perception that the leaders had the same God-given status as El-Banna, since 'they always attributed their behavior and action to Allah.'[116] He elaborated: 'We accordingly always considered them as godly, and that the source of all of their words was God, which meant we could not object to any of their orders.'[117]

Interests and Values

According to psychologists, self-interest is often instrumental in shaping the behavior of those whom we call 'leaders.'[118] El-Banna, as mentioned above, claimed to be oriented toward getting things accomplished for the common interest or collective benefit, which he identified with the utopian project of the realization of Islam in the state and society.[119] This way of thinking was supported through his actions. He was seen as a selfless leader with an austere and simple lifestyle.[120] This has won him some admiration even of those who had disengaged from the group.[121]

[114] 'Eid, *Al-Ikhwan Al-Muslimoon: Al-hader wal mustaqbal*, p. 90.

[115] 'Abdel-Mon'im, *Hekayatii ma' Al-Ikhwan*, p. 195.

[116] 'A.E. (2017).

[117] 'A.E. (2017).

[118] See Miller, D. (1999). The norm of self-interest. *American Psychologist, 54*, 1053–1060. https://doi.org/10.1037//0003-066x.54.12.1053.

[119] Quinn, R. (1996). *Deep change: Discovering the leader within*. San Francisco: Jossey-Bass.

[120] Lia, *The society of Muslim Brothers*, p. 119.

[121] See Aboul-Futouh, A. (2010). *'Abdel-Mon'im Aboul-Futouh: Shahid 'ala al-haraka al-islamiyya* ['Abdel-Mon'im Aboul-Futouh: A witness to the Islamist movement]. Cairo: Alshorouk; Habib, M. (2013). *Al-Ikhwan al-muslemeen bayna al-so'ud wa ta'kul al-shar'iyya* [The Muslim Brotherhood between the rise and the corrosion of legitimacy]. Sama: Cairo.

His intentions, including those to 'sow the seeds of political Islamist movement' that would play such a big role in the history of the twenti-eth and twenty-first centuries, are generally not questioned.[122] This has not been the case with perceiving current leaders.

Exiting members would separate the current leaders from this motiva-tional arrangement. They observed that current leaders did not give up their self-interests for the sake of a specific shared interest such as making Islam the prevailing way of life, or directing the group's efforts toward this utopian project. They denied them the position of selfless leadership serving the collective identity that El-Banna had envisaged in the name of Islam. 'The leaders were only after their own personal interests,' said A.S.R.[123] El-Khirbawy concurred, arguing that those leaders 'only use El-Banna and the sanctity of his teachings to create nepotism, army-like obedience, and to justify the lack of transparency and justice inside the group.'[124] These self-interests of current leaders were regarded as mainly financial. These leaders, benefitting from 'nepotistic connections' to each other, had been involved in the 'corruption and squandering of the resources of the group to open their own business projects such as nurseries or training centers,' said 'Abdel-Mon'im.[125] Or their interests could be organizational, involv-ing promoting members for the sake of their family connections,[126] economic or business prowess and influence.[127] These accusations under-mined the very essence of the ideologically based hierarchical structure of the Brotherhood. This structure was meant to be based on the organiza-tion's meritocratic promotion system and members' progress in 'spiritual purity.'[128] While exiting members did not question the sacrifices made by El-Banna as heavily framed by himself,[129] they do so with current leaders.

---

[122] Pargeter, A. (2013). *The Muslim Brotherhood: From opposition to power*.

[123] A.S.R. (2017).

[124] El-Khirbawy, T. (2012). *Sir al-ma'bad: Al-asrar al-khafiya li gama't Al-Ikhwan al-mu-slemeen* [The temple's secret: The hidden secrets of the Muslim Brotherhood], pp. 54–57.

[125] 'Abdel-Mon'im, *Hekayatii ma' Al-Ikhwan*, pp. 141–144. These accusations are not baseless. Scholars noted that the use of family ties for recruitment, as explained in Chapter 2, 'creates favoritism and nepotism whereby senior leaders can exploit their position in order to help their family,' Al-Anani, *Inside the Muslim Brotherhood*, p. 81.

[126] Al-Anani, *Inside the Muslim Brotherhood*, p. 81.

[127] Aboul-Khalil, H. (2017).

[128] Lia, *The society of Muslim Brothers*, p. 117.

[129] Ibid., p. 93.

THE BATTLE ON GOD: THE *RABANIYYA* FRAME

What all the three abovementioned thematic constructions as represented in frames share is a battle to reshape the relationship with God,
which can be indicated from now on as *Rabaniyya*. [This word derives
from *Rab*, which literally means God.] In the dominant discourse of the
Brotherhood, the group presents itself as the sole one who can help its
members 'get acquainted with God,'[130] obtain the 'satisfaction of God,'
and set it as the 'the purpose and direction of man in life and the final
point of his hopes and endeavors.'[131] By definition, *Rabaniyya* denotes
many meanings that relate to the process of engagement and disengagement, such as the need to give up self-interest, and get rid of 'individual
whims' and 'selfish desires' all for the sake of 'satisfying God.'[132] The
'self' in this conceptualization, as outlined by El-Banna himself, is a negative entity that has to be 'de-materialized,' 'spiritualized,' 'purified,'
and 'elevated' by the *Rabaniyya*.[133] In some ways, this was understood
to be almost the whole purpose of the Brotherhood. As El-Banna put
it, 'God is our goal,' and the Brotherhood's task is 'acquainting people

[130] El-Banna, *majmu't rasayyel al-imam*, p. 125. As part of the recruitment strategy, the
Brotherhood convinces the recruit that it is 'the only Islamic movement he should join' as
it is the one which 'follows the path of the prophet Muhammad and seeks to establish the
Islamic state,' Al-Anani, *Inside the Muslim Brotherhood*, p. 77.

[131] For more, see El-Qaradawy, Y. (2016). *Al-Rabaniyya: Ola khasa'es al-Islam*
[Rabaniyya: The first trait of Islam]. Available via: https://www.al-qaradawi.net/
node/2243. Accessed 2 December 2018.

[132] El-Qaradawy, *Al-rabaniyya: Ola khasa'es al-Islam*. El-Banna wrote that 'What is more
faithful than a man forgetting his self for the sake of realizing his goal,' 'stripping his self
and oppressing its emotions, tendencies and whims' for the sake of 'pure Jihad for the sake
of God,' El-Banna, *majmu't rasayyel al-imam*, p. 61.

[133] El-Banna, *Majmu't rasayyel al-imam*, p. 125. This process would be not altogether
uncommon in a 'Western' context; as such notions found their way into mysticisms and here
it seems a bit made into a 'technological' project, in the sense of the improvement of the
self through a set of techniques. The metaphors here are all familiar in some religious and
'spiritual' discourses. Self-negation was common to Christian mystics in the nineteenth-
century Europe, enough to make it comparable to Rabaniyya. The two concepts order one
to refrain from imposing one's individual will on events and that one has to be anti-egoistic
by showing less attachment to her or his own will; see Janaway, C. (Ed.). (1999). *The
Cambridge companion to schopenhauer*. Cambridge: Cambridge University Press.

with Him.'[134] On the way to this 'goal,' described in the group's literature as 'Da'wa towards Rabaniyya,'[135] the leaders of the group gain their powers, legitimacy as representatives of the Brotherhood as well as representatives of God on the basis of *Rabaniyya*. One main function of *Rabaniyya* in this sense was to act consistently with the 'satisfaction' of Brotherhood leaders, who could show how the two levels of satisfaction, satisfying God and satisfying the leader, are closely related and suggest each other.

Leaders also determine resources or opportunities, or set rewards and punishments on the basis of the concept.[136] For example, on one occasion, Lutfy questioned the speech of one Brotherhood leader, 'who blamed former US president George W. Bush for invading Iraq "all for the sake of stealing its oil reserves".' Lutfy protested and told the other attendees that 'if we think across chapters of history, we would find great empires, including the Islamic one, did the same such as Omar, one of the caliphs did when his forces entered Egypt.' The reaction of both the leader and the attendees was a direct request for Lutfy to enhance his lacking '*Rabaniyya*.' 'They accused me of becoming an "apostate". They asked me to "read Quraan" to dismiss "Satanic ideas in my mind".' In this sense, *Rabaniyya* as framed by the Brotherhood is a tool of exercising 'anti-intellectualism' as thematized above.

The principal of *Rabaniyya* also had the function of establishing the border between those who were *inside* and *outside* of the Brotherhood. The borderline was based on the antithesis of gaining the 'satisfaction of God' versus that of others—or of 'Satan,' often preceded with the definite article, as the figure in Islamic scriptures for the opponent of God, His messages, and His believers.[137] More than one ex-member told me how all ex-members, especially 'Abdel-Moneim Aboul-Futouh, a senior leader in the group until 2011, were literally nicknamed by some leaders in the group 'the Satan' after he exited the group for reasons that

---

[134] Ibid., p. 125.

[135] Ibid., p. 125.

[136] The leaders have extensive powers especially on means of 'punishments' as the rules of the Brotherhood do not 'specify' them; Landau-Tasseron, E. (2010, December). *Leadership and allegiance in the society of the Muslim Brothers*. Hudson Institute. Series 2, paper 5, p. 4.

[137] Ali, K., & Leaman, O. (2007). *Islam: The key concepts*. London: Routledge.

included his criticism of the group's anti-intellectualism.[138] In this way, Aboul-Futouh was deprived of *Rabaniyya* exactly as, legendarily, Satan had been deprived of it by God after he refused to submit to Him. Of course, this meant that the leaders were identifying themselves with divine authority rather directly, and denying the possibility of any uncertainty in the matter.[139] Aboul-Futouh was not alone. Aboul-Sa'd said that he was fired from the Brotherhood because of his support for Aboul-Futouh in the 2012 presidential elections. He felt aghast at the reactions of his fellow members of the group as well as his wife, who quickly accused him of being 'less of a Muslim' and abandoning God's satisfaction, as represented by his membership in the group. 'It was really painful to feel that God will not be satisfied with you after you get out of the Brotherhood, especially as I have long considered the Brotherhood as not a mere group representing Islam. It acts as it is Islam itself.'[140]

The mentions of 'the Satan' that are repeated and frequent across the texts of interviews and autobiographies may be taken as quite an effective tool to stifle the expression of different views or the raising of questions. Harold Laswell, who analyzed religious references to Satan, found them a very effective tool to guarantee adherence and obedience, and stifle any critical attitude. Ideally, this meant for the leaders that members could be guiltily persuaded that their questioning was blocking the 'satisfaction of God,' which was of course identified with the leaders, and bringing them under the influence of the Satan.[141] More importantly, evoking Satan enabled minor disagreements to be treated as fundamental and threatening since they touch down on getting in or out of Islam itself.

---

[138] A.Y. (2017).

[139] Remarkably, this in-group/out-group distinction can also be justified on another meaning of Da'wa. The 'Da'wa towards Rabaniyya' can be historically drawn on Prophet Muhammad and the early Muslim community. The latter made Da'wa by 'converting non-Muslims.' In other words, by describing exiting members as 'Satan' affiliates, the Brotherhood has taken them as targets of Da'wa exactly as Muhammad had done with the Satan-inflicted 'non-Muslims.' The connection is justified as the Brotherhood always linked its Da'wa to that of the prophet (El-Banna, *Majmu't rasayyel al-imam*, p. 141) and also by the thematized meanings in the accounts of several exiting members. The latter argued that they were forced to feel 'being non-Muslims' by their leaders during the journey of disengagement (e.g., Aboul-Sa'd, T. [2017]).

[140] Aboul-Sa'd, T. (2017).

[141] Lasswell, H. (1938). *Propaganda technique in the world war* (p. 77). New York: Peter Smith.

This has pre-empted potential disengagements of many members including El-Qassas. He recalled how for so long he had hesitantly questioned his desire to object to his leaders' decisions, because he was aware of the risk that it could yield a crop of 'Satan-related' indignation and scorn from both leaders and other members.[142] The 'Satan' accusation was in fact not a marginal tool of discipline and punishment,[143] but was pivotal and common, to the extent that a prefect himself warned his Brotherhood family members during a meeting: 'If I ever leave the Brotherhood, do not believe any critique I make, because I would have been tempted by the devil.'[144]

In addition, the threat of 'Satanism' not only brought with it powers wielded by leaders to punish and deter threats. It also allowed those leaders to gain legitimacy, since it conferred upon them a sense of urgent purpose and also had some consensus-building features since group and ideological conformity were also identified. One member was told in response to an objection that all interpreters of the Qur'an agreed on the same interpretation that he, the leader, was enunciating. When the inquisitive member who was told this double-checked, he found no interpretation that fit this claim.[145] The leaders had instrumentalized *Rabaniyya* for political reasons. For example, in 1995, when the Brotherhood boycotted the parliamentary elections, the leaders supported the ruling party's candidate in the Nile town of Damanhour against the leftist candidate, for whom many members wanted to vote. The justification given rested on applying to the leftist candidate the *Rabaniyya* notion of one who 'does not pray, and does not fast.'[146]

Members would resist these uses of the *Rabaniyya* concept in the process of their disengagement by a frame re-alignment process. They sometimes would transform the use of the concept/frame and what it

---

[142] El-Qassas, M. (2017).

[143] Some of the main ideologues of the Muslim Brotherhood stated that disengagement could be explained as an act of the Satan, who has succeeded 'stripping believers of their faith and throwing them into abyss of loss.' Yakan, F. (2005). *Al-mutasaqitoun min al-da'wa: kaifa … wa lemaza* [The dropouts from the daawa: How and why?] (p. 82). Beirut: Al-Rasala leil Teba' wal Nashr.

[144] Cited by Kandil, *Inside the Brotherhood.*

[145] Ibid., p. 26.

[146] 'Eid, S. (2013). *Tajribati fi saradeeb Al-Ikhwan* [My experience in the basements of MB] (p. 5). Cairo: Jazeerat al-Ward.

seemed to identify and group in its scope; at other times, they would reframe it through interpretation, or counter-frame it through refusing it altogether. This is a 'public sphere' that can diversify the actors making arguments about the concept and the whole of Islam. In the autobiographies and books that he began publishing on an annual basis, 'Eid dedicated space to refuting the concept of *Rabaniyya* as not part of Islam. He substantiated claims that it has no actual theological foundations in the religion and is merely a 'punitive measure' to make people like him feel 'ashamed' of their inquisitive nature. Supporting his argument with examples, he told of how a senior Brotherhood figure reacted to his calls for internal reform. '"The *Shaytan* (Satan) enters your mind through your [demand for] reform, he said. My advice to you is to strengthen your relationship with God, and to keep praying, fasting, and grave visiting".'[147] As 'Eid kept asking questions and calling for internal reform, the senior figure asked him to put all of these ideas 'out of mind,' and, for the purpose, 'ordered me to memorize every day a quarter of Qur'an.'[148] Indeed, this answer is typical of one main ideological tendency in the Brotherhood, which was initiated by El-Banna himself: drawing on Sufism, followers were requested to perform a *dhikr*, an activity of action not argument and that involved the repeated and highly emotional invocation of God.[149] It is in this way that El-Banna and the group's leaders, who are all called by the Sufi title of *Murshid* as mentioned above, could ensure the obedience of their followers.[150]

Exiting members counter-frame the concept *Rabaniyya* by uncoupling it with Islam and linking it with other ideologies instead. Some exiting members said that the Brotherhood's ideology was closer to Communism, fascism, or Freemasonry.[151] For example, 'Abdel-Mon'im said that the group is not Islamic in its nature, but 'has literally and

---

[147] 'Eid, *Al-Ikhwan Al-Muslimoon: Al-hader wal mustaqbal*, p. 33.

[148] Ibid.

[149] Lia, *The society of Muslim Brothers*, p. 116.

[150] Ibid., p. 117. El-Banna himself directly made that link when he declared that the 'system of Da'wa' while founding the Brotherhood is 'purely Sufi from the spiritual perspective and purely military from the practical perspective, and the motto of the two perspectives is always (order and obedience) without hesitation, questioning or doubting'; El-Banna, H. (1990). *Majmu't rasayyel al-imam*, p. 397.

[151] This is a repletion of the discourse of critics and opponents who have along associated the Brotherhood with fascism, Nazism, and Communism, see Kamal, A. A. (1989).

efficaciously applied all the tenets of Communist Marxism more literally and rigidly than Lenin himself,' denying its members individual rights, at the expense of the 'society of Brothers.'[152] El-Khirbawy also cited the same association: The group is Communist, he said, because it sanctions 'the use of force' to instill a transformative worldview in the minds of its members 'for the sake of God.'[153] He also linked the Brotherhood to the Freemasons due to its secrecy, and to Machiavelli due to its adoption of the notion that 'the ends justify the means.'[154] Fayez linked the group to fascism, 'which can be easily manifested in the army-like hierarchical organization of the group as set out by El-Banna.'[155] 'Abdel-Mon'im repeated El-Khirbawy's description of the Brotherhood as like the Freemasons because their exclusivist beliefs and practices 'run against the aims of Islam, which in reality adopts inclusiveness regardless of colour, geography, or style of clothing.'[156]

The thinking here indicates not so much opposition to the group and its ideology as a shift in the way these were positioned in the minds of the exiters, as lying in fact outside the very values that were central to it. This meant that exiting members now felt empowered to reinterpret the Qur'an, claiming the satisfaction of God and punishing the Brotherhood's leaders while using the same tools that the latter had once used against rebellious members. They formulated their exit in terms of a rich and expanding literature in Islam that allowed for different interpretations of the Qur'an and variable 'frames of reference,' within which they could in fact constitute their ex-hood as sanctified by Islam and its holy book and on the basis of a semantic pluralism that can shift meanings in favor of their

---

Al-nuqat faqqa al-Hurouf: al-Ikhwan al-Muslimon wa al-nizam al-khas [Dots on letters: The Muslim Brotherhood and the special apparatus] (p. 93). Cairo: Al-zahraa Leil I'lam al-'Arabi; Sadat, A. (2015*). Qissat al-Thawra kamlea* [The whole story of the revolution]. Cairo: Dar al-Hilal.

[152] 'Abdel-Mon'im, *Hekayatii ma' Al-Ikhwan*, p. 209.

[153] El-khirabawi, *sir Al-Ma'bad: Al-asrar al-khafiya*, p. 87.

[154] Fayez, *Janat Al-Ikhwan*, p. 88.

[155] Ibid., p. 15.

[156] 'Abdel-Mon'im, *Hekayatii ma' Al-Ikhwan*, pp. 37–38. Of course, these associations— Lenin, Machiavelli, Freemasons—are wild and do not evince a sharp intellect but ready-to-hand prejudices and clichés. In any case, the language of exiting members in this context is wild, free, and not well-founded, certainly in a precise sense.

new frames.[157] These meanings are not necessarily indicating the adoption of more open or liberal interpretations of Islam than their leaders as much being instruments facilitating the process of disengagement itself.

The reinterpretation is not about opposing or discrediting the text of Quraan per se. It is more to do with resisting and challenging the hegemony of the Brotherhood's leaders over this holy text and over the set of relations and practices normalized and legitimized by it. In this sense, the Quraan and Islam itself is no longer a 'master signifier' as there are 'multiple Islams' and that members of the Brotherhood are no longer attached to themselves or are attached to 'one Islam.'[158] Disengagement thus becomes a struggle over meanings of Islam and Quraan as exiting members seek to accommodate new interpretations that privilege their own relations and practices (including the practice of criticizing the self-proclaimed sanctified leaders).

This frame re-alignment of *Rabaniyya* is related to the process of identity-making, whose two main components are assimilation/accommodation and evaluation (see Chapter 2). Exiting members also transformed the affective associations of *Rabaniyya*, which included practices of shaming. Members could be shamed as lacking *Rabaniyya* if they expressed critical views within the Brotherhood.[159] When members spoke privately to their prefects to express their 'ideological concerns,' prefects would respond by rejecting or downplaying these concerns as

---

[157] Scholars argue for the 'expansiveness of Islam in terms of the textual and rhetorical canon,' which allows Islamist groups such as the Brotherhood having at their disposal 'a rich heritage with historical depth that can be drawn on various junctures with different contexts' Elshaer, A. (2013). Islam in the narrative of Fatah and Hamas. In D. Matar & Z. Harb (Eds.), *Narrating conflict in the Middle East: Discourse, image and communications practices in Lebanon and Palestine* (pp. 111–132 [116]). London and New York: I.B.Tauris. Therefore, exiting members found it feasible to use the same tactic and benefit from this religious mutability to normalize and legitimize their disengagement.

[158] Sayyid, S. (2003). *A fundamental fear: Eurocentrism and the emergence of Islamism* (p. viii). London: Zed Books.

[159] Shame here is broadly defined as 'seeing the self negatively through the eyes of others, such as feeling rejected, unworthy, and inadequate.' As such, and drawing on the work of the pioneers who first theorized the concept, shame is a 'class name' for a large family of emotions and feelings that arise through this seeing of the self negatively through the eyes of others such as fear, embarrassment, humiliation, and rejection, Scheff, T. (2003). Shame in self and society. *Symbolic Interaction, 26*, 239–262 (245, 251). https://doi.org/10.1525/si.2003.26.2.239.

merely signs of God's displeasure, thus evoking shame, which could play a central role in meeting out punishment to those 'potentially rebellious members' expressing such concerns. Feelings of shame, an indicative of negative evaluation of the 'self' or personal identity, were broadly facilitated by the articulation of punishments and reprimands as having religious meanings that the prefects were broadly empowered to pronounce, the commonly used term *ta'zir* (reprimand) having that character.[160] As discussed in Chapter 2, personal emotions such as shame played an important role in keeping members attached to the 'collective identity' of the movement.

What exiting members did was to reverse the shame into shame about being shamed. Exiting members were often ashamed at how they had been manipulated, in part sentimentally, humiliated for expressing their criticisms or concerns, or compelled to conceal their emotions as part of their acquiescence in the face of the Brotherhood's internal control and punitive measures.[161] Now they can stand up to it through writing autobiographies, making TV appearances, and making interviews. During the interview, S.E. took the opportunity and had harsh criticism for those leaders who made use of shaming in this way, as well as for himself for having accepted it: 'They are stupid, arrogant, and repressive, as they have never listened to me or others. It is a shame that they have succeeded in making me feel ashamed of myself, my own questions, and [the] ideas behind them.'[162] This shift in meanings of shame also relates to identity-making as exiting members can now see themselves not solely through the eyes of others, that is, the leaders and their ideology. They now see themselves through their own eyes, in terms of their own sense of self. Within this shift, shame takes a positive empowering force allowing individuals to divest themselves of their 'shameful' past. This explanation coheres well with explanations in previous chapters which identified frames such as 'regaining the I,' 'ending slavery,' and 'gaining emancipation.'

---

[160] Kandil, H. (2015). *Inside the Brotherhood*, p. 28.

[161] Psychologist Gershen Kaufman noted these double sentiments of shame in the American society: 'American society is a shame-based culture, but....shame remains hidden. Since there is shame about shame, it remains under taboo.' see Kaufman, G. (1989). *The psychology of shame: Theory and treatment of shame-based* (p. 4). New York: Springer.

[162] S.E. (2017)

Conclusion

Ideological disengagement from the Brotherhood seems to be about ending an 'ideological contract' between members and the Brotherhood. Under the contract, the group has long enforced a normative allegiance to its ideology and the organization's founder, both sanctified, with their importance bound up with a set of ultimate meanings, or the search for them, that were held to transcend the 'material' aspects of life and lead to a utopia of an 'Islamic' society and state. These meanings have a 'spiritual' and individualistic aspect as it will allow each member to 'free oneself from worldly attachments and imperfections and reach the world of spirit.'[163] Given the centrality of divine authority and commandment in Islam, the Brotherhood frames its mission as requiring each member to submit to a principle like theirs of 'hearing and obedience' all for the sake of reaching what an ideal known by Muslim mystics (adopted and practiced by El-Banna at certain moments of his life) as that of a 'perfected human being.'[164] What exiting members have done is to revoke this contract by reframing it as part of what is referred to in the chapter as the 'frame re-alignment process.' They evaluated the Brotherhood's ideology as a tool of dominance and oppression implemented by its leaders under the guise of alleged sanctification as God's representatives. They showed El-Banna is merely a 'human' who commit mistakes and that current leaders are acting often out of their own material interests.

Exiting members reevaluated the ideology against identity. Ideology blocks the rise of personal identity by acts of anti-intellectualism involving, as we have seen, characteristic features such as 'cognitive closure' and 'authoritarianism.' One way of overcoming this blockage was intellectually stimulating practices such as independent reading. Along with satisfying the need to think freely outside the Brotherhood's imposed system of beliefs, independent reading provided resources and opportunities for the disengagement. The socializing with others that would take place on this basis, including through virtual online forums and reading groups, allowed exiting members the ability to daringly work out new interpretations of the Qur'an (which were sometimes visible in their

---

[163] Saritoprak, Z. (2018). *Islamic spirituality: Theology and practice for the modern world* (p. 1). London: Bloomsbury.

[164] Ibid.

published narratives), and to also neutralize the internalized system of discipline and punishment in the Brotherhood.

The chapter did not contextualize the disengagement within the post-2011 period in Egypt. It is a task which is to be carried out in Chapter 4. Therefore, the findings in this chapter have to tentatively await deeper exploration in the coming chapter. For example, a failure to learn from mistakes and make good strategic calculations after the events of 2011 formed part of the group's ideological failures, against which exiting members justified their individual disengagements.[165] These failures allowed them to consolidate their frames by faulting the group ideologically as 'lack[ing] sophistication and substance,' and showing a willingness to 'sacrifice ideological principles for short-term political gains.'[166] This contextualization would fill in another gap in the above-conducted analysis. Even when the result seems to involve only the linear movement from anti-intellectualism to intellectualism, or some other standard narratival process of modernization, such shifts are rarely simple, linear, or directional, as the recent history in Egypt and the legacy of these ex-members of an 'Islamist' oppositional group, including the still open question of the effects of their published accounts, has shown. Disengagement is a complex process because of the way the organization of ideas in such contexts is necessarily subject to multivalences and ambiguities of meanings, the persistence of some while others change, and the availability of some frames or frames found in experiences and ideas, and the framings of such frames to be spontaneously put to work with or against others. Again, this is what coming chapter has to investigate.

BIBLIOGRAPHY

'Aboul-Futouh, A. (2010). *'Abdel-Mon'im Aboul-futouh: Shahid 'ala al-Haraka al-Islamiyya* ['Abdel-Mon'im Aboul-futouh: A witness to the Islamist movement]. Cairo: Alshorouk.

Ali, K., & Leaman, O. (2007). *Islam: The key concepts.* Milton Park, Oxon and New York: Routledge.

---

[165] See Wickham, C. (2004). The path to moderation: Strategy and learning in the formation of Egypt's wasat party. *Comparative Politics, 36*(2). https://doi.org/10.2307/4150143.

[166] El-Sherif, A. (2014). *The Egyptian Muslim Brotherhood's failures* (p. 12). New York, NY: Carnegie Endowment for International Peace.

Altemeyer, B. (2002). Dogmatic behavior among students: Testing a new measure of dogmatism. *The Journal of Social Psychology, 142,* 713–721. https://doi.org/10.1080/00224540209603931.

Brynjar, L. (1998). *The society of the Muslim Brothers in Egypt.* Reading: Ithaca Press.

Collinson, D. (2005). Dialectics of leadership. *Human Relations, 58,* 1419–1442. https://doi.org/10.1177/0018726705060902.

DeRue, D., & Ashford, S. (2010). Who will lead and who will follow? A social process of leadership identity construction in organizations. *Academy of Management Review,* 35, 627–647 (629). https://doi.org/10.5465/amr.2010.53503267.

Dewey, J. (1938). *Experience and education.* New York: Macmillan.

Dijk, T. (1998). *Ideology: A multidisciplinary approach.* London: Sage.

'Eid, S. (2014). *Al-ikhwan al-muslimoon: Al-hader wal mustaqbal: Awraq fil naqd al-zati* [The Muslim Brotherhood: The present and the future: Papers from self-criticism] (p. 27). Cairo: Al-Mahroussa.

Eigenberger, M., Critchley, C., & Sealander, K. (2007). Individual differences in epistemic style: A dual-process perspective. *Journal of Research in Personality, 41,* 3–24. https://doi.org/10.1016/j.jrp.2006.01.003.

El-Banna, H. (1990). *Majmu't rasael al-imam el-shahid Hassan El-banna* [A collection of epistles of the martyr imam Hassan El-banna]. Alexandria, Egypt: Da'wa.

El-Banna, H. (2012). *Muzakerat al-d'awa wal da'ia* [The memoirs of the preaching and the preacher]. Kuwait: Afaq.

Elshaer, A. (2013). Islam in the narrative of Fatah and Hamas. In D. Matar & Z. Harb (Eds.), *Narrating conflict in the Middle East: Discourse, image and communications practices in Lebanon and Palestine* (pp. 111–132). London and New York: I.B.Tauris.

El-Sherif, A. (2014). *The Egyptian Muslim Brotherhood's failures.* New York, NY: Carnegie Endowment for International Peace.

El-Qaradawy, Y. (n.d.). *Al-rabaniyya: Ola Khasa'es al-islam* [Rabaniyya: The first trait of Islam]. Available via: https://www.al-qaradawi.net/node/2243. Accessed 2 December 2018.

Fairclough, N. (2003). *Analyzing discourse—Textual research for social research.* New York: Routledge.

Grint, K. (2000). *The arts of leadership.* Oxford: Oxford University Press.

Gronn, P. (2000). Distributed properties. *Educational Management & Administration, 28,* 317–338. https://doi.org/10.1177/0263211x000283006.

Habib, M. (2013). *Al-Ikhwan al-muslemeen bayna al-so'ud wa ta'kul al-shar'iyya* [The Muslim Brotherhood between the rise and the corrosion of legitimacy]. Cairo: Sama.

Hall, S. (1996). The Problem of Ideology: Marxism without guarantees. In D. Morley & K. Chen (Eds.), *Stuart Hall: Critical dialogues in cultural studies*. London: Routledge.

Hofstadter, R. (1962). *Anti-intellectualism in American life*. London: Jonathan Cape.

Holloway, I., & Todres, L. (2003). The status of method: Flexibility, consistency and coherence. *Qualitative Research, 3,* 345–357. https://doi.org/10.1177/1468794103033004.

Humphreys, J., Novicevic, M., Smothers, J., et al. (2013). The collective endorsement of James Meredith: Initiating a leader identity construction process. *Academy of Management Proceedings, 2013,* 10021–10021. https://doi.org/10.5465/ambpp.2013.10021abstract.

Janaway, C. (Ed.). (1999). *The Cambridge companion to schopenhauer*. Cambridge: Cambridge University Press.

Jasper, J. (1998). The emotions of protest: Affective and reactive emotions in and around social movements. *Sociological Forum, 13,* 397–424.

Kamal, A. A. (1989). *Al-nuqat faqqa al-Hurouf: al-Ikhwan al-Muslimon wa al-nizam al-khas* [Dots on letters: The Muslim Brotherhood and the special apparatus]. Cairo: Al-zahraa Leil I'lam al-'Arabi.

Kandil, H. (2015). *Inside the Brotherhood*. Cambridge: Polity Press.

Kaufman, G. (1989). *The psychology of shame: Theory and treatment of shame-based*. New York: Springer.

Lakoff, G., & Johnson, M. (1980). *Metaphors we live by*. London: University of Chicago Press.

Lasswell, H. (1938). *Propaganda technique in the world war*. New York: Peter Smith.

Lia, B. (1998). *The society of Muslim Brothers* (p. 114). Reading: Ithaca Press.

Marques, M., Elphinstone, B., Critchley, C., et al. (2017). A brief scale for measuring anti-intellectualism. *Personality and Individual Differences, 114,* 167–174. https://doi.org/10.1016/j.paid.2017.04.001.

Martin, M., & Rubin, R. (1995). A new measure of cognitive flexibility. *Psychological Reports, 76,* 623–626. https://doi.org/10.2466/pr0.1995.76.2.623.

Meindl, J. (1995). The romance of leadership as a follower-centric theory: A social constructionist approach. *The Leadership Quarterly, 6,* 329–341. https://doi.org/10.1016/1048-9843(95)90012-8.

Mellor, N. (2018). *Voice of the Muslim Brotherhood: Da'wa, discourse, and political communication*. London: Routledge.

Miller, D. (1999). The norm of self-interest. *American Psychologist, 54,* 1053–1060. https://doi.org/10.1037//0003-066x.54.12.1053.

Neuberg, S., & Newsom, J. (1993). Personal need for structure: Individual differences in the desire for simpler structure. *Journal of Personality and Social Psychology*, 65, 113–131. https://doi.org/10.1037/0022-3514.65.1.113.

Pargeter, A. (2013). *The Muslim Brotherhood: From opposition to power*. London: Saqi.

Pondy, L. (1989). Leadership as a language game. In H. J. Leavitt, L. R. Pondy, & D. M. Boje (Eds.), *Readings in managerial psychology*. Chicago and London: University of Chicago Press.

Porter, R. (2006). *Ideology: Contemporary social, political and cultural theory*. Cardiff: University of Wales Press.

Quinn, R. (1996). *Deep change: Discovering the leader within*. San Francisco: Jossey-Bass.

Reisberg, D. (2013). *The Oxford handbook of cognitive psychology*. Oxford: Oxford University Press.

Ricoeur, P. (1981). *Hermeneutics and the human sciences* (J. Thompson, Ed. and Trans.). Cambridge: Cambridge University Press.

Rosen, E. (2008). The Muslim Brotherhood's concept of education. *Current Trends in Islamist Ideology*, 7(85), 115–129.

Sadat, A. (2015). *Qissat al-Thawra kamlea* [The whole story of the revolution]. Cairo: Dar al-Hilal.

Saritoprak, Z. (2018). *Islamic spirituality: Theology and practice for the modern world*. London: Bloomsbury.

Scheff, T. (2003). Shame in self and society. *Symbolic Interaction*, 26, 239–262 (245). https://doi.org/10.1525/si.2003.26.2.239.

Shogan, C. (2007). Anti-intellectualism in the modern presidency: A republican populism. *Perspectives on Politics*, 5, 295–296. https://doi.org/10.1017/s153759270707079x.

Weber, M. (1966). *The theory of economic and social organisation*. New York: The Free Press.

Weber, M. (1984). Legitimacy, politics and the state. In W. Connolly (Ed.), *Legitimacy and the state*. Oxford. Basil Blackwell.

Wickham, C. (2004). The path to moderation: Strategy and learning in the formation of Egypt's wasat party. *Comparative Politics*, 36(2). https://doi.org/10.2307/4150143.

Yakan, F. (2005). *Al-mutasaqitoun min al-da'wa: kaifa … wa lemaza* [The dropouts from the daawa: How and why?]. Beirut: Al-Rasala leil Teba' wal Nashr.

AUTOBIOGRAPHIES

'Abdel-Mon'im, I. (2011). *Hekayatii ma' al-ikhwan* [My story with the MB]. Al-hayaa 'Abdel-Mon'im, I. (2011). *Hekayati ma' al-ikhwan* [My story with the Muslim Brotherhood]. Cairo: Al-Hayaa Al-Misriyya Al-'ama leil Kitab.

Ban, A. (2013). *Al-ikhwan al-muslimoon wa mehnat al-watan wal Deen* [The Muslim Brotherhood and the predicament of nation and religion]. Cairo: Al-Neel Centre for Strategic Studies.

Ban, A. (2017). *Ikhwan wa salafiyyon wa dawa'ish* [Brothers, salafists and ISIS loyalists]. Cairo: Al-Mahrousa.

Brown, N. J. (2012). *When victory is not an option: Islamist movements in Arab politics.* Ithaca and London: Cornell University Press.

'Eid, S. (2013). *Tajribati fi saradeeb al-ikhwan* [My Experience in the basements of MB]. Cairo: Jazeerat al-Ward.

'Eid, S. (2014). *Qissati ma' al-ikhwan* [My story with the Muslim Brotherhood]. Cairo: Mahrousa.

'Eid, S. (2014). *Al-ikhwan al-muslimoon al-hader wal mustaqbal: Awraq fil naqd al-zati* [The Muslim Brotherhood: The present and the future: Papers from self-criticism]. Cairo: Al-Mahroussa.

El-'Agouz, A. (2012). *Ikhwani out of the box* [A Muslim Brother out of the box]. Cairo: Dewan.

El-Khirbawy, T. (2012). *Ser al-m'abad: Al-asrar al-Khafiya li gama't al-ikhwan al-muslemeen* [The temple's secret: The hidden secrets of the Muslim Brotherhood]. Cairo: Nahdet Masr.

Fayez, S. (2011). *Janat al-ikhwan: Rehlat al-khuroug min al-gam'a* [The MB paradise: The journey of getting out of the group]. Cairo: Al-Tanweer.

Ramzy, A. (2013). *Dawlat al-murshid wa sanam al-ikhwan* [The state of the guide and the statue of Muslim Brotherhood]. Cairo: Rodiy.

*For Interviewees who are ex-members of the Brotherhood see the appendix Table A.1.

CHAPTER 4

Political Disengagement: Exiting the Brotherhood in 2011 and Afterwards

INTRODUCTION

The year 2011 witnessed a massive popular uprising on January 25, which produced a sea change that no one could have predicted a few days earlier. Looking back at this moment provides a unique opportunity for understanding the Brotherhood, which was engaged in politics at this juncture at three levels. The group had endured many decades of repression from the ruling political elite, by the time of the resignation of Mubarak on February 11, 2011, when it quickly emerged as the country's most powerful civilian actor, though it suffered repression anew at the hands of those associated with El-Sisi, who took power in a 2013 coup. Focusing on this dramatically swift trajectory of power *challenged*, power *gained*, and power *lost*, the chapter is not about narrating what happened or how the Brotherhood took advantage of the tumult of political change that erupted in the wake of this Egyptian 'Spring'; rather, it is about how participants who had left the organization or were at some stage in the process of doing so thought about the events, their role, and that of other actors in them, and the role that such discourses themselves played in the events.

I will divide the chapter into three sections marking these three moments of the group's engagement ('before', 'during,' and 'after' the takeover) and focus on how they *thematically* contributed to shaping and reshaping individual disengagements from the group as both discourse and process. Discourse here will be understood in part as representing

© The Author(s) 2020   121
M. Menshawy, *Leaving the Muslim Brotherhood*, Middle East Today,
https://doi.org/10.1007/978-3-030-27860-1_4

practices and processes understood as involving, or following, shifts in language and power. For example, the 'discourse of ex-hood' was found to be even more resonant, credible, and effective than the dominant discourse of the Brotherhood, which became visibly mired in ambiguity, fragmentation, and contradiction. This came as exiting individuals were able to constitute a counter-power contesting and destabilizing the authority of their leaders. With these mutations of discourses and power dynamics, disengagement can be understood also as process including steps of dis-identification from the group and its attached social, affective, ideological, and socio-political strings. One more argument I made in the chapter is that the challenges to the Brotherhood identity happened not only because it had weakened, but because it had also been put into play. It was partly the group's full engagement in national politics that led to the disengagement of many in its ranks. This transformation was contextually supported by the nature of the revolution itself. Unlike the revolutionary movements that emerged around the world in the 1960s and 1970s, which espoused a powerful 'socialist, anti-imperialist and anticapitalist, and social justice impulse,' the Egyptian revolution was preoccupied with issues that relate to discourse, power, and identity such as 'human rights,' accountability, and attempts at organizational reform.[1] It is in this context that many individual members of the Brotherhood found resources and opportunities to express their desire for personal autonomy from the group as part of many other Egyptians who have taken the events 'personally.'[2] This tendency was also supported by a 'lack of ideology, lax coordination, [and the] absence of any galvanizing leadership and intellectual precepts.'[3]

THE PRE-TAKEOVER DISILLUSIONMENT

Many individuals who disengaged from the Brotherhood contextualize their exit experience partly to the behavior and actions of the group on and after January 25, 2011, when the protests against the regime began that ended with the resignation of President Hosni Mubarak

---

[1] Bayat, A. (2017). *Revolution without revolutionaries: Making sense of the Arab Spring* (p. 11). Palo Alto: Stanford university press.

[2] Soueif, A. (2011). *Tweets from Tahrir: Egypt's revolution as it unfolded, in the words of the people who made it* (p. 10). New York: OR Books.

[3] Bayat, A. (2017). *Revolution without revolutionaries*, p. 11.

on February 11 of the same year. The dominant frame in the texts of interviews and autobiographies is criticism of the Brotherhood as 'non-revolutionary' because it failed to lead, or even fully adapt to, this 'revolutionary' moment. The Brotherhood should have led the protests, as it was the group that was most well-organized and best positioned to do so. It was expected to take the lead, as it was both firmly rooted in Egyptian society and strongly identified with, as the principal opposition group, and with those Egyptians who, having grown weary of Mubarak's authoritarianism, were now driven to rebellion.[4] The group's leaders, having endured many decades of repression at the hands of Mubarak's regime, might have found in the protests a perfect time to react especially as the regime escalated its hostility toward the group. Consequently, many ex-members believed that the group lost at this time an excellent opportunity to take the lead and gain public support as a revolutionary force. They were disappointed that it failed to mobilize its resources to stand by the protestors, whose principal demand was for an end to the rampant police brutality that the Brotherhood itself had long endured. Islam Lutfy, who exited the group in 2011, said that his disillusionment with the group was provoked by seeing it standing on the sidelines throughout most of these initial events.

On January 25, Lutfy joined the tens of thousands of Egyptians who were gathering in Tahrir Square to protest and call for the end of Mubarak's tyranny. Though many members participated, the organization itself, somewhat caught off guard, did not. This reflected in a contradictory and ambiguous discourse constructed by the Brotherhood within this shorter span of a week. On January 20, the Brotherhood said it would not take part in a sit-in in front of the High Court headquarters in Downtown Cairo on January 25.[5] On January 23, it reversed its position.[6] On January 25, as events were escalating to violent clashes with

---

[4] Milton-Edwards, B. (2015). *The Muslim Brotherhood: The Arab spring and its future face* (p. 34). Abingdon-on-Thames: Routledge.

[5] Author, N (2011). *60,000 Nashit iftradi yusharekon fi mudahrat eid al-shurtah* [60,000 virtual activists participate in the demonstration of the police anniversary day]. Available via Bladi-Bladi: http://www.bladi-bladi.com/index.php/news/egypt/614-60.html. Accessed 23 October 2018.

[6] YouTube. (2011). *Doctor El-Erian wa mawkif Al-Ikhwanmin al-musharkah fi yawm 15 yanayer* [Dr. El-Erian and the stances of the Muslim brotherhood toward the participation on January 15]. Available via Youtube: https://www.youtube.com/watch?v=phKSp-95ZITw. Accessed 23 October 2018.

police forces, it refused to announce its participation in the street protests beyond the announced sit-in on claims that 'the body of the movement is too big to be mobilized in such a short time.'[7] On January 27, it
again reversed rhetoric to give a full and unqualified endorsement to the
nationwide protests staged on the next day.[8] However, the Brotherhood
made opposite orders to its members not to escalate on that day, asking them to take part in the token show of support which is sit-ins in
front of mosques, not to assemble in Tahrir Square and also to go home
after 7 p.m.[9] Lutfy, a member for 27 years and a leading figure in the
Brotherhood's University Students Division[10] and a veteran of anti-re-
gime protests on a smaller scale a few years earlier, said: 'I became really
disgruntled. While protestors stayed in the streets and kept flooding it
[the square] by the thousands, we were asked by our leaders to with-
draw by 7pm. Remaining behind and not in step sounded too illogical
for me.'[11]

I asked Lutfy if he thought Brotherhood leaders were right in choosing to be cautious, given the uncertainty about how the situation would
unfold. As Asef Bayat succinctly put it, 'revolution was too abstract to
capture its [the movement's] dynamics,'[12] suggesting that it was concerned only with readily achievable practical goals. From this perspective,
it is reasonably a justified act of cautiousness for the group to await this
'heavy public cover' of mass protests which would make it harder for the
Brotherhood to be 'singled out and pay the price alone as has happened

[7] Beshara, A. (2016). *Thawret Masr: Men jumhuryet yulyu ella thawret yanayir* [The
Egyptian revolution: From Egypt's July revolution to January 25 revolution] (Vol. I,
p. 397). Beirut: Arab Center for Research and Policy Studies.

[8] Tammam, H. (2011). *Al-Islamiyoon wal thawra al-Misriyya: Hidoor wa taradod wa
musharakah* [Islamists and the Egyptian revolution: Absence, hesitation and participation].
Available via Al-Akhbar: https://bit.ly/2Pw2ILn. Accessed 23 October 2018.

[9] Beshara, A. (2016). *Thawret Masr: Men jumhuryet yulyu ella thawret yanayir*, p. 409.

[10] Al-Awadi, H. (2014). *The division 'liaise between the central organisation and its uni-
versity student members' and is mostly overseen by 'recent graduates in their 20s and early 30s*.
Al-Awadi, H. (2014). *The Muslim Brothers in pursuit of legitimacy: Power and political
Islam in Egypt under Mubarak* (p. 233). London: I.B. Tauris.

[11] Lutfy, I. (2017), see Beshara, A. (2016). *Thawret Masr: Men jumhuryet yulyu ella
thawret yanayir*, p. 409.

[12] Bayat, A. (2015). Plebeians of the Arab spring. *Current Anthropology*, 56, S33–S43
(S37). https://doi.org/10.1086/681523.

in history before.'[13] Lutfy reacted fiercely: 'For me, I could only read the behavior as a non-revolutionary act of cowardice and prevarication. It was also more about the narrow interests, deceptiveness, and opportunism of the group's leaders.'[14] The 40-year-old activist and lawyer believed that the justifications offered were not cause for the group to abandon its support for the protests, given their deep-seated causes, including the harshness of the economic situation and the brutality of Mubarak's police forces. The frame of the 'non-revolutionary' character of the Brotherhood was broadly echoed as a trigger or precipitator of disillusionment with the group in the pre-takeover period. The frame even gains credence as the Brotherhood itself repeated it by admitting its 'non-revolutionary' behavior on this occasion.[15]

As the situation was unfolding, one event that happened a week after the eruption of protests triggered further waves of disillusionment with the Brotherhood. The group began to secretly negotiate with Umar Suleiman, the then Vice-President and head of the General Intelligence Directorate (often referred to as the *Mukhabarat*).[16] In the meeting, the group's leaders offered Suleiman their help in trying to deflate the uprising, in return for a 'larger share of the political pie.'[17] News of these negotiations was repeatedly referenced in the interviews and autobiographies as a key 'counter-revolutionary' act triggering or precipitating the disengagement. Haitham Abou-Khalil, a leading figure in the

---

[13] See Tammam, *Al-Islamiyoon wal thawra al-misriyya*. Indeed, the political events after 2011 echo an older political rift in Egypt in which the brotherhood paid the price as part of the splitting of nationalists and Islamists during the rule of Arab nationalist leader Gamal Abdel Nasser (1956–1970), see Gerges, F. (2018). *Making the Arab world: Nasser, Qutb, and the clash that shaped the Middle East*. Princeton: Princeton University Press.

[14] Lutfy, I. (2017).

[15] In 2015, four years after the Tahrir Square protests, the group conducted an internal review from within the organization and concluded that it had been insufficiently 'revolutionary, Brown, N. J., & Dunne, M. D. (2015). *Unprecedented pressures, Uncharted Course for Egypt's Muslim Brotherhood*. Carnegie Endowment for International Peace, 1_19 (2).

[16] Wikileaks. (2013). *Re: Intelligence guidance foredit*. Available via The Global Intelligence Files: https://wikileaks.org/gifiles/docs/12/1263665_re-intelligence-guidance-foredit-html. Accessed 23 October 2018.

[17] Kandil, H. (2014). *Inside the Brotherhood* (p. 137). Malden: Polity Press. The leaders of the Brotherhood refused to disclose the details of the secret meetings even to members of the Shura Council inside the Brotherhood, Beshara, *Thawret Masr: Men jumhuryet yulyu ella thawret yanayir*, p. 505.

group, issued a written statement in March 2011 announcing his resignation to protest the meeting. 'By meeting Suleiman', he wrote, 'the
Brotherhood agreed to give up their participation in the revolution in
return for self-interests such as obtaining a license for creating a new
political party.'[18] Aboul-Futouh, then a member of the Shura Council of
the Brotherhood which is the group's legislative body, even took 'his first
step toward exiting the Brotherhood' when he got no answer after confronting other leaders of the group about the 'secret meeting' which he
or no other members of the Council knew anything about it.[19] Exiting
individuals also tended to think of the Brotherhood's talks with Suleiman
as making it a tool in the hands of the regime,[20] by enabling it to
employ a 'carrot-and-stick' strategy designed to keep the opposition off balance.[21] Ahmed Ban, 50 years old, mentioned the meeting with Suleiman as the main reason for his resignation from the
group in October 2011 after 20 years of membership. He wrote: The
Brotherhood 'shamelessly and un-embarrassingly moved to hold a uni-
lateral deal with the regime,' while at the same time claiming full support
for the protestors.[22] Although the leaders of the Brotherhood retreated
from talks with Suleiman after an initial round, the damage had by then
already been done.

On the other side, the frames of the Brotherhood to justify the talks
with Suleiman created contradictions and confusion among members.
Before meeting Suleiman, the Brotherhood leaders said that they would

[18] Ali, A., & Al-Waziri, H. (2011). *Abu Khalil yastaqeel min al-ikhwan: Al-jama'ah eta-
faqat ma'a Suleiman leinha al-thawrah muqabil hizb wa jameyah* [Abu Khalil resigns from
the Muslim brotherhood: The movement agreed with Suleiman to halt the revolution
in favor of allowing it to create a party and association]. Available via Almasry Al-yawm:
https://www.almasryalyoum.com/news/details/122713. Accessed 4 November 2018.

[19] Beshara, A. *Thawret Masr: Men jumhuryet yulyu ella thawret yanayir*, p. 505.

[20] For example, the meeting was held in the cabinet headquarters where the picture
of Mubarak was centrally hanging high on the hall's wall above all attendees, a symbolic
sign at a time in which tens of thousands were protesting in the Tahrir Square nearby to
demand the 'fall of Mubarak.'

[21] Wikileaks. (2013). *Transition in Egypt: Suleiman's strategy*. Available via Wikileaks:
https://wikileaks.org/gifiles/docs/13/1329987_transition-in-egypt-suleiman-s-strategy-.
html. Accessed 28 October 2018.

[22] Ban, A. (2017). *Ikhwan wa salafiyyon wa dawaish* [Brothers, Salafists and members of
ISIS] (p. 256). Cairo: Al-Mahrousa.

'not hold talks with the regime until the resignation of Mubarak.'[23] After meeting him, the group said it work for ending the sit-in in Tahrir as it adopted Suleiman's position that protestors should stop their sit-in until the end of the 'special security situation.'[24] Facing furor among members of the group, the emphatic position of leaders faltered, and they issued another statement a few hours later announcing that they 'reevaluate its position' on talks with Suleiman and Mubarak's regime.[25]

The frames of the Brotherhood gained further dissonance as the talks even ended 'in failure.'[26] Thus, some argued that the Brotherhood miscalculated its own interests in trying and failing to reach an agreement with Suleiman; had it wanted more, it might have achieved something. 'The Brotherhood did not read the moment of history, as the protests that it sought to abort in the talks with Suleiman eventually led the group to realise its far-fetched dream of taking power,' said Lutfy.[27] The talks were a miscalculation because the regime managed to use the opportunity of meeting with Brotherhood leaders to play the old game of dismissing the protest movement as 'Islamist.' In an interview conducted in Doha, Qatar, Ahmed Nazily, who also located his

[23] Author, N. (2011). *Al-Ikhwanba'd liqa Sulaiman: Muqtrahat al-islah ghair kafeyah* [Muslim brothers after meeting with Suleiman: Proposals of political reform are not sufficient]. BBC. http://www.bbc.com/arabic/middleeast/2011/02/110206_suleiman_meeting_opposition. Accessed 28 October 2018.

[24] Remarkably, the video posted on YouTube of the statements of Sa'd El-Katatny who attended the meetings with Suleiman is symbolically entitled: 'El-katatny after meeting Suleiman and betraying the revolutionaries'; YouTube. (2012). *Alkatatni ba'ad liqa Omar Suleiman wa kheyanat al-thawar* [Al-Katani after meeting Omar Suleiman and betraying revolutionists]. Available via Youtube: https://www.youtube.com/watch?v=F3_D4Tgk13o. Accessed 4 November 2018.

[25] Statements of El-'Erian as quoted in Beshara, *Thawret Masr: Men jumhuryet yulyu ella thawret yanayir*, p. 508.

[26] Ibid., p. 504.

[27] Lutfy, I. (2017). Perhaps Lutfy and other exiting members have in mind the behavior of other political forces and leaders of the revolution who better read the unfolding of events. Wael Ghonim, the most prominent figure representing the revolution, refused to hold talks with the regime out of calculation that the one in control was the 'pulse of the street' driven by a 'revolutionary dreamy generation with no knowledge of politics, no desire to accept half solutions, and it is ready to sacrifice itself for realizing its targets'; Ghonim, W. (2012). *Al-Thawra 2.0: Eza al-sha'b yawman arad al-hayah* [Revolution: 2.0 If the people one day truly aspires to life] (p. 295). Cairo: Dar Al-shorouq.

disillusionment with the group as occurring at the same time (January 25–February 11), called the talks with Suleiman morally wrong, 'tactically ineffective,' and 'strategically erroneous.'[28] The actions could be justified as part of the Brotherhood's 'trademark pragmatism' through which the group can be flexible in its principles for the good of the 'greater case.'[29] However, Nazily described the actions as a mixture of 'stupidity and treason.' They also failed to rise to the occasion as they 'slowed down the dynamic pace of events unfolding in the streets' with the participation of 'many political organizations and individual activists who had invested years of work in forming grassroots networks and mobilizing support for an oppositional movement against the Mubarak regime.'[30] The Brotherhood also 'stabbed in the back Tahrir protestors who were under the attack of state thugs' at the same time of talks with Suleiman.

Certainly, observing the behavior of the Brotherhood to be 'non-revolutionary' or 'counter-revolutionary' can be broadly contextualized within broader contradictions which have led members toward the stage of the 'ideological disengagement,' a stage which could have started before 2011. As detailed in Chapter 3, the group has long promoted itself as 'militant' in a precise sense of possibly modeling such a socio-political struggle that began on January 25 into a kind of 'war,' and it has also long amalgamated its religious and political views in this framework somehow. The rhetoric of its leaders has been always excessive precisely in constructing the group as being war-like, combative, belligerent, or bellicose in its 'struggle' for justice-derived 'Jihad' and insistence on 'full sacrifice.' The events after the eruption of protests in January 2011 proved that the group failed to materialize this rhetoric especially as most of those killed in the first few days were not members of the group.

The disillusionment with the behavior of the group in January–February 2011 can also be argued to be more deeply rooted as it relates to other levels of disillusionment with the ideological base created by the group's founder, Hassan El-Banna (see Chapter 3). El-Qassas said

[28] Nazily, A. (2017).

[29] See Pargeter, A. (2013). *The Muslim Brotherhood: From opposition to power*. London: Saqi.

[30] Nazily, A. (2017).

that the events gave further evidence that the group was flawed on 'the issue of speed.' 'The Brotherhood does not believe in radical change,' he said, 'and this explains the position of its dithering leaders not to join the protestors at an earlier time.'[31] He referred to El-Banna's ideas of the group as having a gradualist or 'evolutionary' rather than 'revolutionary' character.[32] Ban referred to El-Banna as someone who 'did not believe in revolution or in the route of revolution as the ideal way for reform,' Ban wrote.[33] He said that the ideas of a man like El-Banna, who 'only believed in chaining individual members into slavery by their leaders,' could not 'bring on a liberation represented in the revolutionary moment' of 2011.[34]

Identification with the 'National'[35]

As the Brotherhood began to fully participate in the protests, with protestors continuing their sit-in in Tahrir Square, while the talks with Suleiman failed, another element of disillusionment with the Brotherhood emerged. In the changing social and political landscape, members of the Brotherhood found themselves newly identifying as part of a collective identity that had long been rivaled by the Islamist one: a national identity.[36] For, El-Qassas, 42 years old, who had joined the

---

[31] El-Qassas, M. (2017). Late Hossam Tammam, one of the most prolific specialists on the Muslim Brotherhood, put this gradualism rhythmically in the title of his column: 'Absence then hesitation then participation,' see Tammam, H. *al-islamiyoon wal thawra al-misriyya*; On Gradualism, see also El-Sisi, A. (1982). *Hassan El-Banna: mawaqif fi-al-da'wa wa al-tarbiya* [Hassan El-Banna: Situations in da'wa and education] (pp. 138–139). Alexandria: Dar al-Da'wa.

[32] El-Banna underscored the importance of progressing in phases in order to ensure that the movement achieved its objectives. He outlined three main stages: (1) disseminating the group's ideology, (2) recruiting supporters, and (3) implementing work and producing action, see Al-Anani, K. (2016). *Inside the Muslim Brotherhood, religion, identity, and politics* (p. 63). New York: Oxford University Press.

[33] Ban. (2017). *Ikhwan wa salafiyon*, p. 255.

[34] Ibid.

[35] Adopting this posture in analysis is justified as the 'Islamist-nationalist fault line that enraged in the 1950s still exists' during the Arab Spring; Gerges, F. (2013). Introduction: a rupture. In F. A. Gerges (Ed.), *The new Middle East: Protest and revolution in the Arab World* (pp. 1–40 [32]). Cambridge: Cambridge University Press.

[36] See Gerges, Making the Arab world.

Brotherhood 15 years earlier, part of the cause of his disgruntlement was that the Brotherhood 'failed to tip the balance of the national identity against its Islamist identity or at least shift its ideology and discourse to fit in both.'[37] He took part in the Tahrir Square protests from the start, on January 25, when the group was still hesitating about joining. He became a member of the 'Revolution's Youth Coalition,' grouping together Brotherhood members and people identifying with other political groups, including socialists and liberal secularists. El-Qassas said that he felt fully accepted and integrated into this unified and consistent 'political culture' of the Tahrir Square.[38] 'Despite our different political affiliations, we shared the same space, activities, and demands,' he added. The Brotherhood set up in the Square tents for its members in the square, as did other groups, to identify them and keep them together. However, in the final days a mingling between tents occurred, making it harder to identify the political or social affiliations of people present on the Square.[39]

The 'nationalist turn' was not totalizing in nature as it was communicated through a new type of 'revolution' of means of communication which give prominence to what is individual.[40] Many of the Square's individual participants found themselves taking part in political debate and exchanges of ideas that initiated what Nathan Brown calls the rise of a 'republic of debate' in Egypt.[41] This was done from stages with amplification, a wireless network, and an illegal radio station named as 'the

---

[37] Indeed, other Islamist groups such as Hamas, which considers itself a 'wing' of the Muslim Brotherhood, were more adept at dealing with somehow events similarly witnessing rising 'nationalist' sentiments such as the year of its creation in 1987, see Elshaer, A. (2013). Islam in the narrative of Fatah and Hamas. In D. Matar & Z. Harb (Eds.), *Narrating conflict in the Middle East: Discourse, image and communications practices in Lebanon and Palestine* (pp. 111–132). London: I.B. Tauris.

[38] 'A "political culture" usually refers to a set of attitudes held by individuals and aggregated across a national unit,' Brysk, A. (1995). Hearts and minds: Bringing symbolic politics back in. *Polity, 27*(4), 559–585 (562).

[39] El-Sayyed, K. (2018).

[40] Abdellatif, E. (2012). *Balaghat al-hurriya: Ma'rek al-khitab al-siyassi fi zaman al-thawra* [The freedom rhetoric: Battles of political discourse in the time of revolution] (p. 26). Cairo: Altanweer.

[41] See Brown, N. J. (2016). *Arguing Islam after the revival of Arab politics.* Oxford: Oxford University Press, p. 11.

Radio Station of Tahrir' that 'were quickly set up to create an alternative public sphere.'[42] They engaged in a 'multimodal exchange of interactive messages.' This exchange was not from 'one to many'[43] (as had been the case with the censored and hierarchical communication within the Brotherhood, in which the leaders were the sole source of disseminating information to members). It was an exchange from 'many to many,' in which protestors adopted new and autonomous forms of content generation and communication, such as a radio station that included Brotherhood members but not leaders.[44] Speeches made by ordinary Brotherhood members on the stage that was set up in the middle of Tahrir Square were 'self-generated in content' and 'self-selected in reception, with many communicating with many.'[45] The emergence in expression of a national identity—from which an Islamist one might be distinguished, or with which it could also be merged—must be seen as a movement against these dispersive and democratizing tendencies. That there was at work at the same time, and effectively if not explicitly in an opposite direction, a re-formulation of the means of communication and interaction—that would indeed function as part of the individual disengagement process, partly through the refashioning of identities—was also evidenced in slogans.

Slogans are 'deliberate compositions' that can seem to express, and also constitute, the collective will of those using them. They can also reveal something about the sometimes contentious processes of producing meaning at the individual level.[46] The Brotherhood had ordered its members not to use its distinctively Islamist slogans. The protestors mostly focused on expressions of popular will. *'Aysh, Hurriyya, 'Adala Igtima'iyya* (bread, freedom, social justice), was a persistent chant.

[42] Van de Sande, M. (2013). The prefigurative politics of Tahrir Square: An alternative perspective on the 2011 revolutions. *Res Publica, 19*(3), 223–239.

[43] Castells, M. (2007). Communication, power and counter-power in the network society. *International Journal of Communication, 1*, 245–248.

[44] It is an interesting use of a mathematical idea by Castells based on mappings between sets can be one to one, one to many, many to one, or many to many. The simplicity of the idea has an eloquence as 'many to many' can describe several properties of the 'revolutionary moment' in Egypt featured by dispersion and lack of control of messages.

[45] Ibid., p. 248.

[46] Colla, E. (2013). In praise of insult: Slogan genres, slogan repertoires and innovation. *Review of Middle East Studies, 47*, 37–48 (38). https://doi.org/10.1017/s2151348100056317.

As voiced by disparate groups of activists, including many Brotherhood members, it is 'doubtful whether there ever was any agreement about what it meant in concrete terms.'[47] However, and regardless of real intensions shared by forces including the Brotherhood,[48] the mere fact of shouting a slogan (or, sometimes, reading it painted on the walls in the Square) along with others in a repetitious, frequent, and resonant manner seemed to many to represent symbolically a rare moment of unity. Brotherhood members discarded the slogans that they had long repeated in protests staged by the Brotherhood, slogans that reflected the 'Islamist identity' (in phrases typically invoking Islam or its 'glorious' past). Instead, the protestors all now repeated slogans containing words like 'Egypt,' 'the people,' and 'the nation.' Judging by how humans possess a capacity for a unique form of shared or collective 'intentionality' which allows them to construct different forms of reality,[49] protests create with these slogans a new 'we'; that is, the question of the national identity was implicitly being raised, and identified with the people of the nation as represented by those gathered at the present moment in the Square, and so posed as something then partly in the process of being constituted. It was the kind of experience that, as Elliott Colla put it, 'fundamentally altered their feelings and understandings of themselves, their communities and the possible';[50] such events pose the question of the given as something new or up for grabs.

The performativity of the slogans facilitated this duality of individual and collective re-identification. In Tahrir Square and other places of coordinated protest, slogans came to function as 'authorless texts' that could be spontaneously produced and shouted by protestors away from the reach of the leaders of any group that might try to censor or organize their use and dissemination, as the Brotherhood leadership had done before in the group's own protests. Each slogan seemed to 'detach itself from the specific conditions of its initial composition, and to the degree to which it circulates as it were the anonymous expression of a collective will.'[51] For example, when Wael Ghonim, one of the heroes of the

[47] Ibid., p. 38.

[48] See the introduction of Tadros, M. (2012). *The Muslim Brotherhood in contemporary Egypt: Democracy redefined or confined?* London: Routledge.

[49] Searle, J. (1995). *The construction of social reality.* New York: The Free Press.

[50] Colla, E. (2013). *In praise of insult*, p. 41.

[51] Ibid., p. 38.

revolution, gave his first speech in the Tahrir Square on February 8, 2011, he ended it with shouting as 'Egypt is above all,' a call which he repeated four times and which protestors instantly and similarly repeated after him. As Ghonim finished his speech, the Square's internal radio station faded in with a nationalist song that was written and performed in the 1950s under Nasser's era. The song bolstered these heavy nationalist tones by repeating 'Egypt, You are the best name on earth, we love and die for Egypt, long live Egypt.'

Members of the Brotherhood taking part in the protests have got exposed to new discourses that have long been dismissed by their leaders and through which they have gained autonomy from and rebellion against the group. For example, they have to repeat slogans which the Brotherhood would never approve in normal circumstances. On the day that Mubarak resigned, there was one dominant chant in the street protests: 'Lift your head up high; you are an Egyptian.' This slogan implicitly referenced one used by former President Gamal Abdel-Nasser: 'Brother, lift your head up, as the slavery has come to an end.'[52] As borrowing from the Nasser era had long been anathema to the Brotherhood and its Islamist ideology, its use at this time marked the crossing of a boundary. Protestors also borrowed from non-Islamic era as an evocation of a glorious past by calling their actions the 'Lotus Revolution,' in reference to one of the favorite flowers of the Ancient Egyptians. Another type of slogan consisted of negative phrases used comically to mark a certain distance from the Brotherhood's typical caution and hesitancy. Using the *Hijaa*, a type of invective poetry that included insults directed against Mubarak and his regime, had long been abhorred by the Brotherhood especially as some slogans went into 'obscenities' and swear language,[53] which preferred to inculcate humility and 'clean language' (see Chapter 3). However, these rules were now widely being broken in a newly contentious situation in which more profane language seemed well-suited. Slogans also included 'Long Live the Crescent and the Cross' and '[Either You are] A Muslim and A Christian, We are All for Egypt].' These slogans were not only 'avoided' by Islamists but even

---

[52] Indeed, early in the 2011 revolution, protestors compared it to the 1952 revolution led by Nasser; see El-Bendary, M. (2013). *The Egyptian revolution: Between hope and despair:* Mubarak *to Morsi* (p. 3). New York: Algora Publishing.

[53] Abdellatif I., *Balaghat al-hurriya*, p. 48.

'abhorred' and banned as contravening the Islamic law.[54] The very use of such slogans was, even though not directed at it, an act of rebellion against the Brotherhood at the level of language and thought, which had seemed to it so important to control. These linguistic deviances helped transform the square into a place to revise and improvise repertoires of speech contesting the regime, without waiting for any moral authorization, including the Brotherhood.[55]

The Fall of Mubarak: Frames Consolidated

After Mubarak resigned on February 11, 2011, the Brotherhood was much in the minds of exiting individuals. A persistent frame in their accounts continued to be the 'non-revolutionary' or, more strongly put, 'counter-revolutionary,' character of the Brotherhood. Key to this accusation for many was the Brotherhood's having entered into an alliance with the Supreme Council of the Armed Forces (SCAF) and having supported the 'brutality' of security forces against protests.[56] El-Qassas called this an 'act of treason' in departing from the revolution's 'national demands,' to which the group had claimed commitment. The Brotherhood 'sought to serve its own interests,' he said, 'and failed to meet the national interests once shared with other groups during the 18-day sit-in.' The Brotherhood absented itself from some meetings and demonstrations organized by other oppositional groups, though it 'did not hesitate to send its representatives to an officially-sanctioned gathering.'[57] The group lost opportunities to build cross-partisan cooperation and develop the 'ties of trust and true friendship,' as El-Qassas put it. Mohamed Aboul-Gheit, a 28-year-old who exited the group in 2011 after a period of disillusionment that

---

[54] See Tammam, *Al-islamiyoon wal thawra al-misriyya*.

[55] I have witnessed some young leaders of the Brotherhood swearing and shouting in an obscene language in the Square especially during events such as the 'Camel Battle' which marked the fiercest of clashes between the regime loyalists and the Tahrir protestors. Interviewees confirmed the observation.

[56] See Wikileaks. (2011). *H: Intel. Secret offer to El. baradei/Muslim Brotherhood-army alliance.* Hillary Clinton email archive. Available via Wikileaks: https://wikileaks.org/clinton-emails/emailid/12845. Accessed 30 October 2018.

[57] Brown, N. (2011). *The Muslim Brotherhood as helicopter parent.* Available via Foreign Policy: https://foreignpolicy.com/2011/05/27/the-muslim-brotherhood-as-helicopter-parent/. Accessed 30 October 2018.

began a few years earlier, said: 'The Brotherhood really screwed up the revolution. They destroyed it indeed, thanks to their narrow interests leading to their alliance with the SCAF after Mubarak's removal.'[58] Other ex-members repeated the frame in their autobiographies. Cairo-based Ban wrote in his autobiography: 'The crime of the Brotherhood was destroying the revolutionary momentum and dividing up the national unity, because of their deals, maneuvers and conspiracies.'[59] Ban mentions this also in books that he has published as part of his career as a researcher. In one, he writes that the Brotherhood's General Guide should apologize for the 'policies committed by the group,' including 'the early departure from the [Tahrir] Square without a well-defined plan to face the vestiges or remnants of the old regime.'[60] Tareq El-Beshbeshy, 53 years old, who exited the group in January 2013, said the group 'kept its eye on serving its own interests, as it never acknowledged the constitution of the state nor committed itself to the national identity of Egypt.'[61] All these complaints add resonance to the frames already constructed by members as they build up their disgruntlement over the behavior of the Brotherhood from the beginning of the revolution.

Resources and Rising Opportunities

All the frames mentioned above, including those describing the Brotherhood as 'non-revolutionary' or 'counter-revolutionary' and those referring to the rise of rival identities on which these frames are drawn, gain their power through articulation in 'texturing' evidenced what is written or said in autobiographies or interviews. Still, part of this salience is attributed to the operationalization, that is the ability of these frames to take root by benefitting from resources and opportunities which created and sustained them.

In the days leading to the resignation of Mubarak, part of these resources and opportunities had to do with power shifts in the relationship between the Brotherhood and its members. It was part of a shift in power toward the street as a place (the Square, partly as stand-in for the

---

[58] Aboul-Gheit, M. (2017).

[59] Ban, *Ikhwan wa salafiyyon*, pp. 15–16.

[60] Ibid., p. 13.

[61] El-Beshbeshy, T. (2017).

broader political space, at least potentially, of Egypt itself[62]), as an object (the referent of the protests and slogans in the society and the ways it might now be refashioned and transformed), and as a means (the manner of engagement and interaction that these protestors were involved in, and new discourses being engaged in and fashioned). This power of the 'street' created with it a sense of ownership giving voice to the 'voiceless' mainly including those ordinary individuals who could not have been able to find their way to the 'dominant' means of communication controlled and hegemonized by the state and its clientelist institutions.[63] Those 'voiceless' include members of the Brotherhood whose discourse and even response to the dominant discourse have long been falsified, downsized, or silenced.

Some members were emboldened by this to disobedience turning the ownership of the 'street' into an 'ownership of the self'; as such, it involved a 'powerful sense of liberation, and an unprecedented feeling of entitlement.'[64] Without being asked, Nazily showed me photos of himself leading senior members of the Brotherhood into Tahrir Square during the sit-in. 'Without my intervention, they could not get into [the Square],' he told me boastfully. 'Many politicians or group leaders were ousted to keep the revolution leaderless, but we managed to mediate our leaders' access through our connection with other groups organising the protests, and our ability to convince the participants in the protests as well.'[65] Nazily was able to do that because the square introduced a decentralized, horizontal, non-hierarchical form of power that accompanied the sense of personal empowerment and responsibility. Nazily told me that he shouted at one senior Brotherhood figure in the middle of Tahrir Square not to use a Brotherhood-specific slogan, but instead only slogans that had been agreed upon by participants. He admitted that he would not have challenged authority and hierarchy in so daring a manner within the Brotherhood before the revolution. There were occasions

---

[62] Leftist activist Sally Toma (Moore) attributed this foundation of the 'Republic of Tahrir' to the sense of 'ownership' as 'we now have our own Egypt... I felt it like my own Egypt.' Available via, YouTube. (2011). *Sally Moore: Egyptian activist describes life.* https://www.youtube.com/watch?v=3L-ue1e3x3c. Accessed 20 January 2019.

[63] Abdellatif, E., *Balaghat al-hurriya*, p. 56.

[64] Bayat, *Plebeians of the Arab Spring*, pp. 534–535.

[65] Nazily, A. (2017).

in which youth Brotherhood leaders prevented their Brotherhood leaders from giving speeches on the main 'stage' or platform in the Tahrir Square in order not to 'give [too much presence] to the group'[66] and to maintain multiplicity in participation, representation, and communication. This makes sense at a 'revolutionary' moment marked by these opportunities supported by horizontality, an aversion to representation, and decentralized forms of power.[67] It is in this sense that ideology, as such of the Brotherhood and which is associated with 'solid organization and recognizable leadership,' came to be regarded with suspicion.[68]

The power shift which provided exiting members not only made resources and opportunities available to exiting members, but it also deprived the Brotherhood from resources and opportunities that have long attached those members to the group. Part of this had to do with what may be called the politics of prefiguration. The concept of prefiguration names a form of politics rooted in anarchism and central to many of the movements globally in the 1960s. It has been defined as referring to an ideal society that is envisioned by activists as an aspect of the present 'rather than [being realized] at some point in the future when the conditions for building a more equitable society may be more conducive to effecting positive change.'[69] It means that 'political principles are embodied in current behavior, not put on hold until the time is deemed right for them to be deployed.'[70] While the Brotherhood had

---

[66] Drawn on testimonies of other members of the Brotherhood as carried in Beshara, *Thawret Masr: Men jumhuryet yulyu*, p. 503.

[67] For example, part of this 'decentralization' is that as the Brotherhood's traditional hierarchically positioned leaders neither organized nor participated in the protests initially, the 'only link between the group and the protests was through the youth who were members of the Brotherhood and who were simultaneously part of the independent protests movements growing since 2004, and who took part on an individual basis,' see Al-Awadi, *The Muslim Brothers in pursuit of legitimacy*, p. 232.

[68] Bayat, *Revolution without revolutionaries*, pp. 13–14.

[69] Baker, M. (2016). The prefigurative politics of translation in place-based movements of protest. *The Translator, 22*(1), 1–21. https://doi.org/10.1080/13556509.2016.11484 38. This has roots in the twentieth-century philosophy at least in Western Europe. See, for instance, Walter Benjamin on the now-time and the Theses on the Philosophy of History. Some of this thinking draws on Jewish and/or Christian theology; I don't know if similar things have been said within Islamic theology, but I suspect so, perhaps in part because of the role in it of miracles and thus events.

[70] Baker, *The prefigurative politics of translation*.

always promised its members an ideal order to be realized in the future as part of an 'Islamic project' which it envisages and propagates,[71] Tahrir Square by comparison offered a presentist understanding of the meaning of what the protestors were doing that could serve as 'the foundation of a different future.'[72] (That is, the future is located within something already manifest and is not merely desired, pursued, or promised.) Repeating slogans identifying 'people' as agents of change, the protestors found in the Square a partial but actually prefigured 'utopia.'[73] For members of the Brotherhood, the Square was the site of a vision 'in miniature' of the sort of society they wanted to have.

The shifts in power and availability of resources or opportunities related to them grew bigger after the fall of Mubarak. Young members felt stronger due to their decisive role in the 'external' struggle against Mubarak's regime. Now Mubarak is out of power, they began to benefit from this sense of empowerment to internalize the struggle to destabilize levels of power inside their own group. In other words, if they brought about political change in Egypt,[74] they felt they could do that inside the Brotherhood. In March 2011, around 300 members of the group publicly met in one of Cairo's big hotels and held a conference despite the objection of the group's leaders whom no single one of them attended the event. Participants demanded internal reform including promotions on basis of 'meritocracy not loyalty,' an end to the 'hearing and obedience' as 'we have a voice and we want to be heard.'[75] They also countered dominant frames legitimating the group's traditional leaders who had long claimed their role and status as 'victims' bearing the wrath and brutality in the battle with the regime (see Chapter 3) or 'symbolic figures' leading the group and its members toward the realization of the

[71] Wickham calls this the 'Islamist project of ideological outreach,' see Wickham, C. R. (2002). *Mobilizing Islam: Religion, activism, and political change in Egypt* (pp. 119–120). New York: Columbia University Press.

[72] Bayat, *Revolution without revolutionaries*, p. 14.

[73] Azmi Beshara even identified what he also called 'utopia' in Tahrir Square as being of the 'extreme' type as it adopts a radical change of state and society, Beshara, *Thawret masr: men jumhuryet yulyu*, p. 503.

[74] Ibid.

[75] YouTube. (2011). *Mu'atamar shabab Al-Ikhwan* [Conference of Muslim Brotherhoods youth]. Available via Youtube: https://www.youtube.com/watch?v=nKD-9vrrKseU. Accessed 29 October 2018.

'Islamic mission' or protecting it from external dangers and conspiracies. The frame of victimization, used by those leaders even until the very final days of Mubarak's rule, malfunctioned as the perpetrator (i.e., Mubarak) is no longer in power. A young participant said: 'We appreciated their protection of us provided by our leaders against the security harassment. Now this harassment is over we need a moment of opening without limits or borders,' asking their leaders to realize that 'we are living in a new reality and change is a must.'[76] The Brotherhood sought to contain the young members with allowing a youth conference in April in 2013. The Brotherhood made 'empty promises' to those calls and even appointed Khairat El-Shater, framed as the main obstacle to these reforms, to be in charge of instituting them. As expected, 'there was no change since 2011,' and subsequent defections from the organization expanded to include not only revolutionary youth.[77] For example, one resource is represented in political options. Mohamed Habib (born in 1964) applied for the foundation of his party on July 13, 2011, only two days after announcing his resignation from the Brotherhood in which he has been a member for 35 years. Habib 'announced his resignation and joined El-Nahda Party' as combined in the news combining the two elements in the same piece of news.[78] Aboul-Futouh (born in 1956), objecting that the Brotherhood did not field its own candidate in the presidential elections, fielded himself as an independent candidate in them (and he also attracted many other members of the group who were aware they could be expelled or punished for supporting him). Ibrahim El-Za'frany (born in 1952) stepped down in April 2011 and also joined some of these political groupings.

1. The Takeover Disillusionment

A broad disillusionment began as the Brotherhood achieved power by winning the majority of seats in the parliament in November 2011, and the presidency in a separate vote that Morsi, then a leader in the group's

[76] Ibid.

[77] Al-Awadi, *The Muslim Brothers in pursuit of legitimacy*, p. 237.

[78] Hadeyah, S. (2011). *Istiqalat Mohammed Habeeb min Al-Ikhwan wa endhimamih ella hizb al-nahdhah* [Mohammed Habeeb resigned from the Muslim Brotherhood and joined al-Nahdhah Party]. Available via Yawam al-Saba'a: https://bit.ly/2EpSQBO. Accessed 29 October 2018.

Guidance Bureau, won in May 2012. I found the disillusionment among exiting members to fall into three principal categories that act as frames: the Brotherhood's ideology, its policies, and its leaders.

Framing Policies:
The 'Brotherhood's Regime, or Mubarak's?

The equation of the Mubarak regime with the Brotherhood as a frame was generally abstracted from the idea of the Brotherhood as implementing an Islamist project of governance, ideology, and identity. 'When it took power,' remarked Aboul-Sa'd, 'the Brotherhood's rule sounded to me less about realizing the Islamic project or other values related to it, than obtaining and holding power like any self-interested group, and like Mubarak's regime itself.'[79] For the 50-year-old civil servant and 25-year veteran of the group, this realization was largely what drove him to disengage from the group. He found that he could prove to himself and others that he could leave the Brotherhood without being a 'bad Muslim,' as his wife 'had accused me upon exiting the group in early 2011.' Instead, 'I disengaged from a self-interested group, not from Islam.'[80] Ahmed Ramzy made a similar point about ending the confusion between politics and Islam represented by the Brotherhood: Morsi and Mubarak were almost the same, he said, as they both merely wanted to 'dominate power,' and found no need to embrace pluralism.[81] Intissar 'Abdel-Mon'im wrote in her autobiography that the Brotherhood only wanted to 'grab power' and its leaders to 'get part of the pie.'[82] Ban attributed his disillusionment and final exit to the realization that 'the politics of pure interests and sheer lies contradicts with honesty, brotherhood, and sacrifice, among all other sublime meanings in the Brotherhood's dictionary.'[83] In such criticisms, the Brotherhood was

---

[79] Aboul Sa'd, T. (2017).

[80] Ibid.

[81] Ramzy, A. (2013). *Dawlat al-murshid wa sanam Al-Ikhwan* [The state of the guide and the statue of Muslim Brotherhood] (p. 134). Cairo: Rodiy.

[82] See 'Abdel-Mon'im, I. (2011). *Hekayatii ma' Al-Ikhwan* [My story with the MB]. Cairo: Al-Hayaa Al-Misriyya Al-'Ama leil Kitab.

[83] Ban, A. (2013). *Al-IkhwanAl-Muslimoon wa mehnat al-watan wal deen* [The Muslim Brotherhood and the predicament of nation and religion] (p. 14). Cairo: Al-Neel Centre for Strategic Studies.

denied the 'exclusivity of religion' that was its strongest source of legitimacy, appeal, mobilization, and, indeed, existence.[84]

The group's ascent to power could be seen as part of normal power
politics with its strategic and tactical character, including building a coalition with rivals such as the Salafists, or government agencies like the
SCAF and abandoning coalition with 'revolutionary forces.'[85] These
steps could sound legitimate, logical, and even constitutional for any
'responsible' opposition group or party oriented toward governing[86]
especially after the removal of Mubarak. For exiting members, they are
not due to issues to do with discourse. The Brotherhood has long constructed itself not as 'constitutional opposition' taking part in 'game
image' of politics in which the group would perform as an opposition. In
the hegemonic discourse presented to its members, and to further borrow from Sartori, the Brotherhood is 'anti-system opposition'[87] ready to
tear the system apart to make it accord with the Islamic law. Conditions
such as authoritarianism and the one-party system have supported this
construction as they made the Brotherhood a 'permanent opposition'
which, 'far removed from governmental turnover and thereby knows that
it would not be called to 'respond,' is likely to take the path of 'irrespon-
sible opposition,' that is, the path of promising wildly and outbidding.[88]
Accordingly, when approaching and taking political rule unexpect-
edly, the Brotherhood has to take steps that entailed a great deal of
compromise on the 'wild' ideological and religious principles on which

[84]Scholars contend this 'exclusivity of religion' is a legitimating factor and a source of
the distinctiveness that sets the religious group and its ideology apart from other groups.
See Pape, R. A. (2005). *Dying to win: The strategic logic of suicide terrorism*. New York:
Random House Inc. As religious fundamentalism always contains a political component as well, it involves more than simply a religious perception. It is here that scholars
such as Juergensmeyer also link the existence of such groups such as the Brotherhood
to this religious-political identity of presenting 'religious responses to social situations';
Juergensmeyer, M. (2001). *Terror in the mind of God: The global rise of religious violence*
(p. 225). California: University of California Press.

[85]El-Sherif, A. (2014). *The Egyptian Muslim Brotherhood's failures a series on political Islam
in Egypt*. Carnegie Endowment for International Peace. Available via Carnegie: http://carn-
egieendowment.org/files/muslim_brotherhood_failures.pdf. Accessed 6 April 2018.

[86]Sartori, G. (1966). Opposition and control: Problems and prospects. *Government and
opposition*, *1*(2), 149–154 (152). Available via: http://0-www.jstor.org.library.qnl.qa/sta-
ble/44481787. Accessed 9 December 2018.

[87]Ibid.

[88]Ibid.

the group had supposedly been based.[89] This has created a rupture or an irregularity in its long fixated discourse related to it being out of power. The leaders of the Brotherhood did not explain these shifts in policies neither they justify it by rearticulating a different convincing discourse. For T.E., who exited in 2013, it was 'shocking' to see how the group moved away from its Islamist mission in gaining political power, adopting a 'political opportunism' instead of pursuing 'individual, familial, and societal Islamization through changing the hearts and minds of people before ultimately taking over the state.' T.E. remembered certain incidents that substantiated his disillusionment. For example, when the government arrested members of the group in 2005, 'I felt that the regime was fighting Islam, represented in the form of the Muslim Brotherhood. To my mind, it was an attack on Islam, not on members of the group. The group also made us feel so.'[90] As the group moved into politics, T.E. realized that 'I had been wrong and the group is not the same as Islam or even working for Islam. It was simply working for its narrow interests to control power for the sake of power.'[91] He felt that he had been 'manipulated' into taking part in acts merely meant to 'consolidate power,' including the bloody protests that took place outside the presidential palace in December 5, 2012. The protests included clashes between pro-Morsi and anti-Morsi protestors led to the deaths of Brotherhood members in December 5, 2012 after the president surprisingly issued a declaration granting himself broad powers above any court. The organization was ill-equipped to account for this escalation or the orders made to its members to be part of it.[92] Ironically, the credibility

---

[89] El-Sherif, *The Egyptian Muslim Brotherhood's*, p. 12.

[90] T.E. (2017).

[91] Ibid.

[92] Morsi justified the declaration as an attempt to 'protest the transition to constitutional democracy.' However, the rhetoric proved unconvincing to many Egyptians as it made his decisions 'final and unchallengeable,' raising accusations of being a 'power grab' by a 'new dictator.' The declaration drew mass protests, leading Morsi to take one step backward and limit the scope of the declaration to 'sovereign matters' but he still kept many other powers. Still, tens of thousands of people to the streets of Cairo calling for Morsi's downfall. After protests and deadly clashes with members of the Brotherhood, some of them got killed, Morsi bowed to the pressure and rescinded most of his 22 November Decree. Other scholars argue that the decree was 'reasonably and objectively justified' but it was badly presented, which again related to the debate to the efficacy and credibility of the Brotherhood's discourse and its power of persuasion, see Beshara, A. (2016). *Thawret masr: Min al-thawra*

and validity of these frames of exiting members found support from the failure of the Brotherhood to adequately justify its actions through its dominant frames carried by the group's media outlets. Academic scholars Mohammed El-Nawawy and Mohamad Hamas Elmasry systematically analyzed the frames in one of the Brotherhood's media outlets, *Ikhwanweb.com*. The frames, they concluded, demonstrated that the Brotherhood 'behaved as a self-interested political actor... and made decisions based on calculations of self-interest.'[93]

These clashes showed instances of the Brotherhood struggling to rearticulate its discourse or operationalize it for eventual use when it would come into power. The group was unwilling to abandon or transcend such frames as that of the 'victimization' suffered by the group and its members, as it had long been the case that many of its activists were imprisoned or tortured by the regime, though of course this frame seemed incongruous when the group itself was in power. It now had no way to incorporate frame like this to build a new 'national accomplishment-based legitimacy' convincing to both members of the group and Egyptians in general or re-align its narratives with the new facts on the ground.[94] It also adopted the same old tactics of keeping the house in order. When M.'A.Z, 32 years old, who exited the group shortly after the 2011 protests, demanded of his prefect, 'Why did the December 2011 clashes happen? Why have we lost lives [mostly from the Brotherhood members]? What were the targets of this protest?,' the leader's response was typical: He asked him to join a guidance session, which included reading more Qur'an and 'getting closer to God' through prayer. 'I thought my prefect wanted to cover for the mistakes of the Brotherhood as far as I understood them in my mind at the time.'[95] To, thus, give a religious answer to a political question is indicative of a discursive dissonance, which seems to have marked

---

ella al-inqilab [Egypt's revolution: From the revolution to the coup] (p. 284). Beirut: Arab Center for Research and Policy Studies.

[93] El-Nawawy, M., & Elmasry, M. H. (2018). *Revolutionary Egypt in the eyes of the Muslim Brotherhood: A framing Analysis of Ikhwanweb* (p. 146). Lanham: Rowman & Littlefield.

[94] As put by Al-Awadi: 'The Brothers were unable to count on Egyptians' sympathy for their rough treatment at the hands of the Mubarak regime lasting indefinitely, because the revolution changed everything'; Al-Awadi, *The Muslim Brothers in pursuit of legitimacy*, p. 232.

[95] M.'A.Z (2017).

the Brotherhood's participation in power. This characteristically involved members being asked to retreat to a purely individual level of concern while the group itself was expanding outward toward encompassing the state and with it Egyptian society. 'The leaders were the ones committing mistakes in their politics,' insisted M.'A.Z, 'not myself in my relationship with God.'

Exiting members also found that the Brotherhood's discourse also ambiguous, evasive, and contradictory as the Brotherhood took more steps in power. In the 1990s, Essam El-'Irian, one of the group's leaders, argued that '[w]e were the first to call for and apply democracy. We were devoted to it until death.'[96] In the early weeks after Mubarak stepped down and the SCAF took control of the transition, the Brotherhood repeated the same rhetoric. The Brotherhood established its own new political party, the Freedom and Justice Party (FJP), which drew in many thousands of members, and established hundreds of branches across the country. Ex-members found the group abandoning these commitments and values, as the restrictive membership and dynamics of the FJP revealed. Members were asked to join the FJP as part of their duty as Brotherhood members, and were forbidden to join any other political parties. This was despite the fact that leaders of both groups claimed autonomy with respect to the other.[97] This marked a gap between the articulation of discourse and its materialization. For while the Brotherhood pledged itself to make politics in Egypt more 'democratic,' it did not become 'democratic' itself.

Disgruntled over the discrepancies in the group's discourse and emboldened by the liberating mood of the Tahrir protests, many members understandably found it hard to follow the orders of the Brotherhood or to want to join the FJP. Too much was being questioned, and the Brotherhood was as much on the side of the questioned as the questioning. At the same time, disillusionment with the group at this stage was supported by the rise of opportunities to challenge the Brotherhood and counter its discourse.

One of these resources was supplied by Aboul-Futouh, a former Brotherhood leader who exited the group in March 2011 as mentioned

---

[96] Quoted in Abed-Kotob, S. (1995). The accommodationists speak: Goals and strategies of the Muslim Brotherhood of Egypt. *International Journal of Middle East Studies, 27*, 321–339 (325). https://doi.org/10.1017/s0020743800062115.

[97] Al-Awadi, *The Muslim Brothers in pursuit of legitimacy*, p. 239.

above. Much to the Brotherhood's chagrin, many of its members joined his *Misr Al-Qawiyya* (Strong Egypt) Party and became involved in his presidential campaign during the summer of that year. In its very name, Aboul-Futouh's party manifested a link to the rising tide of nationalism that was a feature of the identity of many current and former Brotherhood members in the post-2011 era. The party's inclusion of reference to Islam in its platform made it a more convincing alternative for Brotherhood members not seeking a full 'discursive rupture' with their past. The Brotherhood predictably reacted in anger. It announced that it would not field a candidate of its own. It fired many individuals who had joined Strong Egypt, and employed its traditional tactics of punishment through 'real and imagined kinships' (see Chapter 2). Aboul-Gheit was the leader of Aboul-Futouh's presidential campaign team in the former's hometown Assuit, in southern Egypt. He described the pressure: 'It was like the fall of the sky on earth. One of the seniors, who really brought me up and was considered like my father, threatened that he would come to the office of the campaign and beat me on the legs.'[98]

This reaction is a reminder of the 'affective pressures' that could be mobilized by virtue of the imagined kinship that the group enjoyed (Chapter 2). But it also reveals the limits of the power relations binding members to the organization, and which had to be renegotiated after the eruption of the events that began on January 25. Exiting members, who often found themselves ostracized due to the lack of alternatives in the face of Mubarak's depoliticization measures, could now choose another party that was in ideological proximity to the group and had a serious chance of winning power (Aboul Futouh obtained fourth position with 17% of the votes in the May 2012 elections). Aboul-Futouh's party also provided for many a compensation for the loss of access to alternative social circles, as many members who had been expelled or forced out of the Brotherhood were now able to rejoin other ex-members and rebuild old circles of 'solidarity of ex-hood' and friendships.

Questions of identity seem to have arisen quite naturally in this context. For many, moving away from the FJP and joining another party was partly an attempt to construct a personal identity and further their 'emancipation' (a recurring frame in the discourse of ex-hood, as analyzed in Chapter 2). Aboul-Futouh's party embraced aspects of the

[98]Aboul-Gheit, M. (2017).

revolutionary ethos, including advocating 'personal freedoms.'[99] For
its part, the FJP's platform and bylaws maintained commitment to the
social and ideological entanglements of the Brotherhood. It took as a
focus 'reforming the individual, the family, the society, the government,
and then institutions of the state.' Indeed, reforming individuals and
their families was the traditional mission of the party's parent organization, the Brotherhood itself.[100] It was partly this that exiting members generally sought to be free from (see the discussion of 'real' and
'imagined' kinships in the Brotherhood in Chapter 2). Thus, rejecting
membership in the FJP was not only a matter of disagreement with its
organizational, ideological, or political character. It was also personal
and affective, implicating both one's choice of relationships and sense of
identity.

Framing Leaders: Disengagement Personalized

Personalization is a process that, for disengaging members, depended on
referring frames related to disengagement with the group's ideology or
political decision-making process to the personal qualities of particular
leaders, such as El-Banna, or President Morsi, who ruled the country
for a year. Part of the significance of this personalization is that it con-
solidates earlier frames which identified persons as part of the problems
leading members to disengage from the group (see Chapter 3). Some
exiting members linked their disagreements over the formation of the
FJP with claims that it betrayed the intentions of the founder, El-Banna
himself, who long refused to mix the group's religious missionary activity
with party politics. In the 1930s, El-Banna had the opportunity to form
a political party but choose not to, or so it was said.[101] Current members
who believed in the need to form a party found in this decision an occasion to question the wisdom of El-Banna's views and those of the current leaders, who had long held up El-Banna's position as an inflexible
core of the group's ideology and even of Islam itself. 'We were brought
up in the Brotherhood with the rule of "no *Hizbiyya* [being founders or
members of political parties] in Islam," but all of a sudden our leaders

[99] El-Bendary, *The Egyptian revolution: Between hope and despair*, p. 4.
[100] See Brown, *The Muslim Brotherhood as helicopter parent*.
[101] Al-Awadi, *The Muslim Brothers in pursuit of legitimacy*, p. 238.

changed this rule without even discussing it with us or even offering any satisfying answers to justify this radical change,' said Aboul-Sa'd.[102]

Again, this personalization, attributing their criticism to El-Banna, drew on a discursive dissonance revealing discrepancies in discourses long articulated as part of the group's ideology. The leaders of the group who were not then enthusiastic supporters of *Hizbiyya*, based on the claim that El-Banna had been against it, were the same ones who had defended it, Aboul-Sa'd argued. They had lost opportunities in the past to enable the group to make its voice heard, such as in the parliament, when other political means were blocked, he added. In addition, without the *Hizbiyya* principle, the group might have been able to adapt its ideology to modern realities, such as the nation-state, many years earlier, prior to the formation of the FJP.[103] Leaders who had long linked their legitimacy to El-Banna and his legacy now faced a certain embarrassment. They could not admit that El-Banna had had negative views about forming a political party, or that they had been wrong to present his views on this question as sacred.[104] This embarrassment on the part of the leaders emboldened exiting members in a discourse of ex-hood that conferred legitimacy on the separation of the religious and the political, or Islam and the no longer infallible figure of El-Banna (see Chapter 3). Finding that they could be good Muslims without the Brotherhood facilitated disengagement for many.

Morsi also figured in the narratives of many ex-members in a kind of personalization. He was criticized for both his ideas and his character. All of the exiting members studied considered Morsi a poor performer as leader of either the Egyptian state or the Brotherhood, especially in light of the hopes many of them had had. If 'the simplest message in politics is a human face,'[105] as Manuel Castells argues, the Brotherhood was not so well represented, and many found this disappointing. Yet the Brotherhood sufficiently personalized its politics and relied on its leader's image that the organization suffered in consequence. Lutfy said that he was shocked when he learned of Morsi's nomination. While some took it as a sign of the

[102] Aboul Sa'd, T. (2017).

[103] For debate on the issue of forming a party in 1980s, see Al-Awadi, *The Muslim Brothers in pursuit of legitimacy*, pp. 83–84.

[104] Al-Awadi, *The Muslim Brothers in pursuit of legitimacy*, p. 82.

[105] Castells, *Communication, power and counter-power*, p. 242.

uprising's 'democratic spirit,'[106] Lutfy took it as a step backward. Having worked under Morsi in the Brotherhood's Student Affairs Committee, Lutfy said: 'How can the group choose a man who sounds too dogmatic, non-revolutionary, outmoded, and traditionalist to lead a country under the spell of a revolutionary mood and high expectations?'[107] Morsi maintained a far-from-clear relationship between his role as President and his role in the Brotherhood (as a senior figure and a member of the Guidance Bureau and the Shura Council among other titles[108]), with its secretive and opaque structure.[109] To the extent that that was true, it meant that his failure in office was also that of the group.

Insofar as the legitimacy of a leader is based on what is personal, the 'behaviour and personalities of the occupants of authority and rule are of dominating importance.'[110] Asked to describe Morsi, most of the interviewees limited their description to one quality: 'stupidity.' A.E., a 22-year-old who exited the group in 2016, was the most disgruntled among those studied: 'Morsi was stupid. He was a donkey. He was pushed against the wall by a backward group.'[111] The frame of stupidity accords loosely with the frame of anti-intellectualism (Chapter 3). S.E., once asked about Morsi, said, similarly, 'He is acutely stupid. He missed the unique opportunity to establish democracy and the rule of law in Egypt; he and the Brotherhood trusted the army, the same party which played them up and conducted a coup due to this stupidity.'[112] For A.S.R., Morsi's 'stupidity was coupled with authoritarianism, as he did not give any others the chance to teach him or the leaders of the group how to run the state.'[113] Tareq El-Beshbeshy called Morsi and other current leaders 'the stupidest brothers on earth.'[114] This made

---

[106]Wickham, C. (2013). *The Muslim Brotherhood: Evolution of an Islamist movement.* Princeton: Princeton University Press, p. 154.

[107]Lutfy, I. (2017).

[108]Morsi joined the Brotherhood in 1978 and its political department in 1992. He served in parliament in 2000, see Al-Awadi, *The Muslim Brothers in pursuit of legitimacy*, p. 239.

[109]El-Sherif, *The Egyptian Muslim Brotherhood's*, p. 9.

[110]Eason, D. (1965). *A systems analysis of political life* (pp. 302–303). New York: Wiley.

[111]A.E. (2017).

[112]S.E. (2017).

[113]A.S.R. (2017).

[114]El-Beshbeshy, T. (2017).

Morsi a liability for the group, but an opportunity or resource for exiting members in precipitating and justifying their disengagement.

2. Post-Takeover Disillusionment

A new framing of disengagement began with a sit-in in *Rabi'a al-'Adawiyya* Square, where members of the group began camping on the eve of June 30, 2013, coinciding with the removal of Morsi as president. Judging by the narratives of exiting individuals, this was another 'turning point' precipitating disengagement from the Brotherhood. The 40 nights of the sit-in provided an opportunity for many concerns to be brought up and discussed. Many of these concerns related to the group, its current leaders, or its founder El-Banna.

The leaders of the Brotherhood sought to benefit from the 'prefiguration' marking the events then unfolding. The 'Islamic project' was no longer based on a consequentialist understanding of the pursuit of an 'ultimate end,' but on the idea that, as mentioned earlier, the present was a prefiguration of the end rather than a means to it. For instead of containing the ideal of an 'Islamic state' in the imagination of members, the leaders began to suggest that this ideal state was actually being realized in the encampment, in a manner they defined as a (divine) miracle. Apocalyptic discourses using religious figures were prevalent then, with invocations of figures from religious myths and legends, and of the possibility of divine intervention. During the sit-in, leaders conjured images of the Prophet Mohamed 'sleeping alongside' or praying with President Morsi[115]; they narrated Biblical stories; they made claims that the Archangel Gabriel prayed at the main mosque in the square overlooking the square.[116] They were echoing many of the prophecies that circulated during the sit-in: including that if the members of the Brotherhood kept faith with Morsi, as their predecessors did with Moses, 'a miracle would

[115]YouTube. (2013). *Ezhak ma al-rua'a al-elaheyah fi Raba'ah al-'Adaweyah* [Laugh with God-inspired dreams in Rabea'a al-Adweya. Available via Youtube: https://www.youtube.com/watch?v=6NAyi00COSQ. Accessed 4 November 2018.

[116]YouTube. (2013). *Manasat Rabea'a: Gabriel (alayhe alsalam) dahar fi masjed Rabea'a* [Rabea'a stage: Gabriel (peace be upon him) appeared in Rabea'a mosque]. Available via Youtube: https://www.youtube.com/watch?v=3oOaAbsqVcg. Accessed 4 November 2018.

be shortly at hand.'[117] In this way, the events were imbued with great importance while also being marked as belonging to the possible realization of hopes based on prophetic and utopian ideas long taken up within the Brotherhood as part of its 'imaginary.'[118]

As it happened, security forces broke into the camp, killing thousands of protestors, including many women and children. At this moment, the newly materialized and operationalized religious discourse could be said to disfunction. It was a disillusionment with the divine on which all this discourse is based. The discourse lost two of its main features: credibility and effectiveness. While the demands of the Tahrir Square protest appeared clear and realizable, including the call for the fall of the regime, the protests of *Rabi'a* Square failed to achieve their objectives. *Rabi'a* posed exclusively Islamist demands. When these demands were not met, members of the Brotherhood began to reevaluate their position, and it is no wonder that their first target was their leaders.

Disillusionment with Leaders

The sit-in at *Rabi'a* provided a unique opportunity for direct contact between members and leaders. The latter could no longer maintain the spatial or social distance with members needed to maintain their authority over the interactions. This allowed disgruntled members to seek answers directly from senior leaders, independently of the hierarchical leadership chain that had previously obligated them to first present these questions to their prefects, who would take them to district-level mid-ranking leaders, who in turn would take them to their superiors (see Chapter 5). M.S., who exited the group a few months after the *Rabi'a* protest, said that his disillusionment was first manifested at the campsite as he cut himself off from this chain of hierarchical contact, and began to interact with leaders 'whom I had only seen on TV and whom I had long glorified and revered on the basis of stories circulating about them inside the group.' Upon this direct contact, he said, 'I found them ordinary if not mediocre in their way of thinking or behaving.' When he was

---

[117] Kandil, *Inside the Brotherhood*, p. 2.

[118] The evocation of these tales in the *Rabi'a* sit-in can be taken as part of a general understanding inside the Brotherhood that Qur'an, from which some of these tales are drawn, can provide solutions concerning this crisis and 'every aspect of daily life'; see Al-Hudaybi, H. (1878). *Dusturuna* [Our constitution] (pp. 9–10). Cairo: Dar al-Ansar.

taking part in these protests, M.S. insistently kept asking leaders in the camp about their plans and the aims of the sit-in itself. 'They kept telling me they knew what they were doing, and kept assuring me that the army would never dare to intervene.'[119] When police and army forces began surrounding the camp prior to its evacuation, he confronted the same leaders with the question of what to do in this new situation: 'I was shocked to find that they had no plans. They did not know what to do as a next step. I almost collapsed and felt fooled by those leaders.'[120] The frame got repeated by other exiters and who took part in the sit-in. A.Y. said: 'I remember one leader told me: "Everything is under control. We know what we are doing".' The leaders also were keen to show us those signs of confidence such as 'having men acting as well-trained security guards brandishing their walkie-talkies.'[121] M.H. also framed his exit from the group in 2014 as partly a response to the performance of the Brotherhood at the *Rabi'a* campsite: 'The leaders kept the same patronizing rhetoric always presented to us in the group: "Your Brothers above know what to do next. They know more than you know".'[122] The leaders also committed the same tactical mistake as the Mubarak regime at the time of the Tahrir Square protests: attempting to keep control over information in the face of the 'Twitter revolution.' They were out of sync with the new logic of collective action, which was no longer hierarchical in the way that would have permitted the Brotherhood's leaders to restrict and control the flow of information, as it had done internally in the past. This meant that members could no longer be silenced in the same way. Against attempts by leaders to articulate a single version

---

[119] Ibid.

[120] Ibid.

[121] The author's interview with Ahmed A.Y., Istanbul, August 25, 2017. This sense of security-related readiness as part of the inflammatory promises made by the leaders to have the campsite 'secured,' and to imply to many members that there are 'weapons' enough to defend the protestors in case of any attack (based on my field trip during the first few days of the sit-in), was found to be false. During clashes with police in the break-in, there was a small group with guns who killed eight policemen while defending the camp that day, against over 800 protestors got killed by police forces: Kingsley, P. (2014). Egypt's Rabaa massacre: One year on. Available via *The Guardian*: https://www.theguardian.com/world/2014/aug/16/rabaa-massacre-egypt-human-rights-watch. Accessed 4 November 2018. The variation in figures not only indicate a factual imbalance of power, but it also shows to exiting members the hollowness of reassuring rhetoric of the group's leaders.

[122] M.H. (2017).

of the truth, disillusionment of members with their leaders inside the Brotherhood increased.

As time passed after the 2013 *Rabi'a* event, criticism of the leaders remained predominant among the frames discussed in the interviews and texts. Ex-members framed their disillusionment in terms referencing both the leaders' lack of accountability. As K.F., now living in Turkey, put it, 'The group's leaders need to stand to account.'[123] 'A.G. repeated the same frame: 'The matter is now related to blood slipped on the ground. Those leaders should be held to account. They are partially to blame for this blood,'[124] said 'A.G., who spent ten days camping in *Rabi'a*. Remarkably, most interviewees did not refer to those Brotherhood members killed in the *Rabi'a* as 'martyrs.' They described them as 'casualties' or 'those who got killed.' Once mentioned, it was more of a 'passive martyrdom'[125] in which victimhood inflicted by those security forces as well as leaders who should be held accountable as 'they gave us wrong assurances and swore that there would be no military operation to disperse them and by not taking enough measures of protection.'[126] This refers a discursive shift as martyrdom was not actively chosen by the subject as 'acts of resistance' to Egypt's security forces or the regime ordering them to break the sit-in. Rather, he used the expression to show victimhood for which leaders as perpetrators have to be held accountable.

These frames, which validate other frames mentioned in the stage of 'ideological disengagement' detailed in Chapter 3 such as those comprising the 'anti-intellectualism' theme, all figured prominently among the complaints. In the context of another sit-in that took place at the same time of that of *Rabi'a*, in Al-Nahda Square to the south of Cairo, A.Y., who took part in this sit-in, became disillusioned with the leaders when they refused to respond to any of his enquiries. 'I asked one leader whether the police can break into the sit-in, and he swore by his marriage that the police would not dare. He told me that we would only leave when Morsi is back.'[127] The leader then asked A.Y. to 'prepare a

---

[123] K.F. (2017).
[124] 'A.G. (2017).
[125] See Matar, D., & Harb, Z. (Eds.). (2013). *Narrating Conflict.*
[126] A.Y. (2017).
[127] A.Y.A (2017).

list of all members of the group who were absent from the sit-in so they can be punished.'[128] While the country had witnessed a coup and many people were killed or injured in the sit-in evacuation, 'this leader of the group only cared about the attendance sheet.'[129]

Disillusionment with the leadership continued after *Rabi'a* as the Brotherhood underwent internal a division that developed shortly after the protest and the massacre. The unprecedented schism was very damaging to the group, which had failed to come up with a unified discourse justifying the actions in *Rabi'a*, or falsifying the discourse of exiting members, as it had been able to do in the past. These divisions helped to open the door for an unprecedented pluralism within the organization, which encouraged the expression of dissidence that had previously been suppressed in the name of organizational unity. This new-found pluralism and tolerance also meant that the divergent views of some individual members would be stronger and more coherent, where they had often been fragmentary, transitory, and internally contradictory. Some of the disagreements were related to a power struggle between the Brotherhood's old guard, then in their seventies and early eighties, who dominated its Executive Board, and its middle generation of leaders who were the force behind many of its actions, and sought a greater role in its direction. These disagreements gave substance and credibility to the frames mentioned above including those accusing the Brotherhood of prioritizing 'self-interests' at the expense of values related to either the broader goals of Egypt's 'revolution' or the particularistic goals related to Islam or Islamism propagated by those leaders.

Disillusionment Personalized: The Shater Effect

The responses of ex-members showed that after *Rabi'a*'s break-in, the group's discourse is no longer presumed as true statements pronounced by the leaders in a philosophical or religious context. What survived was a personal authority conferring on the leaders' statements presumptive validity by virtue of their moral character as persons. In some cases, with exiters, this was simply reversed: once presumed to utter necessarily true statements, now their speech was presumed false. The determining values

---

[128] Ibid.
[129] Ibid.

were now things like honesty, sincerity, and respect, as causes or marks of truth, rather than good upbringing, devotion to God, good companionship, and adherence to the 'spiritual contract' on which the leaders had long built their legitimacy and power.[130] In this perspective, the perception of truth becomes more specific, individualized, and context-bound rather than general and universalistic (e.g., that someone is a 'man of God'). This also meant that ex-members could now specify the objects of their blame by identifying 'concrete and specific adversaries.'[131] Within this specification of blame and adversaries, one of the persons most often mentioned was Khairat El-Shater.

A longtime Brotherhood leader, he ran as a presidential candidate on the FJP ticket in the 2012 election, against Morsi (who won), after resigning from the group for this purpose. Arrested during the 2013 coup, he was sentenced to death in 2015 and remains in prison today. Regarded as being in control of the Brotherhood, he was assigned the blame for its failures by many ex-members. 'The Brotherhood could have nominated a non-Brotherhood member for the presidency in coordination with other political groups. Nevertheless, it was the will of Uncle Khairat who pushed events in another direction,' said the 31-year old Shaker. He had joined the group in 2003 and left in May 2014, and was in charge of Muslim Brotherhood students at Alexandria University.

El-Shater was mentioned often, though I mentioned him in none of my questions as I did with Morsi. A.Z., a prefect in a female Brotherhood group in the Al-Behira governorate, attributed a stage of her disillusionment to El-Shater:

I objected to the nomination of El-Shater in one meeting because he is what I then called a 'hardliner and destructive.' All attendees were gob-smacked. They treated El-Shater as a prophet or a God beyond criticism. Some of them began even crying in reaction to my criticism. After that incident, I downsized and stopped my activities.[132]

The description of El-Shater as like a prophet reflected the sanctification process detailed in previous chapters, and from which A.Z.

---

[130]Triandis, H., & Vassiliou, V. (1967). *A comparative analysis of subjective culture* (p. 49). Urbana, IL: University of Illinois.

[131]Vonderford, M. (1981). Vilification and social movements: A case study of pro-life and pro-choice rhetoric. *Quarterly Journal of Speech, 75,* 166–182 (174).

[132]A.Z. (2017).

attempted to distance herself (see Chapter 3). Ban accused El-Shater of introducing 'Stalinism into the Brotherhood, which aborted all attempts to expand the power sharing and monopolization of power that led to the rise of Morsi, who was a representative of the Guidance Office, and its best member because of his obedience and organisational discipline.'[133] He also blamed El-Shater for causing the failure of a moment of opening of the group ideologically and organizationally that paralleled the moment of opening after the January 25, 2011 revolution.

Resources and Opportunities: The Effects of Imprisonment

One of the main resources creating opportunities for disengagement from the Brotherhood in this 'post-takeover' period concerned the effects of state repression and the responses to it on the part of the Brotherhood. Prior to the series of events that began in 2011, the official line within the Brotherhood concerned the frame of 'heroism,' according to which as an opposition the Brotherhood could only be strengthened, as members closed ranks and stood strong against the repression practiced by the regime of Mubarak and preceding regimes. Members have had to obey and revere their leaders whose 'legitimacy' is drawn on many years or sometimes decades they have spent in prison on charges including their 'leadership,' the movement now outlawed by Egyptian authorities.[134] The rhetoric constructed by those leaders and imposed on other members, including 'hearing and obedience' principle, has also evolved into a full-fledged discourse with time as the conditions of power of the state and resistance of leaders by imprisonment giving rise to it have continued. Despite accommodationists' attitudes and polices by the state under Mubarak, the latter maintained its confrontationist side by arresting mainly leaders of the group 'almost on a regular basis every four or five years.'[135] This has granted to the 'imprisonment discourse'

---

[133] Ban, *Ikhwan wa salafiyyon wa dawaish*, p. 337.

[134] See Aboul-Futouh, A. (2010). *'Abdel-Mon'im Aboul-Futouh: Shahid 'ala al-haraka al-Islamiyya* ['Abdel-Mon'im Aboul-Futouh: A witness to the Islamist movement] (p. 75). Cairo: Alshorouk.

[135] Al-Anani, K. (2018). *Transformation of the Muslim Brotherhood in Egypt*. Paper presented at a symposium on the transformation of Islamist parties and movements after the Arab Spring: Contexts, tracks, and consequences. Doha Institute for Graduate Studies, Doha, 7 October 2018.

rootedness, durability, and continuance. It also created another parallel process administering the dynamics of power and resistance inside the Brotherhood, that is dissent and criticism are repressed and controlled on basis of the salience of the 'imprisonment' discourse. In Chapters 2 and 3, exiting members narrated accounts where leaders raised the issue of their many years in prison to claim more roles and status inside the group as the ones 'who know much more than you do and have gone through hardships and situations more than you have been through.'[136] Reform can be deprioritized as it was time to deal with the state's repression, a task undertaken by those leaders who pay the heavy price out of it. Leaders gain further legitimacy as they could claim the task of constructing, mediating, and communicating the imprisonment discourse to garner maximum support and sympathy toward the group from both internal and external agents. This is about showing the Brotherhood as an opposition group falling 'victim' to the regime and also to draw sentiments of abandonment by external powers or actors—including states and human rights organizations—who should protect the group from these 'injustices' and 'violations.' The discursive correlation and its legitimatory power got further empowerment as the Brotherhood adds resonance to it through such features as interdiscursivity. There have been many works of literature produced and published by the Brotherhood's leaders reiterating the same frames accounting how leaders lost years and decades of hardship in prison and tragic loss of freedom, rights, and possessions.[137]

However, that has not always been the case after 2013. Exiting members mostly showed no sympathy for imprisoned leaders, whom they saw as paying the price for their own mistakes. Imprisonment no longer served as a justification to absolve the leaders of their responsibilities, especially as the aftermath of *Rabi'a* saw the detention and torture of thousands of rank-and-file members (which was a new development, since the previous regime had always targeted only the group's leaders

[136] See Aboul-Futouh, *'Abdel-Mon'im Aboul-Futouh: Shahid 'ala al-haraka al-islamiyya.*

[137] Zainab El-Ghazaly, the first leader of the Brotherhood's Sisters' section, dedicated her memoirs to those 'who got tortured' in prison whom she was one of them, El-Ghazaly, Z. (1987). *Ayyam min hayyati* [Days from my life] (pp. 1–10). Cairo: Al-Shorouk. Some publishing houses closely linked or owned by Brotherhood members also produced some of this literature; see Rizq, G. (1978). *Mazabeh Al-Ikhwan fi sujun Abdel-Nasser* [The massacres against the Brotherhood in Abdel-Nasser's prisons]. Cairo: Dar Al-I'tisam.

in its crackdowns). That they might go through the same experiences of detention or torture as the leaders meant that ordinary members saw less need to accord the leaders' special legitimacy on account of their sacrifices.

Released from prison in June 2014, after six months, the 24-year-old M.E. came to Istanbul, had no empathy for those leaders who were in prison. 'The concept of resisting the regime through detention, as I had been told, is so stupid and silly that a ten-year-old child would not understand.'[138] He noted that detention can only make individuals 'backward and mind-deficient.' M.E. ridiculed the argument on basis of his ideological disillusionment with the leaders' anti-intellectualism detailed in Chapter 3: 'How do you reward someone to be the leader when he actually cannot read books or newspapers and is blocked from the developments in the outside world?'[139] I.M.I., who went to prison and spent 20 days in the hospital upon his release as he had been tortured, expressed the same sentiments: 'People were killed and are being killed for the sake of what? ... For the sake of other leaders?! It is worthless, as those leaders should get lost, as they have no vision or even a mind to save the blood of themselves or their supporters.'[140] S.M., who was imprisoned in 2014, and left the group after his release in the same year, similarly said: 'The main problem is that leaders do not admit their mistakes and therefore they found no need for change.'[141] He also found

[138] M.E. (2017).

[139] Ibid.

[140] I.M.I. (2017).

[141] S.M. (2017). On June 29, 2019, the Brotherhood issued a statement admitting that 'we committed mistakes during the revolution and during our rule of Egypt ... which enabled to the counter revolution to [forces] to take over'; https://bit.ly/2YozxPM. Accessed 4 June 2019. Nevertheless, exiting members dismissed the statement as 'too late an admission as it comes six years after the events which the Brotherhood now claim responsibility for', see the statements of exiting leading figure Kamal El-Helbawy, https://www.youtube.com/watch?v=ilHYuWyF9Qw. Accessed 4 June 2019. Furthermore, while the Brotherhood asked in the statement for the 'revolutionary camp' and 'different ideologies' to unite against El-Sisi's regime, it failed to apply the request on itself. A faction led by significant figures in the divided Brotherhood dismissed the statement (issued by the 'the General Office of the Muslim Brotherhood') as not representing them. What also does matter here is how the discourse of the group lacks its distinctive consistency (judged by how all leaders and members repeat the same rhetoric) and coherence (judged by how different parts of this rhetoric have always fit together as a reasonable whole).

them disassociated from reality: 'They only make statements and do not realise what is happening on the ground.'[142] He also complained about the 'unequal distribution of sacrifice,' especially as many leaders and members ended up in other countries, particularly in Europe, Turkey, or Qatar. 'Our Brothers in Europe ask us to stay steadfast and keep Jihad; why would they not come to conduct Jihad in Egypt against injustice, while I have come to where they are and been there for some time?'[143]

The state's intervention helped escalate this shift in conceptualizing the 'imprisonment' frame. The state regained control, against sporadic acts of violence by some sub-groups of the Brotherhood and following the imprisonment of members of the group who had taken part in these acts, also increased the extent of disillusionment with the group and the leaders who ordered these acts. A.E., himself, imprisoned for several months after the *Rabi'a* sit-in, took part in these protests and even in acts of sporadic violence against the state, such as destroying electricity cables. Judging the rationality of actions in terms of costs and benefits, he called this a 'miscalculation.' These actions of sporadic protest or violence involved a huge cost being paid, with little or no benefit gained. It is within this context that many ex-members found their time in detention worthless or counter-productive to their and their leaders' aspirations for political change leading to the return of Morsi to power.

Practically, the imprisonment of the majority of the upper ranks after the *Rabi'a* massacre can be said to be an 'opportunity' for members to have 'emancipation' and empowerment to challenge the social barriers to their disengagement (see Chapter 2). It also weakens the organizational barriers, as these arrests wrecked its chain of command, loosen its strict hierarchy and made it decentralized at the group level.[144] This has offered members more autonomy and a bigger role including the process to decide whether to remain in the group or not. Take the category of female members of the Brotherhood. For example, female members of the group—for years denied an independent role— have been more active participants in street protests for several months after the *Rabi'a* break-in after the imprisonment of mostly male

---

[142] S.M. (2017).

[143] Ibid.

[144] Kingsley, *Egypt's Rabaa massacre.*

leaders.[145] 'We're against the arrests [of our leaders],' Sarah Kamal, a twentysomething member said, 'but without leadership, we have space to think beyond the old routine.'[146] Furthermore, female members can also claim part of the 'heroism' narrative once exclusively reserved for leaders bearing the brunt of the severity of jail terms as the state had arrested some of those female members. It is like more active participation (and the costs incurred by it) requires more representation (and the rewards associated with it). As put by one female member of the group asking to end the male dominance of the group: 'It can't be like before, when we were blindly loyal...We are getting detained, we're getting attacked in the streets – so we must have some say.'[147] Again, these transformative developments carry with them resources that shape disengagement as an opportunity.

However, it cannot be fully said that the state's use of imprisonment helped provide an atmosphere supportive of disengagement. Many ex-members attacked the regime that had replaced Morsi as brutal and murderous. But, in fact, the patterns of language in the interviews and texts showed that criticism of the state was mostly pushed to the sidelines, while criticism of the group's leaders became more prominent. In the transcripts of interviews with ex-members detained and released after 2013, there was a complete absence of mention of El-Sisi and the regime, though I made a point of asking questions comparing the El-Sisi regime with that of Morsi. The individuals being interviewed consistently referred to the Brotherhood leaders as impersonal collective subjects (not objects) grammatically of the statements in which they figured: '*they* told us,' '*they* nominated' a candidate, '*they* changed their views,' '*they* asked us to stay in *Rabi'a*.'

To sum up this section, there is a radical discursive transformation in the relation between the group's leaders and their members. The Brotherhood leaders could no longer generate or utilize the 'victimization' frames as they have long done before to consolidate their internal authority and draw part of their legitimacy.[148] They can no longer

[145] Kingsley, P. (2014). Massacre of Muslim Brotherhood enables sister to emerge from shadows. Available via *The Guardian*: https://www.theguardian.com/world/2014/may/26/massacre-muslim-brotherhood-sisters-egpyt-women. Accessed 20 January 2017.

[146] Ibid.

[147] Ibid.

[148] The media discourse of the Brotherhood before 2011 gave salience to this 'victimization frame' as named in El-Nawawy, M., & Elmasry, M. H. *Revolutionary Egypt in the eyes of the Muslim Brotherhood*, pp. 56–58.

withhold the title of being 'authentic victim subject'[149] and therefore 'rights' including to be obeyed and to be rewarded for their suffering.[150] This is simply because they were the ones who were (or claimed to be) in control of power even after the coup against Morsi. Replacing the 'victimization' frame, and others associated with it as they could bestow on leaders' meanings of 'heroism' and 'resilience,' gave way to frames of 'accountability' associated with others conveying meanings which blame those leaders of miscalculation, misdirection, and inexperienced judgment. Those members can thus claim part of the fragmented 'legitimacy' by being also 'victim subjects' and by also sharing with their leaders the similar commemorative moments of violence meted out by the indiscriminating state security apparatus. The state supported transformations in framing by action. After 2011, tens of thousands of rank-and-file members of the group have suffered from the same destiny and got imprisoned/tortured as the state has adopted an expansionist punitive measure against the group. The El-Sisi regime's durability and continued repression against members adds to this disillusionment with the leaders who have constructed a new discourse claiming their ability to take this regime down and bring Morsi back. This is again a case of the ability to articulate and the failure to operationalize manifesting in earlier cases cited above.

The events which Egypt and the Brotherhood have witnessed in the years following my interviews further vindicate my proposition that the Brotherhood leaders lost this immense power to turn imprisonment an action into unity based on victimization. This is more evident when Morsi died from a heart attack after collapsing in a Cairo court while on trial on espionage stages, on June 17, 2019. Most exiting members did not react with unity or sympathy toward the group or Morsi (who was 67 years old and who had been in jail since being toppled by the military in 2013 after barely a year in power). Take in detail the reaction of Ahmed Ramzy, an ex-member who was 'born as member of the Brotherhood' and exited it in 2013. Ramzy made this publicly shared Facebook post on his page a few hours of Morsi's death: 'Morsi was one of thousands of victims of the

---

[149] Kapur, R. (2002). The tragedy of victimization rhetoric: Resurrecting the 'native' subject in international/post-colonial feminist legal politics. *Harvard Human Rights Journal, 15,* 1–38.

[150] Khalili, L. (2007). *Heroes and martyrs of Palestine: The politics of national commemoration* (Vol. 27, p. 63). Cambridge: Cambridge University Press.

dirtiest movement on earth.'[151] As details of the death kept unraveling, including statements by Morsi's son that authorities were refusing to allow him to be laid to rest in the family burial grounds in his native Nile Delta province of Sharqiya as Morsi himself had wished, Ramzy did not change his critical comments on his page. In another post, he warned that the Brotherhood could 'abuse God' to draw sympathy or resort to 'burning all of Egypt' as a reaction.[152] He wrote another post on the same day to declare his rejection of the description of Morsi as the 'first elected president of Egypt,' and argued that El-Sisi was also 'elected.'[153] The El-Sisi regime came under fire from groups such as Amnesty International which called for 'impartial, thorough and transparent' investigation into Morsi's death as 'Egyptian authorities had the responsibility to ensure that, as a detainee, he had access to proper medical care.'[154] However, Ramzy kept his position with a new post of someone else and which he shared as it contains a warning against showing any sympathy with Morsi or the Brotherhood. The meaning of the post is to prove that if Morsi was an opponent of the Brotherhood, the latter could have described him as 'just an animal.'[155] Some exiting members such as Mohamed 'Affan gave a lukewarm sympathy,[156] but others, including those known for their activism on social media such as Mohamed Aboul-Gheit, ignored the tragic death completely.[157]

CONCLUSION

Joining protestors from other groups and across the ideological spectrum, members of the Brotherhood found in Tahrir Square as of January 2011 a place different from the Brotherhood spaces they knew,

---

[151] https://www.facebook.com/ahmed.ramzy.25/posts/10220003086406994. Accessed 4 July 2018.

[152] https://www.facebook.com/ahmed.ramzy.25/posts/10220004010590098. Accessed 4 July 2018.

[153] https://www.facebook.com/ahmed.ramzy.25/posts/10220004156033734. Accessed 4 July 2018.

[154] https://www.amnesty.org/en/latest/news/2019/06/egypt-must-investigate-mohamed-morsi-death/.

[155] https://www.facebook.com/ahmed.ramzy.25/posts/10220004781089360. Accessed 4 July 2018.

[156] https://preview.tinyurl.com/y5xulaad. Accessed 4 July 2018.

[157] https://www.facebook.com/mohamed.aboelgheit. Accessed 4 July 2018.

marked with exclusion, pure religiosity, and in-group similarity such as the mosque. Rather, Tahrir Square, where epic rallies and demonstrations continued for months, became at times a space of an almost surreal diversity and solidarity. Members of the Brotherhood joined members of secular groups battling the police, building barricades, and dodging tear gas canisters, while sharing primitive tools such as onions, vinegar, and soft drinks to ameliorate the effects. The Brotherhood members were just one element of this heterogeneous 'spatio-political fabric.'[158] These developments not only alienated the group's leaders, but also showed how their discourse had been marked with ambivalence, fragmentation, and hesitancy. Many ex-members described the group's actions as expressions of its non-revolutionary character, or its desire to 'secure self-interests rather than public or national interests.'

Still, the discourse and process of disengagement was still practically occasioned on the availability of resources and opportunities to utilize them for the sake of disengagement. In other words, the events provided members of the Brotherhood, who were now part of an outpouring of anger that galvanized many Egyptians, including many younger members of the group, with cognitive, affective, and material resources facilitating their exiting the group. These resources fell on generational lines. As Carrie Rosefsky Wickham noted, 'Brotherhood youth replaced their elders as the prime movers of events, exhibiting an unprecedented degree of operational autonomy as they tracked new developments and adjusted their tactics in consultation with other youth activists on the ground.'[159] However, as this chapter has argued, the wave of disengagement must be attributed to elements beyond a generation gap as other sub-groups of the Brotherhood also used the resources to disengage such as women and elders. Exiting members as old as 70 have expressed ideas related to practical matters such as the failure to take well-calculated political steps, to outmaneuver rivals or serve the interests of the Brotherhood including its staying in power.

Organizationally, the events caused the locus of political dynamism inside the Brotherhood to shift from formal institutions at the center of the social space to ostensibly marginal sites on the periphery. This shift, as political as it was, was as much about discourse as power. At a time of fluidity and fragmentation created by the events including the lack of 'repressive

[158] Bayat, *Plebeians of the Arab Spring*, p. 540.
[159] See Wickham, *The Muslim Brotherhood: Evolution of an Islamist movement*.

state,' the discourse of exiting individuals found a space to emerge and even contest the power at the center. It was supported by opportunities that, in a manner that social movement scholars have formulated as being important in the calculations of activists, entailed fewer costs (such as imprisonment, physical harm, or job loss) and more benefits, which make these kinds of protests seem like more than just an exercise in futility.

BIBLIOGRAPHY

Al-Hudaybi, H. (1878). *Dusturuna* [Our constitution]. Cairo: Dar al-Ansar.

Abdellatif, E. (2012). *Balaghat al-hurriya: Ma'rek al-khitab al-siyassi fi zaman al-thawra* [The freedom rhetoric: Battles of political discourse in the time of revolution]. Cairo: Altanweer.

Abed-Kotob, S. (1995). *The accommodationists speak: Goals and strategies of the Muslim Brotherhood of Egypt. International Journal of Middle East Studies, 27,* 321–339 (325). https://doi.org/10.1017/s0020743800062115.

Aboul-Futouh, A. (2010). *'Abdel-Mon'im Aboul-Futouh: Shahid 'ala al-haraka al-Islamiyya* ['Abdel-Mon'im Aboul-Futouh: A witness to the Islamist movement]. Cairo: Alshorouk.

Al-Anani, K. (2016). *Inside the Muslim Brotherhood, religion, identity, and politics.* New York: Oxford University Press.

Al-Anani, K. (2018). *Transformation of the Muslim Brotherhood in Egypt.* Paper presented at a symposium on the transformation of Islamist parties and movements after the Arab Spring: Contexts, tracks and consequences. Doha Institute for Graduate Studies, Doha, 7 October 2018.

Al-Awadi, H. (2014). *The Muslim Brothers in pursuit of legitimacy: Power and political Islam in Egypt under Mubarak.* London: I.B. Tauris.

Al-Waziri, H. (2011). *Abu Khalil yastaqeel min al-ikhwan: Al-jama'ah eta-faqat ma'a Suleiman leinha al-thawrah muqabil hizb wa jameyah* [Abu Khalil resigns from the Muslim brotherhood: The movement agreed with Suleiman to halt the revolution in favor of allowing it to create a party and association]. Available via Almasry Al-yawm: https://www.almasryalyoum.com/news/details/122713. Accessed 4 November 2018.

Baker, M. (2016). The prefigurative politics of translation in place-based movements of protest. *The Translator, 22*(1), 1–21. https://doi.org/10.1080/135 56509.2016.1148438.

Ban, A. (2017). *Ikhwan wa Salafiyyon wa Daawaish* [Brothers, Salafists and members of ISIS]. Cairo: Al-Mahrousa.

Bayat, A. (2015). Plebeians of the Arab Spring. *Current Anthropology, 56,* S33–S43 (S37). https://doi.org/10.1086/681523.

Bayat, A. (2017). *Revolution without revolutionaries: Making sense of the Arab Spring*. Palo Alto: Stanford University Press.

Beshara, A. (2016). *Thawret masr: Men jumhuryet Julyu ella thawret yanayir* [The Egyptian revolution: From Egypt's July revolution to January 25 revolution] (Vol. I). Beirut: Arab Center for Research and Policy Studies.

Brown, N. J. (2011). *The Muslim Brotherhood as helicopter parent*. Foreign Policy.

Brown, N. J., & Dunne, M. D. (2015). *Unprecedented pressures, uncharted course for Egypt's Muslim Brotherhood*. Washington, DC: Carnegie Brief, Carnegie Endowment for International Peace.

Brysk, A. (1995). Hearts and minds: Bringing symbolic politics back in. *Polity, 27*(4), 559–585.

Castells, M. (2007). Communication, power and counter-power in the network society. *International Journal of Communication, 1*, 238–266.

Colla, E. (2013). In praise of insult: Slogan genres, slogan repertoires and innovation. *Review of Middle East Studies, 47*, 37–48 (38). https://doi.org/10.1017/s2151348100056317.

Eason, D. (1965). *A systems analysis of political life*. New York: Wiley.

El-Bendary, M. (2013). *The Egyptian revolution: Between hope and despair—Mubarak to Morsi*. New York: Algora Publishing.

El-Ghazaly, Z. (1987). *Ayyam min hayyati* [Days from my life]. Cairo: Al-Shrouk.

El-Nawawy, M., & Elmasry, M. H. (2018). *Revolutionary Egypt in the eyes of the Muslim Brotherhood: A framing Analysis of Ikhwanweb*. Lanham: Rowman & Littlefield.

El-Qassas, M. (2017). Late Hossam Tammam, one of the most prolific specialists on the Muslim Brotherhood, put this gradualism rhythmically in the title of his column: 'Absence then hesitation then participation', see H. Tammam, *Al-Islamiyoon wal thawra Al-Misriyya*.

Elshaer, A. (2013). Islam in the narrative of Fatah and Hamas. In D. Matar & Z. Harb (Eds.), *Narrating conflict in the Middle East: Discourse, image and communications practices in Lebanon and Palestine* (pp. 111–132). London: I.B. Tauris.

El-Sherif, A. (2014). *The Egyptian Muslim Brotherhood's failures' a series on political Islam in Egypt*. Carnegie Endowment for International Peace. Available via Carnegie: http://carnegieendowment.org/files/muslim_brotherhood_failures.pdf. Accessed 6 April 2018.

Gerges, F. (2013). Introduction: A rupture. In F. A. Gerges (Ed.), *The New Middle East: Protest and Revolution in the Arab World* (pp. 1–40). Cambridge: Cambridge University Press.

Gerges, F. (2018). *Making the Arab world: Nasser, Qutb and the clash that shaped the Middle East*. Princeton: Princeton University Press.

Ghonim, W. (2012). *Al-Thawra 2.0: Eza al-sha'b yawman arad al-hayah* [Revolution 2.0: If the people one day truly aspires to life]. Cairo: Dar al-Shorouq.

Juergensmeyer, M. (2001). *Terror in the mind of God: The global rise of religious violence*. California: University of California Press.

Kandil, H. (2014). *Inside the Brotherhood*. Malden: Polity Press.

Kapur, R. (2002). The tragedy of victimization rhetoric: Resurrecting the 'native' subject in international/post-colonial feminist legal politics. *Harvard Human Rights Journal, 15*, 1–38.

Khalili, L. (2007). *Heroes and martyrs of Palestine: The politics of national commemoration* (Vol. 27). Cambridge: Cambridge University Press.

Kingsley, P. (2014). Egypt's Rabaa massacre: One year on. Available via *The Guardian*: https://www.theguardian.com/world/2014/aug/16/rabaa-massacre-egypt-human-rights-watch. Accessed 4 November 2018.

Kingsley, P. (2014). Massacre of Muslim Brotherhood enables sister to emerge from shadows. Available via *The Guardian*: https://www.theguardian.com/world/2014/may/26/massacre-muslim-brotherhood-sisters-egpyt-women. Accessed 20 January 2017.

Milton-Edwards, B. (2015). *The Muslim Brotherhood: The Arab Spring and its future face* (p. 34). Abingdon-on-Thames: Routledge.

Pape, R. A. (2005). *Dying to win: The strategic logic of suicide terrorism*. New York: Random House Inc.

Rizq, G. (1978). *Mazabeh Al-Ikhwan fi sugun Abdel-Nasser* [The massacres against the Brotherhood in Abdel-Nasser's prisons]. Cairo: Dar Al-I'tisam.

Sartori, G. (1966). Opposition and control: Problems and prospects. *Government and Opposition, 1*(2), 149–154 (p. 152). Available via: http://0-www.jstor.org.library.qnl.qa/stable/44481787. Accessed 9 December 2018.

Searle, J. (1995). *The construction of social reality*. New York: The Free Press.

Soueif, A. (2011). *Tweets from Tahrir: Egypt's revolution as it unfolded, in the words of the people who made it* (p. 10). New York: Or Books.

Tadros, M. (2012). *The Muslim Brotherhood in contemporary Egypt: Democracy redefined or confined?*. London: Routledge.

Tammam, H. (2011). *Al-Islamiyoon wal thawra al-Misriyya: Hidoor wa taradod wa musharakah* [Islamists and the Egyptian revolution: Absence, hesitation and particpation]. Available via Al-Akhbar: https://bit.ly/2Pw2ILn. Accessed 23 October 2018.

Triandis, H., & Vassiliou, V. (1967). *A comparative analysis of subjective culture*. Urbana, IL: University of Illinois.

Van de Sande, M. (2013). The prefigurative politics of Tahrir Square: An alternative perspective on the 2011 revolutions. *Res Publica, 19*(3), 223–239.

Vonderford, M. (1981). Vilification and social movements: A case study of pro-life and pro-choice rhetoric. *Quarterly Journal of Speech, 75*, 166–182.

Wickham, C. (2013). *The Muslim Brotherhood: Evolution of an Islamist movement*. Princeton: Princeton University Press.

Wickham, C. R. (2002). *Mobilizing Islam: Religion, activism, and political change in Egypt* (pp. 119–120). New York: Columbia University Press.

AUTOBIOGRAPHIES

'Abdel-Mon'im, I. (2011). *Hekayatii Ma' Al-Ikhwan* [My story with the MB]. Al-Hayaa Abdel-Mon'im, I. (2011) Hekayati ma' Al-Ikhwan [My story with the Muslim Brotherhood]. Cairo: Al-Hayaa Al-Misriyya Al-'ama leil Kitab.

Ban, A. (2013). *Al-Ikhwan Al-Muslimoon wa Mehnat Al-Watan wal Deen* [The Muslim Brotherhood and the Predicament of Nation and Religion]. Cairo: Al-Neel Centre for Strategic Studies.

Ban, A. (2017). *Ikhwan wa Salafiyyon wa Dawa'ish* [Brothers, Salafists and ISIS Loyalists]. Cairo: Al-Mahrousa.

'Eid S. (2013). *Tajribati fi Saradeeb Al-Ikhwan* [My experience in the basements of MB]. Cairo: Jazeerat al-Ward.

'Eid, S. (2014). *Qissati ma' Al-Ikhwan* [My story with the Muslim Brotherhood]. Cairo: Al-Mahrousa.

'Eid, S. (2014). *Al-Ikhwan Al-Muslimoon Al-Hader wal Mustaqbal: Awraq fil Naqd Al-Zati* [The Muslim Brotherhood: The present and The future: Papers from Self-Criticism]. Cairo: Al-Mahroussa.

El-'Agouz, A. (2012). *Ikhwani Out of the Box* [A Muslim Brother out of the box]. Cairo: Dewan.

El-Khirbawy, T. (2012). *Ser Al-M'abad: Al-Asrar Al-Khafiya li Gama't Al-Ikhwan Al-Muslemeen* [The Temple's secret: The hidden secrets of the Muslim Brotherhood]. Cairo: Nahdet Masr.

Fayez, S. (2011). *Janat Al-Ikhwan: Rehlat Al-Khuroug Min Al-Gam'a* [The MB Paradise: The Journey of Getting Out of the Group]. Cairo: Al-Tanweer.

Ramzy, A. (2013). *Dawlat Al-Murshid wa Sanam Al-Ikhwan* [The State of the Guide and the Statue of Muslim Brotherhood]. Cairo: Rodiy.

OTHER INTERVIEWEES

El-Sayyed, Khaled, a left-wing activist, Doha. 6 November 2018.

*For Interviewees who are Ex-members of the Brotherhood see the appendix Table A.1.

CHAPTER 5

Pre-2011 Disengagement: A Comparative Analysis of Change and Continuity

INTRODUCTION

The previous three chapters traced disengagement from the Brotherhood as both *process* and *discourse*. The process is one of stage-based gradualism. Over the course of their lives, the individuals studied moved through forms, or stages, of disengagement that can be characterized as affective, ideological, and political. The *discourses* involved were ways for individuals to *articulate* and *operationalize* their disengagement,[1] while, within these discourses, the uses of certain frames and the meanings of the concepts involved tended to change as the situation of the individuals involved also changed. Certain terms came with a baggage of meanings, within which they might continue to develop and take on new shades of meaning as people's situations and their understanding of them changed. So, to understand the meaning of a term, it is important to grasp the context of its use. And the semantic changes that could be observed over time were indices of changing realities, as well as of the history of meanings in relation to which words and expressions always exist in 'dialogical' relationships with others.

The analysis, as well-structured and logically organized since it starts from what is 'micro' (affective and psychological) and then moves to

---

[1] By 'language,' I mean its functionality as a 'particular view of the world' characterized by 'its own objects, meanings, and values'; Bakhtin, M. M. (1981). *The dialogic imagination* (p. 292). Austin: University of Texas Press.

© The Author(s) 2020   167
M. Menshawy, *Leaving the Muslim Brotherhood*, Middle East Today,
https://doi.org/10.1007/978-3-030-27860-1_5

what is 'meso' (organizational and ideological) and 'macro' (political developments). Nevertheless, such analysis still suffers from a major gap: It does start 'in the middle.' In other words, one of the things which makes the Brotherhood an interesting case study is that joining the movement is a considerable life event, requiring internal and external reorientations of belief and behavior that could continue for years if not decades. The previous analysis thus does not consider this process, beginning with the decision to exit or to think of exiting.

This chapter seeks to fill in this gap by capturing meaningful temporal changes through a combination of *retrospective* and *real* analysis. It considers disengagement to be an entity that exists in the present but is in dialogue with the past. This is true of language itself, which has discrete terms indicating things whose existence is as dynamic as it is static, since meanings are constructed and have a history, or exist in time. We saw in the case studies discussed in previous chapters that many members recognized that their motivations and dispositions, and their uses of language and ways of thinking, had evolved through a set of events and experiences leading to disengagement. This was never the response to a mere judgment about something actual that was happening then or had just happened, but always the end result, even if this could only be grasped retrospectively, of a process. Or at least given an account of how their disengagement seemed to them. The discourse of the ex-members revealed a process, and that process was dependent on a discourse. This chapter adds a layer of verification to this finding by discussing in detail three cases of exiting in the years before 2011, and it finds a similar pattern. This comparison will enable me to look more closely at the understanding by ex-members of their disengagement, partly in search of broader formal and thematic discursive patterns, as I try to shed further light on the intelligibility and meaning of departures from the same organization, in terms of what appeared to be similar in kind but occurring at rather different moments in time.

In this chapter, I look at two cases of disengagement from an earlier time. They are the brother and sister pair of Mahmoud El-Tahawy (who left in 1987) and Miral El-Tahawy (who left in 1995). Their accounts reveal that their processes of disengagement, and the development of discourses that served as part of these processes, were not always directional, or cumulative, as was the case largely with the exiting members in the period of 2011 and after discussed in previous chapters. Mahmoud and Miral both express enough hesitancy and inconsistency that one can wonder if their disengagement was not only open-ended but tentative and even reversible.[2] Both seemed to have disengaged without giving their disenchantment and departure a specifically 'political' character. They also did not have the opportunity to benefit from the rich political discourses that were in the air during the 2011 events and after, nor from the open sharing of these frames with many others, or the opportunity for recognition and being heard that was made possible for later ex-members by TV appearances, online activism, and the publication of their testaments. No doubt this contributed to the more hesitant and tentative character of their thinking. Mahmoud's discourse and thinking remained occulted for 30 years, and only saw the light of day through my own intervention in the form of a long interview, which provided him with his first opportunity to narrate his experience for a public. In other words, Mahmoud and Miral share similar details in the 'process' of disengagement from the Brotherhood with the post-2011 ex-member. However, they differ on discourse. Both brother and sister have failed to 'frame' their past as they simply did not narrate it in the first place. Being kept hidden, all potential frames on disengagement have not found the opportunity to be articulated consistently and coherently through repetition or frequency. They also have not found the opportunity to be effectively operationalized by benefitting from the changing surrounding reality conductive to their construction as 'frames' resonating with this reality. Their disengagement is not a combination of 'discourse' and 'process.' Judging by falsifiability, the findings of my long interviews with the sibling, Mahmoud and Miral, prove my findings on all other ex-members.

---

[2] I sent the chapter to El-Tahawy one year after the interview and as part of a 'respondent validation,' a process whereby a researcher provides the individuals on whom he or she has conducted research with an account of his or her findings for the sake of 'corroboration or otherwise of the account that the researcher has arrived at' (Bryman, A. [2016]. *Social research methods* [p. 391]. Oxford: Oxford University Press). The findings occasioned a defensive reaction on the part of El-Tahawy, who refused words such as 'reversal' and 'hesitancy.' Nevertheless, his defense carried some of my concluding remarks as he described his case as 'a state of nostalgia to a paradise lost that is not about regret or hesitance. It is rather about missing some entertaining moments that have irrevocably passed' (El-Tahawy Ma 2018).

THE MAHMOUD EL-TAHAWY CASE: 'AFFECTIVE DISENGAGEMENT'

Mahmoud went through an 'affective disengagement' in the process of departing from the Brotherhood. Indeed, kinship relationships played an important role in his decisions both to engage in the group and disengage from it. 'My Brotherhood friends represented all of my life,' he said. 'They are the ones who taught me how to talk to people, especially as I had been an introverted character, how to go out, and with whom to interact.'[3] Asked about his biggest loss after his disengagement, Mahmoud's answer followed a pattern that would be typical of post-2011 ex-members: 'friends.'[4] He said that 'getting out of my social shell was devastating enough that I still bitterly feel its consequences. It was really hard to lose my friends as parts of this shell.[5]' In their reaction, the Brotherhood's leaders took advantage of this same theme, getting his friends to join a 'campaign to isolate me, tarnish my character and even suspect my intentions as sinister and destructive.'[6]

During his disengagement, Mahmoud employed a coping strategy of assimilating into alternative social circles providing similar friendships. He depended on circles of ex-members, interacting with them via a common language based on sharing the same past. Mahmoud considered this assimilation as 'emancipating' in relation to the group's restrictive measures, which had included a 'no touch policy with exiting members, who were always demonized and condemned in the dominant rhetoric of the Brotherhood.'[7] It was within this coalition of the despised that Mahmoud found solidarity with, and support from, others who had experienced 'the same level of orphaning, shock, and injury after their disengagement.'[8] He called this a joint attempt to 'heal wounds and minimize losses.' This solidarity of ex-hood was manifest in Mahmoud's friendship with Ahmed Abdullah, who is now a Professor of Psychiatry at the Faculty of Medicine at Zaqaziq University in *Zaqaziq* (in the Nile Delta region of Egypt, and where Mahmoud also studied).

[3] El-Tahawy Ma (2017).
[4] Ibid.
[5] Ibid.
[6] Ibid.
[7] Ibid.
[8] Ibid.

Mahmoud attributed the beginning of his disengagement to the start of his friendship with Abdullah, after the latter moved into the same neighborhood. This was effectively a geographical re-spatialization that ameliorated for him the consequences of the 'boycott and rejection' and other punitive measures he suffered at the hands of the Brotherhood. It was their sharing of an ex-hood mentality that also drove Abdullah out of the Brotherhood shortly afterwards.

Ideological Disengagement

Mahmoud's disengagement was 'affective' and personal, but of course also ideological. He described it a 'search for my mind.' 'Mind' and related terms were repeated often in his discourse; I counted it 15 times in his answers to my questions, along with similar repetitions of associated words like 'thinking' (mentioned 7 times). Mahmoud spoke of his losses in the 'affective stage,' compensated by gains in the 'ideological stage.' He called his journey 'a battle of heart and mind,' or a 'conflict between painful emotions and a clear ideological vision,' adding, 'While my heart keeps telling me I should stay in the Brotherhood, my mind says otherwise.'[9] As he tipped the balance in favor of his mind.

Mahmoud had many experiences to share about his 'search for his mind.' One experience, which he regarded as the main trigger of his disengagement, was a momentary interaction during a conference in Cairo on the topic of dialogue between Islamists and nationalists. Mahmoud then had the chance to be exposed to another Islamist discourse, presented by leaders of other Islamist movements, such as the Tunisian intellectual and political leader Rachid El-Ghannoushi. He was so impressed that he went to the hotel where El-Ghannoushi was staying, hoping to discuss with him some of the ideas that interested him. 'I really admired his way of thinking, including his talk about the need for Islamist groups to apply internal reforms and reorganising tactics.'[10] This admiration was drawn on a comparison: 'I could not stop comparing this progressive and reformist Islamist with our leaders in the Brotherhood, who then sounded to me simplistic and traditionalist.'[11] The opportunity

---

[9] Ibid.
[10] Ibid.
[11] Ibid.

to interact and compare thoughts with this 'other' Islamist became the main stop on an intellectual journey of soul-searching and introspection. Mahmoud turned to another intellectual habit conducive to many other disengagement experiences (see Chapter 3): critical reading. He went through the basic literature of Islamism from the past, and found there the means to describe the organization's present leadership as plagued by 'stagnation and ideological rigidity.' His sustained and growing disillusionment drew crucially upon his reading of the writings of the group's founder El-Banna himself. Mahmoud began to discuss his criticisms and concerns with other disgruntled members including Abdullah.

Mahmoud's explanation for his close relationship with Abdullah was replete with reference to the concept of 'mind': 'What drew me to him was that he had a different mind'; 'his mind ended up distancing my mind as well from the whole of the Brotherhood's mind.' This relationship of like 'minds' was reflected in their shared exposure to independent readings and intellectual debates. He said that these activities led to his rebellion against the Brotherhood's 'traditionalism,' its 'stereotypical way of thinking,' and its wish to keep members as 'closed boxes.'[12] Mahmoud, then a university student, at first wrote down his questions and criticisms in the form of two papers. One paper called for 'independence and freedom' for the Brotherhood's university students 'to choose our student leaders and carry out our activities on campus independently of the supervision and dominance of the leadership of the Brotherhood.' The other paper called for 'restricting the unlimited authority of middle and upper leaders of the group, creating in laws to overview complaints and disputes inside it and reforming the contradictory curriculums and outdated cultural patterns adopted.'[13] Mahmoud brought the two papers to his prefect, in a commonly encouraged Brotherhood practice of confession, in which members would tell their leaders what was on their minds (see Chapter 3).

The reaction of Mahmoud's prefect was counter-productive, as it increased Mahmoud's sense of disillusionment with the official ideology. It seemed to him that they had sought to close an 'ideological opening' with a social closure:

[12] Ibid.
[13] Ibid.

All of a sudden, I got excluded from all of the activities that I had been carrying out on the university campus as part of the tasks as a Brotherhood activist. To make it worse, they did not tell me of these changes or provide answers why they took them. I even felt ostracized as some other members began to show caution and suspicion in the way they talked to me.[14]

When he tried to reach his direct leaders to ask about this, but did not hear back from them, Mahmoud took his case to 'those who are above.' He finally got a response from a leader of the East Delta region. The leader sent back this reply, written on a small piece of paper, including a few lines that Mahmoud said he still remembered: 'To a Brother who is still at the beginning of the road, you have to know that only those who are truthful reach the end of this road.'[15] This answer resembled those to the effect that 'your brothers above you know more than you know,' which was repeatedly cited by other ex-members after the 2011 events, in response to their own similar requests.

Mahmoud's leaders reacted to his ideologically driven questions by citing the same frames repeatedly mentioned by post-2011 exiting members in response to their dissident views or enquiries. 'The leaders accused me of falling under the influence of *El-Shaytan* [the Satan] and abandoning *Da'wa* [call to God]'. They asked Mahmoud to 'repent by improving his relationship with God' through more prayers and further doses of the Qur'an. This is the same response mentioned by Sameh 'Eid, another exiting individual, in his autobiography: 'My leaders asked me to pray more and read more Qur'an, as my questions were all part of Satan's workings.' The then-religious Mahmoud said he was devastated by the suspicions thrown onto his relationship with God and level of commitment to Islam. This was another example, common in post-2011 cases of ex-hood, of hegemony being 'produced and reproduced in discourse,'[16] and substantiated with Qur'anic references. What Mahmoud had attempted to do was to contest a hegemonic discourse using a counter-discourse partly of his own fashioning, and a counter-process of interacting with other Islamist leaders outside his given, proper Brotherhood milieu.

[14] Ibid.
[15] Ibid.
[16] Fairclough, N. (1992). *Discourse and social change* (p. 9). Cambridge: Polity Press.

AWAY FROM DISCOURSE AND THE POLITICAL

While Mahmoud's example is perhaps one of the more remarkable cases of disengagement from the Brotherhood since the 1960s, his experience was not known to many at least prior to my own study, nor had he come out as a Brotherhood dissident. Both before and after leaving the organization in 1987, he did not write about his experience for publication, nor make any media appearance or online declaration. At the time, he only sought to pursue internal avenues of grievance and change instead of 'texturing' them as many since the 2011 events have done. The putting of emotions and thoughts (the main components of the affective and ideological stages of disengagement) into texts, which is called 'texturing,' is an essential part of activities like disengagement from groups like the Brotherhood. It has provided exiting individuals with the resources to *articulate, expose,* and make *cohere* scattered and fragmented meanings of ex-hood experience into a whole 'discourse of ex-hood.' Attached to the availability of 'resources' manifested in texturing is another availability attached to 'power,' that is, making interviews or writing autobiographies communicative events by themselves means that those exiting members could challenge and resist the dominant texts through which the Brotherhood has long imposed on them its 'hegemony' at the level of discourse. The lack of closure of Mahmoud's experience prevented him from using these valuable 'resources.'

Remarkably, Mahmoud's experience was only exposed and articulated through the medium of texts of post-2011 exiting members, another bit of evidence showing how the latter have made best use of the resources available, including those concerning pre-2011 experience such as Mahmoud's, to bolster their disengagement discourse. I only learned of his case through a book written by a post-2011 ex-member, Haitham Abou-Khalil. In fact, he uses the example of Mahmoud marginally but instrumentally to build a case for disillusionment with the Brotherhood in general. Abou-Khalil did not interview Mahmoud, and only mentions him marginally. When he began publishing a series of newspaper articles before turning them into a book, Abou-Khalil mentioned the reform initiatives that Mahmoud had once presented to his leaders, as mentioned above. It was only after the publication of this book that Mahmoud introduced himself to Abou-Khalil. After the 2011 revolution, Abou-Khalil became a TV host and a renowned activist, using both online and offline platforms, where he has repeated the same arguments against the Brotherhood. Mahmoud kept his distance. He did not wish to share 'ownership' of the discourse manifested by dozens of members of the Brotherhood who disengaged and wrote autobiographies confirming each other's views. While post-2011 exiting members would 'enact' this discourse of disengagement as part of their way of positioning themselves within the Egyptian polity and society, Mahmoud held himself aloof from such efforts.

Mahmoud's discourse was only articulated and materialized in a discreet and private form through our online chat, his preferred means of communication, and a short phone conversation leading up to it. Through many hours of online conversations, eventually filling 100 pages, he agreed to talk to me not necessarily as a researcher but as an interested stranger. Our discussions followed what he called the 'therapeutic' purpose of coming to see truths that had been hidden for decades. On his Facebook page, he has never referred to his past as an ex-member of the group. Thus, if the Brotherhood wanted the story of Mahmoud to remain hidden, falsified, or minimized, they succeeded. For example, when I asked Mahmoud for a copy of his 'significant' document, the reform initiatives which he had presented to his leaders and which caused his disengagement from the group (it is considered a significant historical artifact in the discourse of ex-hood), he said that he had not kept a copy of them. He suggested I ask Abou-Khalil, as 'he was the one who published these initiatives and he could have a copy.'[17] This makes Abou-Khalil, the author of the book, not only an *owner* of the discourse, but also its *gatekeeper*, in contrast to Mahmoud who clearly lacked these two characteristics.[18]

All of this limited the effectiveness of Mahmoud's discourse. Its effectiveness could also be judged by how his narrative moved from individuated and personalized statements to connecting with a collective or shared discursive form, as with open and published ex-members, who also tended to form social networks with others with similar experiences.

---

[17] El-Tahawy Ma (2018).

[18] Unlike Abou-Khalil, Mahmoud himself disowns his discourse on disengagement as 'outdated since it relates to events that occurred 20 years ago.' Also unlike the discourse of post-2011 ex-members, who add consistency and frequency by repeating their stories of disengagement even in more than one autobiography, Mahmoud showed a sense of 'burn-out' as 'I am already fed up repeating some concepts [taken up by the narratives of recent other ex-hood cases]' (El-Tahawy Ma 2018).

In other words, Mahmoud did not make a shift that would allow his disengagement to be part of a practice shared, pooled, and even contested within networks of ex-members or other members of the society. For example, he did not share spaces or means of production that allowed other ex-members to support each other in publishing or circulating their autobiographies, finding a career path drawn on a 'solidarity of ex-hood,' or even helping each other relocate to a geographical areas more conducive to this solidarity (which are all elements of forming a new identity as an 'ex,' as detailed in Chapters 2 and 4). Post-2011 exiting members mostly abandoned the single centralized authority of the Brotherhood (which had also controlled the publishing efforts of its members) and resorted to alternative 'authoritative power networks.' (Their autobiographies were published by state printing houses as past of a shift of meaning based on a shift in the communicative process or means of production.[19])

The absence of political disengagement is not only concluded on the absence of texts or the failure to benefit from politically shaped means to communicate or circulate them. It has to do also with the kind of lacking elements that could have made Mahmoud's discourse more materially grounded and promoted, such as undertaking politically driven activities. When Aboul-Futouh formed his party and announced his presidential campaign in 2011, Mahmoud did not join, as other exiting members did. He felt that all 'political solutions and partisan belonging could not offer answers to my problems [that were] mainly related to a societal and intellectual change.'[20] Mahmoud's abstinence from political engagement meant that he lost opportunities both to articulate and operationalize his discourse of disengagement, as Aboul-Futouh did (through founding his political party, targeting many other ex-Brotherhood members to join his party, forming coalitions with political groups founded by other ex-Brotherhood members, and also having his own autobiography published by Egypt's leading printing house, *Shorouk*).

Such missed opportunities for political disengagement were not limited to the post-2011 era. Indeed, in 1980s, Mahmoud found no opportunities to relate his criticisms and disgruntlement over the Brotherhood with any outside resources or actions that can shape and resonate with

---

[19] For more on 'recontextualization,' see Linell, P. (1998). *Approaching dialogue: Talk, interaction and contexts in dialogical perspectives.* Amsterdam: John Benjamins.

[20] El-Tahawy Ma (2017).

his experience. As Nathan Brown put it, in the 1980s, there was a 'vacuum of politics' in terms of arguments and discussions,[21] and it was exactly within this vacuum that Mahmoud kept his narrative inward to himself or within a very limited circle of friends. In the 1990s, Egypt underwent a period of some political liberalization as part of 'politics reborn,'[22] with Mubarak opening windows of opportunity for the Brotherhood as well as for some of its disgruntled members who decided to depart from it at the time. Some members took the opportunity to express their disillusionment with the group loudly and emphatically. They were supported by 'alternative' routes for participating in Egyptian public life. In 1996, Aboul-Ella Madi, a prominent exiting Brotherhood member, who challenged the Brotherhood's rejection of political parties, and founded a moderate Islamist party, the *Wasat* [the middle] party, seeking to 'assist in the building of a democratic civil society.'[23] Opposing, he said, the exclusionary nature of the Brotherhood, Madi built wider circles of ideological and social solidarity, partly by attending to the rights of women and the status of the Copts, as well as the question of national unity, the scope of artistic activity and expression, and relations with the West.[24] Madi repeatedly sought official authorization for founding his party, and obtained it after the 'revolution' in March 2011. The party espoused an 'ideological and political pluralism,' and called for the establishment of 'democracy, reforms, and freedoms.' Having said that, Mahmoud neither followed the route of Madi nor joined the latter's efforts or activities benefiting from the windows of political opportunity made available in the 1990s and which gave other exiting members such as Madi a privileged entry into public sphere.[25]

[21] Brown, N. J. (2016). *Arguing Islam after the revival of Arab politics* (p. 11). New York: Oxford University Press.

[22] Ibid., p. 12.

[23] Wickham, C. R. (2004). The path to moderation: Strategy and learning in the formation of Egypt's Wasat party. *Comparative Politics, 36*, 205–228 (216).

[24] Ibid., p. 220.

[25] For example, I do remember when Madi came to visit the headquarters of IslamOnline, a popular website based in Cairo, in 2001 for a full interview that included his optimism over his ability to benefit from these rising political opportunities outside the orbit and influence of the Brotherhood. Strikingly, that same workplace also employed Brotherhood ex-members of the early 2000s' waves such as journalist/blogger 'Abdel-Mon'im Mahmoud.

With further situations (by which I mean resources and opportunities) made available across time, the Brotherhood underwent a new wave of disengagement in the 2000s, Mahmoud still kept his distance from this opening. As part of changes in the structures of 'political arguments,' which witnessed older hierarchies and structures of authority 'undermined' and 'limited,'[26] exiting members found the opportunity in this rising 'spirit of activism' to construct meaning from their disengagement. As they were discussing broader 'public affairs' as part of this moment of 'political arguments,' they also went inward to *argue* on the Brotherhood-related affairs and reevaluate their positionality in and relations with the group. They used such modern communicative tools as blogs (see Chapter 3). Mahmoud also did not join their interactionist activities to operationalize the group's discourse by active participants in 'demonstrations; online forums' and the adoption of 'ideas of personal freedom learnt from abroad—even from Hollywood movies.'[27] Mahmoud admitted that he was at a disadvantage by what he called the 'technological backwardness' of the time. 'For example, the ways which we used to communicate and circulate our ideas were very primitive in comparison with the blogging world. We wrote a statement, and then moved to the house of a colleague who had an electric writing machine. Once written, we would then photocopy the statement, and limitedly send it to others inside the group. As we got no or a slow response to all this effort, we really felt disappointment.' In addition, Mahmoud added, the communications also were causing a loss of potential support from 'disgruntled members who were hesitant and afraid to express their views, which again is the opposite from the emboldening sense of what social media can currently create as members could interact with and hear from each other.'

As he did more recently, as the Brotherhood lost power and suffered again from state repression beginning in 2013, Mahmoud also found no reason to join other exiting members who found in this event an opportunity to vindicate themselves or their cumulative sense of disillusionment with the group. He also did not benefit from the state's limited acquiescence in the disengagement discourse when El-Sisi came to power. Other exiting members hypocritically applied the disengagement

[26] Brown, *Arguing Islam*, p. 12.

[27] Quoted in Brown, N. J., & Dunne, M. (2015). *Unprecedented pressures, uncharted course for Egypt's Muslim Brotherhood* (p. 5). Carnegie Endowment for International Peace.

discourse in a different setting by justifying or finding excuses for El-Sisi's campaign against the Brotherhood. Not joining this recontextualization, in which texts on disengagement got incorporated into the state-run texts circulating 'coercion and persuasion' against the Brotherhood, left Mahmoud's discourse further de-articulated and de-materialized, and detached from useful opportunities in the political sphere.

Judging by the texts, Mahmoud's discourse lacked somewhat in coherence and consistency. He expressed both nostalgia for his previous Brotherhood ties and satisfaction at abandoning them for quite different ones, and his evaluations of his own strategies of identity-transformation outside the group combined with negative self-descriptions so as to underscore his ambivalence. As he put it:

> Sometimes I yearn for this comforting stage of psychological stability.... Sometimes I cry over what is missed ... Sometimes I feel sad that I lost this sweat dream... Sometimes, I tell myself: "I wish I had not thought, used my mind or thought of internal reform for the sake of not losing this enjoyable feeling of being comfortable by sharing the group identity."[28]

Mahmoud's ways of framing his experience were similarly contradictory, ambivalent, and sometimes confusing for Mahmoud himself, as he appeared to fumble about in his narrativization. Within the same short space of text, frames of defeatism, and regret about 'losing friends,' followed empowering ones of gaining friends. Textually, this made his narrative lose some of its 'cohesion,' which may be defined in terms of how clauses are linked together into sentences, and sentences in turn linked to form larger units such as paragraphs.[29] His speech involved constant interruptions and cuts between distinct thoughts marring the sequential and linear qualities of the discourse and narrative. When contrasted to the discourses and narratives of post-2011 ex-members, the hesitant and uncertain character of Mahmoud's discourse may have been a consequence of the absence then of a broad movement legitimating the discourse of disengagement, or of stronger social networks supporting it. The latter was evident in a recent conversation Mahmoud forwarded to me. I quote from fragments of it:

---

[28] El-Tahawy Ma (2018).
[29] See Halliday, M. A. K., & Hasan, R. (2014). *Cohesion in English*. London: Routledge.

Mahmoud: The Brotherhood has broken me.
A female friend: You are a great person, so you cannot be broken.
Mahmoud: They [The Brotherhood leaders] bet I would be perplexed, confused, and weakened by the exit. They were everything in my life ... Can I tell you something?
The female friend: Go ahead.
Mahmoud: I have to admit that I failed to begin a new life after I exited the group... I miss this 'dream' of living with the friends who belong to the Brotherhood. I miss the safety, warmth, and peacefulness I had always felt in their company.[30]

Thematically, Mahmoud also did not frame his disengagement in terms of self-empowerment, as was common with post-2011 ex-members. They often even used the somewhat hyperbolic language of moving from 'slavery' to 'emancipation.' To the contrary, Mahmoud said, 'I regret getting out of the group. I have thought at several times of going back into its ranks.' Disengagement for him was painful, and he spoke of having gotten 'over it,' and of being a 'defeated person whose paradise and dream got lost.' He describes his feeling isolated and excluded before his exit as 'amputation.' Mahmoud also told me that it was a 'relief talking to you,' mentioning the 'therapeutic' effect of uncovering his past. Mahmoud complained that he 'still feels at every time of narration the same level of tension bordering on a panic attack.'[31] This was a direct contrast to the sense of empowerment most later ex-members claimed to experience, in part because of the opportunity to criticize the group. Mahmoud also had a lot to say, and sometimes would provide up to ten pages of detail in answer to a single question about his disengagement. He also would sometimes write to me days or weeks after the interview to add some thoughts or more fully express his feelings about the Brotherhood, which he had left fully 30 years earlier. On every occasion of talking, the Mahmoud's narrative remained full of references to his conflicted perceptions of the group: 'I adore the Brotherhood the group, but I abhor the Brotherhood the ideology... I am relieved of getting out of the Brotherhood which is poor in thoughts, but I miss the Brotherhood which is rich in social relations.' It is hard to know to what extent Mahmoud's understanding of his own experience is typical

---

[30] El-Tahawy Ma (2018).
[31] El-Tahawy Ma (2018).

of others at that time, or due to his own psychology. However, what does matter is not its representativeness, which can allow us to generalize. Rather, it is about how the situations available and the environment with which Mahmoud had to interact contributed to his ability to *process* and *discourse* his disengagement.

MIRAL EL-TAHAWY

Evidence of my claim that disengagement is incomplete if exiting members do not articulate and operationalize their discourse is also provided by the case of Mahmoud's sister, Miral El-Tahawy. Like her brother's disengagement, that of Miral was mainly affective and ideological. She had joined the Brotherhood in the late 1980s, during her first years at the university, and exited it in 1995. In her narrative, I found the same frames as in that of Mahmoud. In a soft, melancholy voice, Miral described her engagement as mainly 'affective.' Living in a small village in the *Sharqiya* governorate, Miral joined the group after an experience that was for her an emotional shock, the death of her father. In this context, she said:

> The Brotherhood became my real family. Members were very supportive, and they treated me as one of their family. I recall these many visits which I had conducted to the house of Mohammed Morsi [living in the same governorate until he became President] as if I were a member of his family.[32]

It was thus a search for a sense of belonging with sympathetic others that drove Miral further into the Brotherhood and its activities. She began to feel a 'unique sense of solidarity' after demonstrating a prolific talent as a writer. The Brotherhood sponsored the publication of her first novel, *The Memoirs of A Muslim [Brotherhood] Sister*, accounting for her experience of becoming involved in the group. The book was introduced by Zainab El-Ghazaly, historically one of the most (if not the most) significant woman leaders in the Brotherhood. Miral said that the support she had received contributed to her sense of self-worth. 'I still remember a gift from the publisher, Salah Abdel-Maqsoud [who became Information Minister when the Brotherhood took power]. I was on the moon, as it felt great to be a proper author. I asked her the same question that I had

---

[32] El-Tahawy Mi (2017).

posed to all of the exiting individuals with whom I met: "Why then did you decide to disengage from the group?"[33]

Miral said that it was a process in which an ideological disengagement overran all affective considerations. Like others, she framed her journey along the lines of 'regaining the I' that had been lost in a 'me/we' identification within the Brotherhood. Miral attributed the 'turning point' in her exit to her attempt to escape the group's censorship strategies, which included its changing big chunks of her writings in order to make them accord with the 'Islamic vision.' She said this acted as a heavy form of censorship, since the 'changes made to the text made it not mine and beyond my recognition.' To her, the organization's justifications involving 'submission to the will of God' were merely a reflection of its 'cognitive inflexibility.' She was also subjected to ostracism by other group members, who severed their contacts with her and engaged in a 'smear campaign' against her. 'It was really shocking,' she reported, 'that those friends propagated rumors and directed accusations of what they called my ingratitude towards them and the group.'[34] It was like, she added, 'a complicated marriage in which I was seeking a divorce and in which the partner refuses my decision to do so.'[35] These are the same punitive measures in which the Brotherhood has employed its affective and ideological capital to face down almost all cases of disengagement.

Like other exiting members, Miral depended on 'coping' mechanisms to avoid the punitive measures of the Brotherhood, alleviate their consequences, and to form a new identity drawn on a search for the 'I' and abandonment of the 'we.' She formed an alternative network of friends. Indeed, she attributed her disengagement to forming friendships outside the ranks of the Brotherhood with Ahmed Abdullah and Heba Raouf Ezzat, the latter known for her progressive Islamist writings. They helped her more clearly see the anti-intellectualism and other deficiencies of the group's leaders and their ideology. Remarkably, Abdullah was the same 'new friend' who also played a pivotal role in helping Miral's brother complete his disengagement through assimilation, as mentioned above. 'My new friends,' she said, 'gave me the space to think and to read in different directions,' and after her exit, they 'supported me by

[33] Ibid.
[34] Ibid.
[35] Ibid.

getting me out of the psychological crisis that I went through.'[36] They also introduced her to the literary circles that helped her in her writing career. As the leaders reacted to her new friendship and initiatives with rejection, and 'my prefect told me that "those new friends are not part of us",' Miral did not heed their advice but got closer to her new friends.

Like her brother, Miral did not articulate her disengagement from the Brotherhood. The lack of articulation can be seen in a lack of texturing, as well as an ambivalence, and a lack of consistency or coherence in what she had said and written on the group. While speaking of 'emancipation' from the group, she said she remained 'emotionally captivated' by the solidarity and support, which she now missed. And despite her criticism of the Brotherhood's 'rigidity' and 'cognitive inflexibility,' she thought that the members she knew 'were really humans,' and said that the expressions of cynicism toward leaders of the group 'personally hurts me.'[37] In her interview, she repeatedly evoked frames of 'nostalgia' and 'sweet memories.' These contradictory frames combined with her failure to benefit from the supportive operationalization of them in resources and situations made available to her through her career and media presence. Asked in a BBC interview why she left the Brotherhood, she presented her disengagement as having been motivated partly by relatively personal issues of gender. She spoke of the 'marginalization and manipulation of women' to serve the group's interests. The interviewer tried in vain to get her to focus on more general concerns about democracy, and I also failed to elicit them from her. In the BBC interview, she did not discuss the affective side of her disengagement at all. Without these personal details, her views remained what Foucault would call a 'disinterested statement about an objective order'[38] of things in the Brotherhood and from which she had become detached. Ironically, Mahmoud himself criticized this lack of consistency and coherence. 'In narrating her Brotherhood story, Miral sometimes diverts into topics such as gender,' he said. Miral's political views, including those on the Brotherhood, 'are also hasty and immature. Therefore, I advised her to focus on literature,' he said.[39] Miral apparently heeded this advice, as some of her other

---

[36] Ibid.

[37] Ibid.

[38] Foucault, M. (1972). *The archaeology of knowledge* (p. 47). London: Routledge.

[39] El-Tahawy Ma (2017).

interviews literally include not one single mention of the Brotherhood or her experience as a former member of it.[40] This criticism again set the disengagement discourses of both Mahmoud and his sister as incoherent or intertextually complementary.[41] By criticizing her in an interview with myself, he was not supplementing her discourse through frequency of repetition as a form of intertextual connectivity. It was a moment of discursive dissonance built on contradictions or disagreements (unlike most cases of post-2011 exiting members).

Nevertheless, Miral did operationalize her discourse as she gave voice to her disengagement in her published writings. In her novel, the *Blue Aubergine*, the main theme is a 'search for the I,' as the heroine moves through a series of unsettling adventures. She changes her dress, leaving behind the Islamic *hijab* in exchange for the flowing hair and tight clothes of an 'emancipated young graduate' student, in what her publisher described as an 'ever more desperate and ultimately failed search for tenderness and affection.'[42] The novel focuses largely on the sufferings of a young woman who is emotionally scarred by the events of her childhood and her difficulties with her non-Brotherhood parents. Still, the novel does not focus on the heroine's time in the Brotherhood; instead, its plot interweaves her growing into womanhood with Egypt's defeat in the 1967 war with Israel, and the upheavals of the final decades of the twentieth century. The heroine is identified only as an Egyptian woman, referred to as 'she,' interacting with her generally oppressive surroundings, both Islamic and otherwise.

Still, all these references to her experiences, as essential as they are, remain random and fragmented. They are coupled with the fact that Miral's autobiography does not describe her disengagement and so did not, as Fairclough puts it, 'texture' it.[43] She reported that many

---

[40] El-Hamamsy, M. (2010). *Miral El-Tahawy: Kabertu wal-ghruba hararatny* [I grew and living abroad liberated me]. Aljazeera. Available via: https://bit.ly/2CbK9J0. Accessed 21 October 2018.

[41] Texts are 'constructed through other texts being articulated in particular ways.' Fairclough, *Discourse and social change*, p. 9.

[42] Al-Tahawy, M. (2006). *Blue Aubergine*. Cairo: American University in Cairo Press.

[43] Fairclough defines texturing as 'social agents draw[ing] upon social structures (including languages) and practices (including orders of discourse) in producing texts.' Fairclough, N. (n.d.). *Critical discourse analysis*. Available via: https://bit.ly/2RYFjo1. Accessed 1 November 2018.

people still identified her on the basis of her previous connections with the Brotherhood. A searching for her name on Google brings up her book, 'Memoirs of a Muslim [Brotherhood] Sister,' narrating her journey in the Brotherhood, released by a publishing house owned by the Brotherhood. That her memoir is not about departing from the group entailed a 'discursive imbalance' in relation to the expectation that one would. Nor was she part of any network of exiting members who were authors. Still, she found writing about her experiences, if indirectly, liberating. As a well-known novelist, she could have given the discourse a boost by leveraging her prominent status in Arab and international literary circles. Benefitting from this 'literary capital,' she might have 'discursively' supported less known exiting members (such as by writing introductions for their autobiographies as older exiting members had done with younger ones after 2011). This might have consolidated the general disengagement discourse and perhaps induced hesitant and disgruntled members of the Brotherhood into joining the trend as potential ex-members. This textual and contextual solidarity among other exiting members created what I consider a 'genre' with distinctive features building a well-knit discourse of ex-hood (see Chapter 6).[44] These resources made available and used by exiting members not only to construct their own discourses, but also to challenge and resist the hegemony of the Brotherhood by shifting the 'order of discourse.' By contributing to this 'genre' consistently, frequently, and resonantly, exiting members would also demonstrate how their discourse could be widely accepted and even naturalized. Mahmoud and Miral did not do so. By their absence from the 'struggle on discourse,' they allowed the Brotherhood's discourse to remain hegemonic.

To sum up, Miral's disengagement also did not have an explicitly 'political' character, involving other exiting members who found opportunities and resources empowering them to resist and challenge the group and its discourse. Nor did she take part in the 2011 revolution or engage politically afterward. She said that she belongs to a 'generation preceding the revolution's generation.' She admitted, 'my generation

---

[44] Genre is defined by Bakhtin as a way that 'certain features of language [lexicological, semantic, syntactic] will knit together with the intentional aim, and with the overall accentual system inherent in one or another genre: oratorical, publicistic, newspaper and journalistic genres.' Bakhtin, *The dialogic imagination*, p. 288.

was disappointing as it has always sought to distance itself.'[45] She said her role as a novelist has more to do with being a 'good observer,' as she could not be a 'good participant' in events such as those of the 2011 revolution. In addition to not joining in the 'discursive solidarity' of exiting members, who published narrations of their experiences with the Brotherhood, she also did not join them in any particular activities of political engagement in which their disengagement desires evolved and were consolidated. The fact that many exiting members also shifted careers by being novelists without losing interest in these 'political' activities and narrated their ex-hood experiences as part of their identification (see Chapter 3) shows how the contrast between the two types is glaringly striking.

CONCLUSION

This chapter has shown that the post-2011 wave of disengagement from the Brotherhood shares a number of procedural elements with cases of disengagement from the same group at an earlier time. The sequence of events, actions, and activities unfolding over time in the context of dissociation from the Brotherhood were similar in both cases, before and after 2011. It was also seen that individuals, dissociating in different times and contexts or at different levels of organizational affiliation, experienced roughly the same affective and ideological processes of disengagement. However, those departing after 2011 tended to be more emboldened, perhaps because the context was more favorable in the sense of disengagement being a phenomenon of some popularity. This meant that later ex-members tended to better articulate and operationalize their individual disengagements into more collectivized forms, and more consistent, coherent, and resonant 'discourses of disengagement.' The focus on process and on discourse meant that exiting the Muslim Brotherhood tended to lose its identification as an essentially religious phenomenon specific to Islam or Islamism or some form thereof. This could mean that ex-members from non-Islamist groups tended to go through the same sequencing of events in the process of their departure

[45] El-Koumy, W. (2011). *Miral El-Tahawy: Ma yuktab al-an fi tarekhana am mema katabna* [Miral El-Tahawy: What is written now in our history is more important than what we had written]. Available via: https://bit.ly/2PBeAM1. Accessed 10 December 2017.

and their accounting to themselves and others for it. (This will be discussed in future projects and will be briefly mentioned in the concluding remarks of Chapter 6).

BIBLIOGRAPHY

Al-Tahawy, M. (2006). *Blue Aubergine*. Cairo: American University in Cairo Press.
Bakhtin, M. M. (1981). *The dialogic imagination: Four essays* (M. Holquist, Ed., C. Emerson & M. Holquist, Trans.). Austin: University of Texas Press.
Brown, N. J. (2016). *Arguing Islam after the revival of Arab politics*. New York: Oxford University Press.
Brown, N. J., & Dunne, M. (2015). *Unprecedented pressures, uncharted course for Egypt's Muslim Brotherhood*. Carnegie Endowment for International Peace.
Bryman, A. (2016). *Social research methods*. Oxford: Oxford University Press.
El-Hamamsy, M. (2010). *Miral El-Tahawy: Kabertu wal-ghruba hararatny* [I grew and living abroad liberated me]. Aljazeera. Available via: https://bit.ly/2CbK9J0. Accessed 21 October 2018.
El-Koumy, W. (2011). *Miral El-Tahawy: Ma yuktab al-an fi tarekhana am mema katabna* [Miral El-Tahawy: What is written now in our history is more important than what we had written]. Available via: https://bit.ly/2PBeAM1. Accessed 10 December 2017.
Fairclough, N. (1992). *Discourse and social change*. Cambridge: Polity Press.
Fairclough, N. (n.d.). *Critical discourse analysis*. Available via: https://balticpractice.hse.ru/data/2015/04/13/1094925608/Critical%20discourse%20analysis_THEORY_FAIRCLOUGH.pdf. Accessed 1 November 2018.
Foucault, M. (1972). *The archaeology of knowledge*. London: Routledge.
Giddens, A. (1979). *Central problems in social theory: Action, structure and contradiction in social analysis*. London and Berkeley: University of California Press.
Halliday, M. A. K., & Hasan, R. (2014). *Cohesion in English*. London: Routledge.
Linell, P. (1998). *Approaching dialogue: Talk, interaction and contexts in dialogical perspectives*. Amsterdam: John Benjamins.
Wickham, C. R. (2004). The path to moderation: Strategy and learning in the formation of Egypt's Wasat party. *Comparative Politics, 36*, 205–228.

*For Interviewees who are ex-members of the Brotherhood (departing from the group before 2011) see Table A.7 in the appendix.

CHAPTER 6

Conclusion

The extant literature on disengagement is largely preoccupied with understanding it as a process (i.e., stages and turning points leading to the final point of one's announcing his or her departure from a certain group). This book departs from the recognition that this *process* always involves *discourse*, without which group members could not articulate and operationalize their departure. Exploring the parallel developments of process and discourse, I adopted a multidisciplinary approach. Critical Discourse Analysis (CDA) was used to unpack what is linguistic and what extra-linguistic in disengagement; Identity Process Theory (IPT) showed how disengagement relies upon dis- and re-identification through assimilation and evaluation; Social Movement Theory presents the role of a frame de-alignment process in individuals' detaching themselves from the Brotherhood; and symbolic interactionism offers a way to show how this detachment involves looking inward to replace the 'me' or 'we' with the 'I' and find reinterpretations to cohere within this replacement.

Individuals could only disengage from the Brotherhood with the help of language that can *represent, describe*, or even *become* the reality of disengagement. The language of ex-hood manifests in discursive formations produced by regularities, orders, correlations, and similar thematic choices systematically identified and analyzed in the texts through the pattern recognition of repetition, frequency, and resonance. This patterning exists within each text and across texts including, repeating, excluding, or confining certain words, phrases, or sentences relating to meanings of the idea of disengagement from the Brotherhood.

© The Author(s) 2020   189
M. Menshawy, *Leaving the Muslim Brotherhood*, Middle East Today,
https://doi.org/10.1007/978-3-030-27860-1_6

The interview or writing of each exiting member was analyzed in terms of its consistency and coherence in the narrativization of ex-hood. At the same time, against that unity, there were also *disunities* in experience as differences of age, sex, geographic locality, and timing of departure. Consider, for example, the description of participation in the group as 'slavery.' Most exiting members repeated the same description, but also brought to it their own associations such as 'imprisonment' or visualized Hollywood-styled comparison with 'Shawshank Redemption.' Sometimes this involved what we can call 'counter-interdiscursivity': referring, from a critical standpoint, to texts and narratives of the Brotherhood that use the same description of slavery to consolidate the group's dominant discourse.

The relationality drawn on textual similarities may be more than coincidence. Discursive formations exist within extra-lingusitic shifts of *rules* and *relationships* that are partly ones of power, including interactions between individuals, the groups, and institutions that they belong to or must interact with, reinterpretations, and geographic re-spatializations. All of these factors can play a role in disengagement by bringing aspects of the discourse into existence, maintenance, modification, durability, and even absence.

Still, texts have to be considered as 'surfaces of emergence' that are undergirded by layers of legitimation and validation, evidenced in a contextual relationality enabling experiences, by causing them to be written, edited, spoken, filtered, or circulated enough to accord them the status of 'discourse.' For example, after 2011, exiting members consolidated their position as actors due to the organizational and political changes that both the Brotherhood and Egypt had by then undergone or were undergoing. Such changes created *resources* and *opportunities* involving the disengagement process and discourse that facilitated exiting the group and narrating this experience. For example, the new arrangements of the 'interaction order' at recent years meant that each ex-member became more active in his or her use of language, more of a speaker or writer than a mere listener or reader as they had been when subject to the group's rules for communication and restrictions on the dissemination of writings. Becoming themselves as text producers and narrators *of* their own experience was a significant change in activity, role, and self-understanding. Politically, the post-2011 period involved a 'prefigurative' politics and a horizontality in which individuation became an important accomplishment. The events involved a repositioning of the hierarchical Brotherhood system with leaders no longer 'people above you' who 'know more than you do,' these notions being excuses long used to block internal debate and desires to exit the group. Examples abound in the book's chapters illustrate this. Tahrir Square stood as an alternative 'secular ideal' providing exiting members with both a physical ability (freedom of movement away from leaders) and a cognitive one (learning, thinking, experimenting, and communicating) that facilitated disengagement. In the *Rabi'a* sit-in in 2013, the events caused the Brotherhood to enter a state of shock and disorientation. The group failed to adapt or to provide alternative discourses for members to re-check and reinterpret reality. The leaders of the group tentatively filled the vacuum with nostalgic fantasies about some golden past. This was terrifying for members, especially when thousands of them were killed or injured after police broke into the camp against the assurances of their leaders that this would not happen. Such events were opportunities from the point of view of developing disengagement as they inhibited the investment of authority in their leaders, who now appeared too callous or ignorant to place continued faith in the Brotherhood. And in losing faith in the group and what it represents, exiting members relied more upon a strengthened sense of self as taking responsibility, and judging what is right or true in a way that requires doubting or questioning and checking again. The accountability of leaders was also affirmed.

Still, disengagement is not always a directional or linear process or path. Residues of the past bring with them conflicts and moments of hesitancy drawn on struggling, for example, to get rid of cult-like real and imagined kinships. Another hurdle to overcome relates to religion. Exiting members dismantled the Brotherhood's sanctified links to Islam by throwing doubts on its claims to be its sole representative. Events after 2011 showed it to be a mere 'interest group' representing 'another face of Mubarak,' as various frames in the texts demonstrate. They thus framed their disengagement as an attempt to retain Islam without an Islamism that they saw as masking narrow material interests and a hunger for power. Accordingly, the role and status of leaders were also shaken, as they were no longer considered as saints providing absolute answers that every member had to unquestionably accept. The debunking process even reached the group's legendary founder, the late Hassan El-Banna. Even in events as recent as 2013, El-Banna stood as the main target of blame for the actions and reactions of the group even 70 years after his assassination. Many ex-members called attention to mistakes and shortcomings in his ideas. El-Banna and other leaders are no longer a 'higher' power taking care of and protecting the group. There are fresh and blood mortals who can be held responsible for whatever they do or do not do.

As attributional links and relations pertaining to disengagement have to draw on broader changes in agency and power, state authority inevitably also played a role. It could codify processes like disengagement by constituting their discourse as part of a 'body of knowledge.' As I write this conclusion, I keep reading Facebook posts of exiting Brotherhood members announcing their winning the state's highest awards, returning from a state-paid trip to Europe to promote their literary works, writing for state-sponsored newspapers, or serving as board members of leading cultural institutions.

One final thought drawn from the analysis of exit experiences is that discursive formations, relations, and rules of and on disengagement from the Brotherhood after 2011 have given an unprecedented shape to the production, circulation, and communication of discourse to the extent of turning it into a 'culture.' As most disengagements take an open, well-coordinated, *textured* (emerging in texts such as interviews autobiographies, TV appearance, Facebook post, or even informal chats with other exes in a café), and widespread shape, they become a 'shared knowledge,' which is one of the elements that is said to define a culture.[1] It is a 'shared knowledge' in which exiting members can survive as exes and even foster communication among themselves and with others. Many social media pages identify as groups of exiting members of the Brotherhood and explain their identity and views as 'exes.' Members even announce their disengagement in public and sometimes live on television.

The sharing of knowledge operates today through an active multi-platform multi-dimensionality. You can access the culture of ex-hood through reading hard copies of several autobiographies, watching frequent appearances on TV stations, reading columns by ex-members in Egypt's widely circulated newspapers, or subscribing to their YouTube channels. This multi-dimensionality is also adaptive to the changing environment of circulation and communication. In the early 2000s, exiting members, including 'Abdel-Mon'im Mahmoud, shared their accounts

[1] Wurzel, J. S. (2004). *Towards multiculturalism*, IRC.

of ex-hood experiences as knowledge disseminated through blogs that were in vogue at the time. After 2011, they shared them also through other formats such as Facebook, which I found an important resource in my research. They would share this knowledge in work situations (the pre-2011 exiter, Mahmoud, has many post-2011 exiters as colleagues as they both work at the same London-based satellite TV channel). This is a globalized knowledge-sharing even beyond the control of exiting members themselves. For example, Osama Dorra, who exited in 2011, told me that he himself does not keep a copy of his autobiography, which was published in a few copies by a small and lesser-known publishing house. However, I went online, and found it available in an 'open file' made available by someone on Google. I sent the link I found back to Dorra, and he was grateful. Even with no copy of his book, Dorra added to his ex-hood narrative in the book by writing four online articles for his blog, to explain his journey of disengagement, by posting on Facebook further chapters of his post-disengagement soul-searching. It is in this climate of communications drawn on an absence of restriction of the movement of individuals and their ideas that the Brotherhood lost much of its previous ideological power, to hijack any critical thinking about the group, to discredit disgruntled members rather than engage in a discussion with them, or to punish dissenters by censorship and isolation.

This multi-dimensionality of knowledge-sharing, as a constituent of culture of ex-hood, is not marginalized, arbitrary, or random. It may come as a variable yet concentrated content within the same platform itself. Take the world of printing in hard copies. You can read the story of Sameh 'Eid's disengagement in two autobiographies, and you can read his views drawn on his experience in three more print books published within shorter spans of time. In these books, he maintains his focus: Narrating his individual experience of departing from the group, developing an effective and credible counter-discourse against the Brotherhood's dominant discourse in its various shapes. Part of his effectiveness and credibility has to do with language: he reiterates the same frames in all of them, deepening the sense of consistency and coherence. He also links these frames with others reiterated by other exiters who have adopted the same tactic. You can also read Ahmed Ban, who has four books published drawing on his experience as a former member of the Brotherhood. If you want to explore a more high-level case of disengagement, you can read Mohamed Habib's articles in some of

Egypt's leading and wide-circulating newspapers, as well as his books, also narrating his experience as a former leader of the Brotherhood. These authors' intensive acts of narrativization help sustain the culture of ex-hood, especially as they wield the 'power of expert,' introducing many parts of the group's secrets to us as shared knowledge.

Disengagement from the Brotherhood became itself a culture, as sharing creates *commonality*, which makes ex-hood more ordinary, more a 'way of life.' Indeed, exiting members are still a minority of dozens or hundreds against thousands, or even hundreds of thousands, of committed members of the Brotherhood who espouse and operate with another hegemonic culture that systematically and hierarchically circulates within the Brotherhood's ranks. Nevertheless, this commonality of the opposite and 'marginalized' objects of discourse does not make the personal individual accounts less of a culture. To borrow from Raymond Williams, a 'culture' is about common meanings and is the product of a 'whole people,' but at the same time it can emanate from 'individual meanings' and 'the product of a man's whole committed personal and social experience.'[2] If anything, these personal accounts constitute a 'subjective culture,' that is, the way members of a society understand themselves and their environment. Still, within these self-perceptions, an 'objective' part of culture can be born and thrive, as the narratives are always susceptible to being collectivized and thematized as a 'common entity' represented in categories and associations or even genres such as books, Facebook pages, blogs, or TV programs.[3] As linguistic constructs get into cycles of repetition and frequency, what is subjective gains more objectification through a de-personification invested by the power of sharing.

In this sense, the stories of exiting members stand as part of a broader and internationally established cultural repertoire normalizing the status of being an ex-. In these transformations, individuated disengagements are no longer hidden, falsified, or downsized. They can also be celebrated as *appropriate* or *normalized* behavior. In one interview, 'Eid sat proudly along with his wife, who exited from the Brotherhood a few

---

[2]Williams, R. (n.d.). *Culture is ordinary [1958]*, p. 96. Available via University of Warwick: https://bit.ly/2A382RA. Accessed 2 November 2018.

[3]See Kluckhohn, C. (1954). Culture and behavior. In G. Lindzey (Ed.), *Handbook of social psychology* (Vol. 2, pp. 921–976). Cambridge, MA: Addison-Wesley.

years later, while giving an interview to the pan-Arab TV channel *Al-Arabiyya* (owned by Saudi Arabia, a key ally in the campaign against Egypt's Brotherhood). Tareq Aboul-Sa'd had posted his photos of their informal gatherings at a café on social media while sharing thoughts of their experiences as part of a new community defined by shared features and habits.[4] Dorra posts on Facebook glimpses of his 'Islamist' past, attempts to date girls, cherishing responsibility for all of his tasks including his attempts to lose weight. Mindful of all of the doubts that could make the disengagement phenomenon less absolute or uncritical, he sought to redefine himself as an 'ordinary' being rather than a Brother. He knows he is not lost or doomed, as the Brotherhood always warned those who exit from it would be. He survives and thrives outside the orbit of the Brotherhood. I believe that within this normality, and commonality, that more exiting members will come forward to disengage from the Brotherhood and identify themselves as 'ex-Brothers.' This means further cycles of dissemination and sharing of experiences whereby exiting members can resonate with similar experiences, repeat the same kind of discourse, and go through the same stages of disengagement. As leading exiting members have told me that many thousands of the Brotherhood members have departed from the group over the past few years, scholars have the task to turn attention from who and what is *inside* the group as the march toward ex-hood becomes unstoppable.

At the level of the group, these desires to exit could lead to major transformations not only to resist, but also to accommodate these desires. Censorship by the self or others inside the group is passé. Gone are the days of questions with no answers or answers without questions. Members have already learnt to think for themselves and ask questions instead of blindly obeying 'holy' leaders and hidebound answers. They can outperform the group and retain a secure edge as they keep gaining more and more of these skills of learning, and communicating them through different media. Leaders are partially aware of these changes, including claims that they and they alone are the sole custodians of a sanctified truth. They no longer accuse disgruntled members of being 'apostates' once the latter criticize them. Indeed, many steps have been taken by the group to engage in an internal discussion about the problems and future of the group, and it has stopped using some old tactics

[4]Facebook. (2014). *Mukhtar Nouh with Sameh'Eid and Tareq Aboul-Sa'd*. A Photo Caption. Available via: https://bit.ly/2QDg1zf. Accessed 18 December 2018.

that stem from intolerance of any criticism directed at it or its leaders. As the group has long been able to reinvent itself in earlier crises, we still need time to wait and see how it can deal with this crisis at hand.

BIBLIOGRAPHY

Kluckhohn, C. (1954). Culture and behavior. In G. Lindzey (Ed.), *Handbook of social psychology* (Vol. 2, pp. 921–976). Cambridge, MA: Addison-Wesley.
Williams, R. (n.d.). *Culture is ordinary [1958]* p. 96. Available via University of Warwick: https://bit.ly/2A382RA. Accessed 2 November 2018.
Wurzel, J. S. (1988). *Toward multicuturalism: A reader in multicultural education*. Yarmouth, ME: Intercultural Press.

APPENDIX

Table A.1 Interviewees who are ex-members of the Brotherhood

Name	Date of joining MB	Date of exiting MB	Age	Profession	Interview place
Ghandi Antar	2000	2012	35	Journalist and political researcher	Turkey
A.E.	2000	2006	20	Documentary maker	Turkey
T.E.	2000	2009	35	Journalist	Turkey
M.'A.Z	2002	2012	32	Journalist	Turkey
I.M. I.	1987	2011	30	Lawyer	Egypt
A.S.R.	1998	2012	31	Arabic teacher	Egypt
A.Z.	1993	2012	51	Housewife	Egypt
R.S.	2003	2014	31	Cameraman	Egypt
S.E.	1990	2011	28	Journalist	Egypt
S.M.	2006	2014	31	Merchant	Egypt
Tareq Aboul-Sa'd	1985	2011	50	School Vice-Principal	Egypt
Tareq El-Beshbeshy	1984	2013	53	Government employee	Egypt
'A.E.	1984	2011	52	Engineer	Egypt
M.I.'A.	2010	2013	26	Engineering student	Egypt
'Emad Ahmed 'Ali	2002	2017	33	Student	On Skype
A.G.	1986	2014	32	Pharmacist	Turkey
I.'O.	2012	2015	24	Political science student	Turkey
Haitham Aboul-Khalil	1989	2011	49	Media practitioner	Turkey
Mohamed Aboul-Gheit	1989	2011	28	Journalist	Britain
Mohamed El-Qassas	1987	2011	42	Deputy Chairman of Strong Egypt Party	Egypt (On phone)
Islam Lutfy	1984	2011	40	Lawyer	Britain

© The Editor(s) (if applicable) and The Author(s),
under exclusive license to Springer Nature Switzerland AG 2020
M. Menshawy, *Leaving the Muslim Brotherhood*, Middle East Today,
https://doi.org/10.1007/978-3-030-27860-1

197

Name	Date of joining MB	Date of exiting MB	Age	Profession	Interview place
Ibrahim Rab'	1979	2013	53	Government employee	Egypt (On phone)
Ibrahim El-Za'frany	1965	2011	66	Physician	Egypt (On phone)
Kamal El-Helbawy	1951	2012	79	Writer	London
Ahmed 'Abdel-Gawwad	1977	May 2011	41	Secretary General of Strong Egypt Party	Egypt (on phone)
K.F.	1999	2015	39	Writer and researcher	Turkey
M.S.	2007	2013	33	Owner of a construction company	Turkey
A.Y.	2001	2013	34	Journalist	Turkey
Ahmed Nazily	1983	2011	40	Businessman	Qatar
Mohamed 'Affan	1998	2011	38	Academic researcher and writer	Turkey
M.H.	2005	2013	29	Ph.D. student	Turkey
M.E.	2010	2014	23	Student	Turkey

Table A.2 The profession of interviewees conducted in Egypt, Turkey, the UK, and Qatar

Job title	Frequency	Percent
Journalist/writer	12	37.5
Student	5	15.6
Civil servant	3	9.4
Other	7	21.9
Politician	2	6.3
Businessman	2	6.3
Housewife	1	3.1
Total	32	100.0

Table A.3 Duration of staying as a member inside the Muslim Brotherhood

Category of years	Frequency	Percent
1–10	9	28.1
11–20	8	25.0
21–30	11	34.4
31+	4	12.5
Total	32	100.0

Table A.4 The time of joining the Muslim Brotherhood (divided by decades)

Decade	Frequency	Percent
1960s	1	3.1
1970s	2	6.3
1980s	10	31.3
1990s	5	15.6
2000s	13	40.6
1950s	1	3.1
Total	32	100.0

Table A.5   Age groups at the time of joining the Muslim Brotherhood (divided by ages and stages of development from children to youth and beyond)

Age group	Frequency	Percent
0–16	14	43.8
17–24	17	53.1
25+	1	3.1
Total	32	100.0

Table A.6   Location of the interviews (by country)

Country	Frequency	Percent
Turkey	13	40.6
Egypt	15	46.9
UK	3	9.4
Qatar	1	3.1
Total	32	100.0

Table A.7   Interviewees who are ex-members of the Brotherhood (departing from the group before 2011)

Name	The date of joining the Brotherhood	The date of exiting the Muslim Brotherhood	Age	Profession	Place of the interview	Time of the interview
Mahmoud El-Tahawy	1981	1987	52	Associate professor of Hepatology and Gastroenterology (Egypt)	Over phone and facebook	5/6/7 June 2017 12/13/15 May 2018 20/21 January 2019 and 12/13 February 2019
Miral El-Tahawy	1989	1995	50	Associate professor at Arizona State University, the US and Novelist	Over phone and facebook	18 September 2017

INDEX

© The Editor(s) (if applicable) and The Author(s),   201
under exclusive license to Springer Nature Switzerland AG 2020
M. Menshawy, *Leaving the Muslim Brotherhood*, Middle East Today,
https://doi.org/10.1007/978-3-030-27860-1